D1140685

A HISTORY OF
WORLD
FOOTBALL

A complete history of the beautiful game and its greatest players

igloobooks

A HISTORY OF
WORLD
FOOTBALL

A complete history of the beautiful game and its greatest players

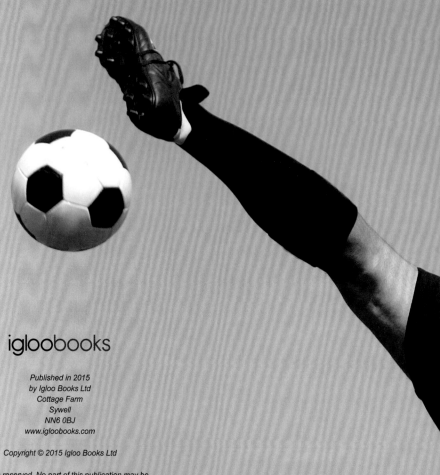

igloobooks

Published in 2015
by Igloo Books Ltd
Cottage Farm
Sywell
NN6 0BJ
www.igloobooks.com

Copyright © 2015 Igloo Books Ltd

All rights reserved. No part of this publication may be
reproduced, stored in a retrieval system, or transmitted
in any way or by any means, electronic, mechanical,
photocopying, recording or otherwise, without the prior
written permission of the publisher. Information and
statistics are correct as of time of writing.

Cover images: bottom left (Bobby Moore, Kenny Dalglish)
© Mirrorpix; all other images © Getty Images

SHE001 0715
2 4 6 8 10 9 7 5 3 1
ISBN: 978-1-78440-206-8

Printed and manufactured in China

CONTENTS

THE ORIGINS

HISTORY OF FOOTBALL

Modern football is only a century-and-a-half old, but competitive ball-kicking games can be traced back much earlier. FIFA recognizes the ancient Chinese game *tsu-chu* (or *cu-ju*) as modern football's oldest ancestor.

Tsu-chu was popularised around 200–300BC as an exercise in the army. In one variation, players kicked a feather-filled ball into a 12–16 inch (30–40cm) net hung between two 30 foot (9m) high bamboo poles. In AD600, the Japanese game *kemari* was invented. Players passed a small, grain-filled ball between themselves without letting it touch the ground.

Early versions of football in Europe came from the Greek and Roman empires. These games were more similar to rugby than modern football, with players able to use their hands as well as their feet. The Roman version, known as *harpustum*, grew into *calcio*, a notoriously violent Renaissance game, which gives its name to modern Italian football.

MEDIEVAL FOOTBALL

Records of medieval football (called fute-ball) in France and Britain tell of violent mobs charging through towns, using anything from a pig's bladder

RIGHT Gabriele Bella's painting of a game of football in Venice in the eighteenth century

to the head of a defeated Danish prince as a ball. Football was so competitive, popular, and disruptive that it caused riots. Both the Lord Mayor of London in 1314 and Henry VIII in 1540 attempted to ban the sport, despite Henry having his own pair of football boots.

RULES AND REGULATIONS

By the 19th century, football, or soccer, as it was also known from its earliest years – had started to take a more recognisable shape as part of the British public school curriculum. Two unofficial sets of rules, one from Cambridge University and another developed by clubs in the north-east of England, were established to govern the game.

The English Football Association (FA) was formed in 1863 and published the first consolidated set of formal laws. Rebel schools, which wanted to permit running while holding the ball, abandoned association football and launched rugby football.

AN INTERNATIONAL GAME

Football quickly spread around the world as sailors, engineers, bankers, soldiers, and miners introduced it wherever they went.

Clubs were formed in Copenhagen, Vienna, and Genoa, with British colonial outposts further aiding the spread of the game. In 1891, Argentina became the first nation outside the UK to establish a football league and British sailors helped to popularize the game in Brazil. Even the United States had its own 'soccer' teams as far back as the 1860s. By the end of the century, leagues – albeit not necessarily national ones at this early stage – were running in England, Scotland, Italy, Holland, and pre-communist Russia.

The first international match took place the year after the inaugural FA Cup, when England played Scotland in 1872, at Hamilton Crescent, Partick, Glasgow. The British Home Internationals quickly became a regular fixture.

ABOVE Members of Harrow School's Soccer Eleven, 1867

THE ORIGINS

HISTORY OF FOOTBALL

THE CREATION OF FIFA

By the start of the 20th century, national football associations had been formed in countries across Europe and South America, including Uruguay, Chile, Paraguay, Denmark, Sweden, Italy, Germany, Holland, Belgium, and France.

Carl Anton Wilhelm Hirschman of Holland suggested convening an international meeting of football associations to the English FA's secretary, F. J. Wall. The English FA was initially positive, but left the call unanswered. Robert Guerin from the French Sports Association didn't want to wait indefinitely and, at a match between France and Belgium in 1904, he invited the European associations to join together.

This time the English FA made it clear it was not interested. However, the others agreed and FIFA (Fédération Internationale de Football Associations) came into being on 21 May 1904, in Paris, when representatives agreed a list of

FOOTBALL FACTS

300–200BC *tsu-chu* popularised in China
AD600 *kemari* developed by the Japanese aristocracy
1100s both women and men took part in huge games in England
1314 'football' banned by the Lord Mayor of London
1530 a famous *Calcio* game takes place during the siege of Florence
1848 'Cambridge Rules' published by Cambridge University
1863 English Football Association founded with a set of codified laws for modern football

RIGHT Crowds build at the 1923 FA Cup 'White Horse Final' between West Ham United and Bolton Wanderers

regulations, including playing matches according to the English Football Association's law book. Represented at the meeting were France, Belgium, Denmark, Holland, Spain, Sweden, and Switzerland. The seeds were sown for the World Cup, with Article Nine stipulating that FIFA would be the only body with the authority to organise such an international tournament.

Although none of the British nations attended the founding meeting of FIFA, they joined two years later and England's D. B. Woodfall became president.

ENGLAND'S INFLUENCE

The English game remained revered around the world in those days, proof of which is to be found in the English clubs names which survive far and wide. Clubs named after Arsenal are to be found in countries as far apart as Ukraine and Argentina and the famous amateur team, the Corinthians, saw their name adopted by what is now one of Brazil's greatest clubs.

In Italy, the English legacy is still evident in the names of clubs such as Milan and Genoa – not the Italian 'Milano' and 'Genova' – while the fervent Basque supporters of Athletic Bilbao in northern Spain maintained a private insistence on "Atleti" despite the Franco dictatorship imposing the Spanish-language 'Atletico' label.

Students who came to England for an education also took home with them more than the latest developments in engineering, finance, and commerce. One such was Charles Miller, whose Scottish father, a railway engineer in Sao Paulo, had sent his son 'home' for an English boarding school education. Young Miller returned to Brazil in 1894 with two footballs in his baggage and sparked a passion which resulted in a record five World Cup triumphs.

Jimmy Hogan, William Garbutt, and Arthur Pentland were outstanding among English football coaches who taught the finer points of the game on the continent in the first half of the 20th century. Hogan worked in Hungary and then in Austria, whose national team he coached in their famously narrow 4-3 defeat by England at Stamford Bridge in 1932.

THE ORIGINAL LAWS OF THE GAME

(as adopted by the Football Association on December 8, 1863)

1. The maximum length of the ground shall be 200 yards, the maximum breadth shall be 100 yards, the length and breadth shall be marked off with flags; and the goal shall be defined by two upright posts, eight yards apart, without any tape or bar across them.

2. A toss for goals shall take place, and the game shall be commenced by a place kick from the centre of the ground by the side losing the toss for goals; the other side shall not approach within 10 yards of the ball until it is kicked off.

3. After a goal is won, the losing side shall be entitled to kick off, and the two sides shall change goals after each goal is won.

4. A goal shall be won when the ball passes between the goal-posts or over the space between the goal-posts (at whatever height), not being thrown, knocked on, or carried.

5. When the ball is in touch, the first player who touches it shall throw it from the point on the boundary line where it left the ground in a direction at right angles with the boundary line, and the ball shall not be in play until it has touched the ground.

6. When a player has kicked the ball, any one of the same side who is nearer to the opponent's goal line is out of play, and may not touch the ball himself, nor in any way whatever prevent any other player from doing so, until he is in play; but no player is out of play when the ball is kicked off from behind the goal line.

7. In case the ball goes behind the goal line, if a player on the side to whom the goal belongs first touches the ball, one of his side shall be entitled to a free kick from the goal line at the point opposite the place where the ball shall be touched. If a player of the opposite side first touches the ball, one of his side shall be entitled to a free kick at the goal only from a point 15 yards outside the goal line, opposite the place where the ball is touched, the opposing side standing within their goal line until he has had his kick.

8. If a player makes a fair catch, he shall be entitled to a free kick, providing he claims it by making a mark with his heel at once; and in order to take such kick he may go back as far as he pleases, and no player on the opposite side shall advance beyond his mark until he has kicked.

9. No player shall run with the ball.

10. Neither tripping nor hacking shall be allowed, and no player shall use his hands to hold or push his adversary.

11. A player shall not be allowed to throw the ball or pass it to another with his hands.

12. No player shall be allowed to take the ball from the ground with his hands under any pretence whatever while it is in play.

13. No player shall be allowed to wear projecting nails, iron plates, or gutta-percha on the soles or heels of his boots.

THE
WORLD CUP

The World Cup is the planet's greatest sports event. In terms of competing nations, television viewers and finance, it dwarfs every other tournament. Uruguay were the first hosts, and first winners, in 1930, and since, it has travelled and entertained all around the world, with tournaments in South America, Europe, North America, Asia and Africa. The most successful country, winning the title of World Champion five times, is Brazil.

THE WORLD CUP

FIRST TOURNAMENTS

After a string of false starts, the World Cup was launched in 1930. The inaugural international tournament was the British Home Championship, but FIFA's first attempt to launch a truly international championship in 1906 had fallen flat. Switzerland agreed to host the tournament and even made a trophy, but no one turned up.

PAGE 10 Italy score the first goal in the 1982 World Cup final

PAGE 11 Italy's Fabio Cannavaro lifts the 2006 trophy

THE RESULT 1930

Location: Montevideo
Final: Uruguay 4 Argentina 2
Shirts: Uruguay white, Argentina light blue-and-white stripes
Scorers: Dorado, Cea, Iriarte, Castro; Peucelle, Stabile

URUGUAY

Ballesteros

Nasazzi   Mascheroni

Andrade Fernandez Gestido

Dorado Scarone Castro Cea Iriarte

M Evaristo Ferreira Stabile Varallo Peucelle

Suarez   Monti   J Evaristo

Paternoster   Della Torre

Botasso

ARGENTINA

England, who joined FIFA in 1905, organised the first large-scale international football tournament as part of the 1908 London Olympic Games.

FIFA became a genuinely international body as countries from North and South America started to join. The Olympic football tournament continued, and from 1914 FIFA took a lead role in it, officially designating it the 'World Championship of Amateur Football.'

Yet FIFA still harboured ambitions of launching its own tournament. Not only was the status of football in the Olympics insecure – it was almost dropped entirely from the 1932 Games at Los Angeles – but interest was hampered by the sudden spread of professional teams.

URUGUAY WIN ON HOME TERRITORY

In the 1920s, two Frenchmen, FIFA President Jules Rimet and French Federation Secretary Henri Delaunay, set up a steering committee. In 1928, the FIFA Congress in Amsterdam voted to support a first World Championship and Uruguay's bid to host the event easily beat off European competition. As part of the country's centenary celebrations, the event was guaranteed financially by the government. The Uruguayans boasted an impressive pedigree as double Olympic champions

– in 1924 they won in France and four years later they triumphed in Amsterdam – and built the massive Centenario Stadium in Montevideo.

Lucien Laurent of France scored the first-ever World Cup goal in the 4-1 victory over Mexico, but Uruguay's generosity in hosting the tournament was rewarded with ultimate victory, when 80,000 fans packed the Centenario Stadium to witness their 4-2 win over Argentina in the final.

RIGHT Czech goalkeeper Planicka punches clear in the 1934 final

THE RESULT 1934

Location: Rome
Final: Italy 2 Czechoslovakia 1
(after extra time)
Shirts: Italy blue, Czech red
Scorers: Orsi, Schiavio; Puc

ITALY

Combi

Monzeglio   Allemandi

Ferraris   Monti   Bertolini

Guaita   Meazza   Schiavio   Ferrari   Orsi

Puc   Nejedly   Sobotka   Svoboda   Junek

Krcil   Cambal   Kostalek

Ctyroky   Zenisek

Planicka

CZECHOSLOVAKIA

WORLD CUP 1934

Italy were both hosts and winners of the first finals to be staged in Europe. Dictator Benito Mussolini wanted to put on a show to impress his international visitors. But World Cup title holders Uruguay stayed away because they feared their top players would remain in Europe.

Vittorio Pozzo, Italy's manager, included three Argentinian-born players in his squad, while his best home-grown players were forwards Giuseppe Meazza and veteran Angelo Schiavio.

Spain became Italy's most awkward opponents. The heroics of the legendary Spanish goalkeeper Ricardo Zamora held the hosts to a 1-1 draw in the quarter-finals. However, Zamora took such a battering from Italy's over-physical forwards that he was not fit enough to play in the replay.

Italy won 1-0 and then defeated Austria, Europe's other top nation, by the same score. In the final they beat Czechoslovakia 2-1, but only after extra-time, with Schiavio scoring the winner.

ABOVE Leonidas (left) leads Brazil to their victory over Sweden in 1938

WORLD CUP 1938

Four years later, Italy won a second time, this time in France. The atmosphere was very different compared to 1934, when Pozzo's team had benefited from home advantage, generous referees, and home support. In France they were jeered by fans angered by Italy's fascist politics.

England, had boycotted FIFA since World War 1, but were invited to compete at the last minute in place of Austria, which had been swallowed up by Adolf Hitler's Germany. However, England's Football Association declined the invitation, even though they had thrashed Germany 6-3 in Berlin shortly before the finals.

The favourites included Brazil, following their astonishing first round match against Poland. Brazil won 6-5 in extra time: Brazil's Leonidas and Poland's Ernst Wilimowski both scored hat-tricks.

Brazil were so confident of beating Italy in the semi-finals that they rested Leonidas to keep him fresh for the final, but their gamble misfired because they lost 2-1. Italy went on to defeat Hungary 4-2 in the final to become the first-ever back-to-back World Cup winners.

THE RESULT 1938

Location: Paris
Final: Italy 4 Hungary 2
Shirts: Italy blue, Hungary cherry red
Scorers: Colaussi 2, Piola 2; Titkos, Sarosi

ITALY

Olivieri

Foni   Andreolo   Rava

Serantoni   Locatelli

Biavati   Meazza   Piola   Ferrari   Colaussi

Titkos   Zsengeller   Sarosi   Vincze   Sas

Lazar   Szucs   Szalay

Biro   Polgar

Szabo

HUNGARY

1950s

"All I remember was

everyone in tears."

PELÉ RECALLS THE 1950 FINAL

A nation was traumatised when the host, and one of the favourites, Brazil lost to Uruguay in the climax of the first post-war World Cup. The competition ended not with a one-off final but a four-team group, a format not used since.

1950

The closing match, in front of a record crowd of nearly 200,000 in Rio's Maracana Stadium, proved decisive as Uruguay claimed their second title.

Free-scoring Brazil needed only a draw to win their first World Cup, and looked to be on their way when Friaça fired them into the lead. But underdogs Uruguay, captained and marshalled by defender Obdulio Varela, stunned the hosts with late goals by Juan Schiaffino and Alcides Ghiggia. Brazilian fans were furious with their team's failure, with much of the blame heaped on unfortunate goalkeeper Barbosa.

The defeat marked the very last time that Brazil wore an all-white kit, which was believed to be so unlucky that it was replaced by the now famous yellow shirts. Because of the result, the Uruguay players remained in their dressing room for hours after the final whistle until it was safe to emerge.

The final was not the only shock of the tournament – England had been humbled in the first round by the United States. England lost 1-0 at Belo Horizonte, courtesy of a goal from Haiti-born Joe Gaetjens.

1954

When runaway favourites Hungary thrashed under-strength West Germany 8-3 in their opening round group game, no one expected these sides to meet again in the final – let alone for the West Germans to triumph.

West Germany's coach Sepp Herberger rested several key players for their first game, while Hungary's captain Ferenc Puskás suffered an ankle injury that was meant to rule him out of the rest of the tournament. Yet Puskás, as the star player, was controversially brought back for the final and even gave his Magical Magyars a sixth-minute lead. Left-winger Zoltan Czibor scored again almost immediately, with another rout looking likely.

RIGHT 1954 souvenir postcard featuring the Maracana Stadium and views over Rio de Janerio

THE RESULT 1950

Location: Rio
Final: Uruguay 2 Brazil 1
Shirts: Uruguay light blue, Brazil white
Scorers: Schiaffino, Ghiggia; Friaça

URUGUAY

Máspoli

Gambetta   Gonzáles

Andrade   Varela   Tejera

Ghiggia Julio Pérez Míguez Schiaffino Morán

Chico   Jair   Ademir   Zizinho   Friaça

Danilo   Bauer   Bigode

Juvenal   Augusto

Barbosa

BRAZIL

THE RESULT 1954

Location: Berne
Final: West Germany 3 Hungary 2
Shirts: West Germany white, Hungary cherry red
Scorers: Morlock, Rahn 2; Puskás, Czibor

WEST GERMANY

Turek

Posipal   Liebrich   Kohlmeyer

Eckel   Mai

Rahn Morlock O Walter F Walter Schaefer

Tóth   Puskás Hidegkuti Kocsis Czibor

Zakarias   Bozsik

Lantos   Lantos   Buzánszki

Grosics

HUNGARY

LEFT Brazil's 17-year-old Pelé shoots for goal in the 1958 final

THE RESULT 1958

Location: Stockholm
Final: Brazil 5 Sweden 2
Shirts: Brazil blue, Sweden yellow
Scorers: Vavá 2, Pelé 2, Zagallo; Liedholm, Simonsson

BRAZIL

Gilmar

D Santos   Bellini   Orlando   N Santos

Zito   Didi

Garrincha   Vavá   Pelé   Zagallo

Skoglund Liedholm Simonsson Gren Hamrin

Parling   Börjesson

Bergmark Gustavsson Axbom

Svensson

SWEDEN

But the Germans made a spirited comeback. Led by captain Fritz Walter and two-goal hero Helmut Rahn, the Germans battled back for what is known in footballing history as 'Das Wunder von Bern' – the miracle of Berne.

Hungary entered the tournament as Olympic champions and overwhelming favourites, but remarkably the final would be their only defeat between 1950 and early 1956.

They thought they had done enough to take the match into extra time, only for an 88th-minute Puskás strike to be controversially disallowed for offside by Welsh linesman Mervyn Griffiths.

The competition produced an amazing 140 goals over 26 matches, including the World Cup's highest-scoring match during Austria's thrilling 7-5 triumph over Switzerland.

1958

Brazil finally ended their wait for their first World Cup crown, with a little help from their latest superstar, Pelé, in Sweden. The 17-year-old Santos prodigy had to wait until Brazil's final group game to make Vicente Feola's starting line-up, with mesmerising winger Garrincha also given his first opportunity at the finals.

The pair proved irresistible by setting up Vavá for both goals to beat the Soviet Union, before Pelé grabbed a hat-trick in the 5-2 semi-final success over France. Brazil defeated hosts Sweden by the same score in the final, including two goals by Pelé, who broke down in tears at the end.

Yet Brazil were not the only ones to impress. French striker Just Fontaine scored 13 goals, a record for a single World Cup tournament that no one has since come close to emulating. The 1958 finals were also the only time that all four of the UK's Home Nations qualified, although England had lost Duncan Edwards and several other international players in the Munich air disaster.

West Germany lost a bitter and violent semi-final to Sweden. Captain Fritz Walter was fouled out of the game and could not be replaced because substitutes were not allowed at the time.

THE WORLD CUP

1960s

Even without Pelé at the helm, Brazil were unstoppable as they comfortably retained their title in South America. Pelé scored in Brazil's first game but was injured in the next match, so he played no further part in the tournament.

RIGHT Garrincha (left) and Amarildo celebrate Brazil's equaliser against Czechoslovakia in the 1962 final

THE RESULT 1962

Location: Santiago
Final: Brazil 3 Czechoslovakia 1
Shirts: Brazil yellow, Czechoslovakia red
Scorers: Amarildo, Zito, Vavá; Masopust

BRAZIL

Gilmar

D Santos   Mauro   Zozimo   N Santos

Zito   Didi   Zagallo

Garrincha   Vavá   Amarildo

Jelínek   Kvasnak   Scherer   Pospíchal

Masopust   Kadraba

Novák   Popluhár   Pluskal   Tichý

Schrojf

CZECHOSLOVAKIA

1962

Pelé's deputy was Amarildo from Botafogo of Rio de Janeiro. Known as 'the white Pelé,' he made an immediate impact by scoring two goals in the 2-1 win over Spain in their decisive concluding group match. Amarildo also notched an equaliser in the final, but the undisputed star of the tournament was Garrincha, nicknamed 'the Little Bird.'

Garrincha, the world's greatest-ever dribbler, was the two-goal man of the match as Brazil saw off England 3-1. He even overcame the embarrassment of being sent off in the 4-2 semi-final win over hosts Chile.

Brazil managed to persuade the disciplinary panel not to ban their star player, so he played in the final. The defending champions suffered an early shock when midfielder Josef Masopust shot the Czechoslovakians into an early lead. However, mistakes by goalkeeper Vilem Schroif helped

Brazil hit back to register a 3-1 victory. Masopust's consolation, months later, was to be voted as the European Footballer of the Year.

Chile's preparations had been marred by an earthquake two years earlier, yet they surpassed expectations not only off the pitch but on it as they clinched a deserved third place.

The Chileans caused a quarter-final upset by knocking out the highly rated Soviet Union, despite the outstanding efforts of legendary goalkeeper Lev Yashin.

1966

A historic hat-trick hero, a Soviet linesman, and a dog named Pickles were all made famous by the World Cup hosted in England.

West Ham's Geoff Hurst, who started the finals as a reserve striker, became the only man ever to score three goals in a World Cup final as the hosts beat West Germany 4-2 at Wembley Stadium.

But his second strike was one of the most controversial in football history. West Germany levelled through Wolfgang Weber's 89th-minute goal to take the final into extra time. In the first half of extra time, Hurst produced an angled shot that struck the underside of the crossbar and went down behind the goal line before bouncing back out again for the Germans to clear it to safety.

England claimed they had scored and, despite West Germany's protests, linesman Tofik Bakhramov told Swiss referee Gottfried Dienst that the ball had indeed crossed the line. Hurst, who fell while shooting at goal, was unsighted. However, fellow striker Roger Hunt was so certain that the ball had crossed the line that he did not bother even following up to put it back into the net. The controversial goal left the Germans deflated and Hurst capped his performance by claiming his hat-trick – and England's greatest footballing triumph – with virtually the last kick of the contest.

Alf Ramsey's hard-working side, nicknamed the 'Wingless Wonders,' had edged past Uruguay, Mexico, France, Argentina, and Portugal en route to the final. However, there were some complaints that England had been able to play all their matches in their stronghold of Wembley Stadium.

Their quarter-final against Argentina proved to be the most bitter. Visiting captain Antonio Rattin was sent off for dissent by German referee Rudolf Kreitlein but initially refused to leave the pitch and eventually had to be escorted by police.

The tournament had been boycotted by African nations, who were unhappy at their 'winner' having to qualify via a play-off with the champions of Asia or Oceania.

BRAZIL MISS PRESENCE OF PELE

For the second successive World Cup finals, Pelé limped out of the tournament early on after being the victim of relentlessly tough tackling. His ageing teammates were unable to raise their game without their star player, and Brazil surprisingly crashed out in the first round.

It was also a story of woe for former champions Italy, whose squad were pelted with rotten vegetables on their return home. They suffered a 1-0 defeat to the minnows of North Korea, whose winner was drilled home by dentist Pak Doo-Ik. The Koreans raced into a 3-0 quarter-final lead over Portugal, before Mozambique-born Eusébio inspired the Portuguese to a 5-3 comeback and slotted home four goals.

Eusébio, dubbed the "Black Panther" for his goal-scoring prowess, ended the tournament as top scorer with nine goals but was denied a place in the final by Bobby Charlton's two goals, which guided England to a 2-1 semi-final success.

Less than four months before England captain Bobby Moore accepted the Jules Rimet trophy from Queen Elizabeth II, it had been stolen from a London exhibition. Fortunately, a mongrel dog called Pickles dug up the trophy from a South London garden and was promptly rewarded with a lifetime's supply of pet food.

ABOVE Pickles, the dog who found the stolen World Cup

LEFT England captain Bobby Moore holds aloft the Jules Rimet trophy

THE WORLD CUP

1970s

"Brazil on that day were on a different planet."

ITALY'S GIACINTO FACCHETTI

This was the first World Cup to be broadcast in sun-soaked colour around the world. Nothing could match Brazil's famous yellow shirts as Mario Zagallo showcased arguably the most dazzling attacking side in footballing history.

THE RESULT 1970

Location: Mexico
Final: Brazil 4 Italy 1
Shirts: Brazil yellow, Italy blue
Scorers: Pelé, Gerson, Jairzinho, Carlos Alberto; Boninsegna

BRAZIL

Felix

Alberto Brito Piazza Everaldo

Clodoaldo Gerson Rivelino

Jairzinho Tostao Pelé

Riva Boninsegna
(Rivera)

De Sisti Mazzola Bertini Domenghini
(Juliano)

Facchetti Rosato Cera Burgnich

Albertosi

ITALY

1970

Spearheaded by Pelé, Jairzinho, Rivelino, and Tostão, Brazil were allowed to keep the Jules Rimet trophy after becoming the first country to win three World Cups. Pelé became the only player with a hat-trick of victories, although in 1962 he had been injured very early in the tournament.

Brazil featured in a classic first round contest, when they defeated England 1-0. However, both sides qualified for the quarter-finals. England's title defence came to a dramatic end when West Germany avenged their 1966 final defeat to bounce back from a two-goal deficit to register an extra time 3-2 win over Sir Alf Ramsey's men. The effort of overcoming England undermined the Germans in their semi-final against Italy, and West Germany ran out of steam and lost another epic, to be edged out 4-3.

Brazil wrapped up the tournament with a 4-1 triumph over Italy in Mexico City. Brazil's fourth goal was the finest of the tournament, and one of the most memorable ever scored in a final. A smooth passing move, the length of the pitch, was finished off by captain Carlos Alberto. Manager Mario Zagallo became the first man to win the World Cup both as a player and a manager.

1974

Franz Beckenbauer achieved the first half of his own leadership double when he captained hosts West Germany to victory over Holland. The final was played in Munich's Olympic Stadium, the footballing home to Beckenbauer and his FC Bayern teammates – goalkeeper Sepp Maier,

defenders Hans-Georg Schwarzenbeck and Paul Breitner, and strikers Uli Hoeness and Gerd Müller.

Yet the dominant personality of the finals was Holland's forward Johan Cruyff who, as captain, epitomised their revolutionary style of total football, characterised by a high-speed interchange of playing positions.

Hosts West Germany surprisingly stuttered in the first round but managed to qualify despite suffering a shock defeat to East Germany, who had emerged through the Berlin Wall for the first and last time in World Cup history. Jürgen Sparwasser made a name for himself with a historic strike in the 77th-minute to secure a slender 1-0 success.

West Germany topped their second round group ahead of Poland – qualifying victors over

RIGHT Holland's Johan Cruyff holds off a West German defender

England – while Holland topped the other group ahead of an over-physical Brazil.

English referee Jack Taylor awarded the first World Cup final penalty – Cruyff had been fouled in the opening minute at Munich. Johan Neeskens stepped up to put the Dutch ahead before the hosts had even touched the ball.

West Germany soon levelled matters through a penalty kick and went ahead decisively, courtesy of Müller, just before the half-time interval.

1978

Holland had to settle for second best again, this time without the inspirational Cruyff, who refused to travel to Argentina, amid kidnap fears.

Cruyff's absence was particularly missed in the final as the hosts clinched their inaugural World Cup 3-1 after extra time. Argentina's only European-based player, Mario Kempes, finished as top scorer, with six goals, including two goals in the final.

A ticker-tape assisted storm of home support carried manager César Menotti's Argentina through the first round and to the second group with a tricky meeting against Peru. Needing to win by at least four clear goals, Menotti's men ran out contentious 6-0 winners to deny Brazil a final berth. Instead, Brazil settled for a 2-1 win over Italy in the third place play-off.

In the final, Holland went behind to a Kempes strike before half-time and equalised through substitute striker Dick Nanninga. On the verge of the full-time whistle, Rob Rensenbrink's effort was denied by the post and proved a costly miss as Argentina pulled away in extra time with further goals from Kempes and Daniel Bertoni.

Scotland failed to progress beyond the first round and were shamed by Willie Johnston being kicked out of the tournament after failing a dope test. The dazzling left-winger protested his innocence, insisting he was taking Reactivan tablets to treat a cold, but he was banned from internationals and his playing career fizzled out.

ABOVE Jairzinho scores Brazil's third goal against Italy

THE WORLD CUP

1980s

The competition swelled to 24 sides in 1982, as Spain played hosts for the first time. Italy ended a 44-year wait for their third title, with captain Dino Zoff becoming the oldest player to win a World Cup at the grand age of 40.

THE RESULT 1982

Location: Madrid
Final: Italy 3 West Germany 1
Shirts: Italy blue, West Germany white
Scorers: Rossi, Tardelli, Altobelli; Breitner

ITALY

Zoff

Scirea Gentile Bergomi Collovati Cabrini

Conti Oriali Tardelli

Rossi Graziani
(Altobelli) (Causio)

Rummenigge Fischer Littbarski
(H Müller)

Dremmler Breitner B Förster
(Hrubesch)

Briegel K Förster Stielike Kaltz

Schumacher

WEST GERMANY

1982

Toni Schumacher, West Germany's goalkeeper, was fortunate to have been playing in the final. Despite having knocked unconscious France's Patrick Battiston with a brutal foul during a thrilling semi-final in Seville, he somehow escaped punishment.

In the final, Schumacher faced a spot kick from Antonio Cabrini and the Italian left-back made history by becoming the first player to miss a penalty in the title decider. In the same match, German Paul Breitner wrote himself into the annals of history when he became the first player to score a penalty in two separate finals.

But second half goals from Paolo Rossi, Marco Tardelli, and Alessandro Altobelli handed Enzo Bearzot's attacking side the trophy. Rossi's hat-trick in a 3-2 win had earlier knocked out a Brazil team that included Falcao, Socrates, and Zico.

Rossi finished up as the tournament's six-goal leading marksman to claim the Golden Boot. This was an astonishing achievement because the Juventus striker had returned to top-class football only six weeks earlier, following a two-year suspension for his role in a match-fixing scandal.

Holders Argentina struggled from the outset and they introduced their new hero, 21-year-old Diego Maradona, who had narrowly missed out on a place in their previous World Cup squad. Yet Maradona was stifled in the opening match, beaten 1-0 by Belgium, and then sent off for retaliation during a second round defeat by Brazil.

Spain were one of the more disappointing World Cup hosts out on the pitch, sensationally beaten by Northern Ireland in their opening match and later eliminated after finishing bottom of a three-nation second round group behind West Germany and England.

A further change of format saw the knockout semi-finals restored. Italy defeated Poland 2-0 in Barcelona to make the final, then West Germany saw off France in Seville, courtesy of the first penalty shoot-out in World Cup history. A magical match swung one way, then the other: Germany opened the scoring but trailed 3-1 before battling back with two goals to force extra-time. Schumacher went from villain to hero by stopping the crucial last French penalty from Maxime Bossis.

RIGHT Claudio Gentile and skipper Dino Zoff celebrate in Madrid

1986

After his previous World Cup disgrace, Maradona jumped into the spotlight when, virtually single-handedly, he won Argentina their second World Cup by combining audacious skills with equally audacious law-breaking.

The world saw the best and worst of Maradona in a five-minute spell of Argentina's quarter-final contest against England. Although the Argentinian captain punched the ball into the back of the net, Tunisian referee Ali bin Nasser allowed the goal to stand (this was his first and last World Cup game as a referee).

Maradona claimed the goal was 'a little bit of Maradona, a little bit the hand of God,' a boast that accompanied him for years to the delight of a nation that considered the trick a belated answer to Argentina's military and naval defeat by Britain in the 1982 Falkland Islands conflict.

However, no one could dispute the majesty of Maradona's second strike. A solo slalom took him the full length of the England half, before he swept the ball past embattled goalkeeper Peter Shilton with his left foot, for one of the best-ever goals. Just to prove this had been no accident, maverick Maradona scored a similar solo goal in the 2-0 semi-final victory over Belgium.

Despite being closely marked by West Germany's Lothar Matthäus in the final, Maradona escaped long enough to provide the defence-splitting pass that set up Jorge Burruchaga's late goal to once more clinch World Cup success. The Germans had clawed their way back from a two-goal deficit and looked to be heading toward extra time, before the glittering run and pass from match-winner Maradona.

Franz Beckenbauer, a World Cup winner with West Germany in 1974, was in charge of the national team. Yet even his magic touch off the pitch was simply no match for the genius of Maradona on it.

England's consolation was that striker Gary Lineker went on to win the Golden Boot as the tournament's leading scorer with six goals. His tally included a hat-trick in England's first round defeat of Poland, which sent them to the quarter-finals against Paraguay. England had struggled initially, losing their opening game 1-0 to Portugal, and in the scoreless draw against Morocco they lost key players – Ray Wilkins was sent off and captain Bryan Robson was helped off with an injury.

European champions France sneaked past Brazil on penalties in their quarter-final, but, for the second successive World Cup, fell in the semi-final to West Germany. The Germans simply cruised into the final against Argentina, courtesy of goals from Andreas Brehme and Rudi Völler.

ABOVE Diego Maradona sends Peter Shilton the wrong way

THE RESULT 1986

Location: Mexico City
Final: Argentina 3 West Germany 2
Shirts: Argentina blue and white, West Germany green
Scorers: Brown, Valdano, Burruchaga; Rummenigge, Völler

ARGENTINA

Pumpido

Cuciuffo   Brown   Ruggeri

Giusti Burruchaga Batista Olarticoechea Enrique
(Trobbiani)

Valdano   Maradona

Rummenigge   Allofs
(Völler)

Brehme   Eder   Magath   Matthäus
(Hoeness)

Briegel K Förster Jakobs Berthold

Schumacher

WEST GERMANY

THE WORLD CUP

1990

West Germany overcame Diego Maradona and Argentina, gaining revenge for their 1986 final defeat, which meant Franz Beckenbauer joined Brazil's Mario Zagallo as the only other man to win a World Cup as player and coach.

Victory in the Stadio Olimpico saw history made as Franz Beckenbauer became the first man to have won separate World Cups as coach and captain (Zagallo had not captained Brazil), while Argentina saw red and paid the penalty for their negative tactics in the final. Beckenbauer stepped down after the triumphant return home and was promptly succeeded by his former assistant Berti Vogts. However, the Germans didn't win another World Cup until 2014.

Unlike four years earlier, the final showdown of Italia '90 was a dull defensive game. Settled by Andreas Brehme's controversial late penalty, it was marred by red cards for Argentina's Pedro Monzon and Gustavo Dezotti. This was the first time that a player had been sent off in a World Cup final.

The 1990 finals were later considered as one of the poorest tournaments in the event's history, partly because of the inferior quality of refereeing. Sepp Blatter, then the general secretary of world governing body FIFA and later its president, decided then and there to launch a campaign to improve refereeing standards.

CAMEROON BRING AN AFRICAN BEAT

Argentina were not a patch on the team who had won the World Cup for the second time in their history just four years earlier. Inspirational captain Diego Maradona was carrying a knee injury and in their showpiece opening match they were pulled apart by nine-man Cameroon, the African surprise package. The Africans, making their debut in the World Cup finals, beat the holders 1-0, thanks to a

historic strike from François Omam Biyik. Cameroon's secret weapon was veteran striker Roger Milla. He provided some of the tournament's highlights but Cameroon were let down by their indiscipline. The Africans led England, managed by Bobby Robson, 2-1 in their quarter-final contest in Naples, but slack defending opened up gaps, which prompted them into conceding two penalties. Both were converted by Gary Lineker, who helped drive England through to their first semi-final appearance for 24 years.

But England's fortune with penalties ran out when they faced West Germany. England finished 1-1 after extra-time, but lost the penalty shoot-out 4-3 after Stuart Pearce and Chris Waddle missed their spot-kicks.

England, managed for the last time by Robson, who was moving to PSV Eindhoven, lost to hosts Italy in the third place play-off. By then, the Tottenham midfielder Paul Gascoigne had become a national icon, both for his performances as well as for the tears he shed after being shown a yellow card in the semi-final defeat by the Germans. The card was Gascoigne's second of the tournament, which meant he would have missed the final had England reached that stage. Later, Gascoigne returned to Italy to play for Lazio.

England were not the only nation to suffer the pain of penalty punishment. In the second round, Romania fell in the shoot-out to the Republic of Ireland, who were making an impressive debut under manager Jack Charlton, and Argentina edged past both Yugoslavia in the quarter-finals and hosts Italy in the last four through penalty kicks.

The finest match in the tournament was arguably

THE RESULT 1990

Location: Rome
Final: West Germany 1 Argentina 0
Shirts: West Germany white, Argentina blue
Scorers: Brehme (pen)
Sent Off: Monzón, Dezotti

WEST GERMANY

Illgner

Augenthaler

Berthold   Kohler   Buchwald   Brehme
(Reuter)

Hässler   Matthäus

Littbarski   Völler   Klinsmann

Maradona   Dezotti

Lorenzo   Basualdo   Troglio   Burruchaga
(Calderón)

Sensini   Serrizuela   Ruggeri   Simon
(Monzón)

Goycochea

ARGENTINA

the second round duel between old rivals Holland and West Germany. Tension surrounding the game was exacerbated in the first half by the expulsions of Holland midfielder Frank Rijkaard and German striker Rudi Völler. Ultimately, West Germany won 2-1, thanks to a sensational performance by striker Jürgen Klinsmann — possibly the best of his career — who scored one goal and made the other.

Argentina's new hero, especially in the shoot-outs, was goalkeeper Sergio Goycochea. The first choice, Nery Pumpido, was injured in Argentina's opening group game against the Soviet Union, so Goycochea played instead.

MARADONA AT HOME IN NAPLES
The duel between Italy and Argentina was staged in Naples, where Maradona was plying his trade at club level. His appeal for Napoli fans to cheer for Argentina backfired, yet they still won.

The downside for Argentina was that their outstanding winger, Claudio Caniggia, received a yellow card for a second time in the tournament and so was suspended from playing in the final.

Maradona had played remarkably throughout Italia '90, considering his injury. But in the final his luck ran out, and he pointed the blame at everyone except himself, including FIFA's Brazilian president João Havelange.

The final straw for Maradona was the controversial award of a late penalty to West Germany for a foul on striker Völler. Lothar Matthäus was the designated German penalty taker. But, citing a muscle strain, the captain handed over the responsibility to Brehme, who made no mistake in shooting past Goycochea.

RIGHT Andy Brehme celebrates his World Cup-winning penalty against Argentina

THE WORLD CUP

1994

After missing out to Mexico in 1986, the United States finally hosted a World Cup and proved better than expected on the pitch by reaching the second round before bowing out to the eventual champions – Brazil.

RIGHT Diana Ross launches the World Cup party in Chicago

THE RESULT 1994

Location: Los Angeles
Final: Brazil 0 Italy 0 (after extra time; Brazil 3-2 on penalties)
Shirts: Brazil yellow, Italy blue

BRAZIL

Taffarel

Jorginho   Aldair   Márcio Santos   Branco
(Cafu)

Mazinho II   Dunga   Mauro Silva   Zinho
(Paulo Viola)

Romário   Bebeto

R Baggio   Massaro

D Baggio   Albertini   Berti   Donadoni
(Evani)

Maldini   Baresi   Mussi   Benarrivo
(Apolloni)

Pagliuca

ITALY

The Americans had set themselves a goal of staging the event back in the late 1960s. They had failed with a bid to host the finals in 1986, but won FIFA approval through both their commercial potential and a promise to build a solid professional league.

Bora Milutinovic, a freelance Yugoslav coach, was hired to build a national team on the strength of his work in guiding Mexico, as hosts, to the quarter-finals in 1986. His 'Team America' reached the second round before narrowly losing to Brazil, the eventual winners.

The finals proved surprisingly successful, with the average attendance for the tournament reaching its highest-ever figure of 69,000. The total attendance of 3.6 million became the then highest attendance in World Cup history.

The tournament was also the most attended single sport sporting event in US history, and featured the first-ever indoor match in the World Cup finals, when the US hosted Switzerland in the Pontiac Silverdome in Michigan, Detroit.

The competition kicked off at Soldier Field Stadium in Chicago with another penalty miss, when veteran pop star Diana Ross rolled a pretend spot-kick wide during a glitzy opening ceremony in front of US President Bill Clinton.

The opening match saw holders Germany edge past Bolivia 1-0, courtesy of Jürgen Klinsmann's strike on the hour mark. Ultimately, the Germans, playing for the first time as a unified team since the collapse of the Berlin Wall, were dethroned 2-1 by Bulgaria in the quarter-finals.

One of the favourites to win overall had been Colombia, led by their maverick frizzy-haired playmaker Carlos Valderrama, who was dubbed 'El Pibe' – the kid. The Colombians had been tipped for great things by no less a judge than Pelé, after an incredible 5-0 win away to Argentina during the qualifying competition, in which winger Faustino Asprilla exploded onto the international scene. Unfortunately, their campaign proved both short-lived and tragic. They failed to progress beyond the first group stage, when central defender Andrés Escobar scored an own goal in their 2-1 defeat by the United States.

Colombia's squad returned home to a furious reception from fans and media. The furore was cut short within days, after Escobar was shot dead after an argument near his home. His killer was later jailed for 43 years, but served only 11 years of the sentence before being paroled.

MARADONA MAKES HASTY EXIT

Diego Maradona's final World Cup also proved controversial and short-lived. In 1991 he had fled Italy in disgrace after failing a dope test for cocaine and was banned for 15 months while playing for Napoli. He made a comeback in Spain and then Argentina, playing his way back into the national squad in time for the World Cup finals.

However, after scoring and starring in an opening win against World Cup newcomers Greece, Maradona then failed a further dope test for the stimulant ephedrine, following Argentina's 2-1 win over Nigeria, and was immediately expelled from the tournament. Maradona later blamed the dope test failure on the weight-loss drugs he had been taking prior to the World Cup finals.

His shocked team-mates were not long in following him home to Buenos Aires after their unexpected 3-2 exit at the hands of Romania in the last 16 knockout stage. The Romanian side was built around the creative midfield talents of Gheorghe Hagi, known as the 'Maradona of the Carpathians.'

For the first time since the four British Home Nations returned to the FIFA fold after World War II, none of them qualified for the finals. However, the Republic of Ireland – largely built around English league players – emerged impressively from a first round group that featured Italy, Mexico, and Norway. They fell at the next hurdle, soundly beaten 2-0 in the last 16 by Holland at the Citrus Bowl Stadium in the midday humidity of Orlando, Florida.

BRAZILIAN BLEND FAITH AND FLAIR

Brazil, despite lacking the flair of some of their previous sides, boasted the most effective strike partnership of the tournament in the European-based pair of Bebeto and Romario. But a disappointing final against Italy ended scoreless, making it the first in the history of the World Cup to be settled by a penalty shoot-out.

The decisive kick was missed by Italian forward Roberto Baggio, whose goals had been crucial in taking his country all the way to the final at the Rose Bowl Stadium in Los Angeles, California.

Mario Zagallo, the assistant manager of Brazil to Carlos Alberto Parreira, became the first man to be involved in four World Cup winning teams, 20 years after his first attempt at gaining this distinction. Zagallo had been an invaluable outside left in Brazil's victorious teams at Sweden in 1958 and four years later in Chile. He successfully managed Brazil in 1970, but four years later his side crashed out to finish fourth.

ABOVE Consolation for Italy's Roberto Baggio after his decisive penalty miss

THE WORLD CUP

1998

Zinedine Zidane's distinctive balding head won France their first World Cup. The midfielder's headed goals, either side of half-time, were overshadowed by a Brazilian side subdued by striker Ronaldo's pre-match collapse.

THE RESULT 1998

Location: Paris
Final: France 3 Brazil 0
Shirts: France blue, Brazil yellow
Scorers: Zidane 2, Petit
Sent Off: Desailly

FRANCE

Barthez

Thuram Leboeuf Desailly Lizarazu

Petit Deschamps Karembeu Zidane
(Boghossian)
Djorkaeff
(Vieira)
Guivarc'h
(Dugarry)

Ronaldo Bebeto

Leonardo Rivaldo Dunga César Sampaio
(Denilson)   (Edmundo)

Carlos Baiano Aldair Cafu

Taffarel

BRAZIL

Internazionale striker Ronaldo had been a member of the 1994 Brazil squad, but did not play a game. Yet, by 1998 he was the team's key player and goal-scorer. But crucially, on the morning of the World Cup final, he collapsed in the hotel room that he shared with Roberto Carlos, and was taken to hospital for an emergency check-up.

Manager Mario Zagallo, not expecting Ronaldo to be available to play, named an official line-up that featured Edmundo in Ronaldo's place. Surprisingly, Ronaldo appeared in the line-up after being given the medical all-clear. Zagallo swiftly obtained FIFA clearance to alter the team line-up and later denied that he had been pressured into including Ronaldo by FIFA officials and/or sponsors. Although Ronaldo did play the entire match, he was never a force in the game and rarely threatened to add to his personal tally of four goals scored during the previous rounds.

Zidane's double and a last-minute third goal from midfielder Emmanuel Petit provided France with a comfortable victory in Saint-Denis, north of Paris. The 3-0 triumph was astonishing because the French side were reduced to ten men after defender Marcel Desailly was sent off.

Desailly's red card cost Thierry Henry an opportunity to make an appearance in the final. The striker had played in all the previous games and as a substitute was expected to play a part. But manager Aimé Jacquet opted to bring on a replacement defender for Desailly instead.

An earlier red card, in England's second round loss to Argentina, had already made David Beckham notorious. England had reached the finals by qualifying from a tough group that included Italy. Under the management of former international midfielder Glenn Hoddle, England had beaten Tunisia and Colombia in their first round group but finished in

RIGHT Referee Kim Milton Nielsen sends off England's David Beckham

second spot because of a 2-1 reversal to Romania. It proved a costly slip-up because it meant England had to tackle old rivals Argentina in the second round instead of Croatia.

England's Michael Owen, the outstanding new Liverpool striker, scored a superb solo goal, but early in the second half Manchester United midfielder Beckham was sent off by Danish referee Kim Morten Nielsen for flicking a retaliatory foot at the Argentinian midfielder Diego Simeone. England, without the influential Beckham, fought bravely and even had a potential winning 'goal' by defender Sol Campbell contentiously disallowed before they eventually succumbed in the lottery of a penalty shoot-out.

Argentina's midfielder Ariel Ortega was given his marching orders during their next game against Holland. Being reduced to ten men meant the same ultimate outcome of defeat. Holland progressed to the semi finals with a 2-1 win, courtesy of a superb winning goal from Arsenal striker Dennis Bergkamp – later voted the best goal of the finals.

WINNING FORMULA

Dutch luck finally ran out. In their semi-final they lost on a penalty shoot-out to Brazil while hosts France, gathering speed and confidence, sneaked past Croatia thanks to the first and second goals of defender Lilian Thuram's international career. France won despite finishing with ten men after Laurent Blanc was sent off after a tussle with Slaven Bilic.

Croatia went on to finish third on their debut at the finals, less than a decade after the country had gained independence out of the wreckage of the former Yugoslavia. Star striker Davor Suker ended up as the tournament's six-goal leading marksman to crown a remarkable season and win the coveted Golden Boot. Less than two months earlier, Suker had became a European club champion with Real Madrid following their slender 1-0 victory over Juventus in the Champions League final.

France went on to defeat Brazil and duly celebrate the triumph for which they had been waiting since fellow countryman Jules Rimet had launched the inaugural World Cup 68 years earlier. Thousands of delirious fans poured into central

Paris to celebrate, and the victorious team undertook an open-top bus parade the following day down the Champs-Elysées. Manager Aimé Jacquet, a former international midfielder, was delighted with the manner of victory because he had been subjected to a barrage of relentless criticism for his tactics and team selection by the daily sports newspaper *L'Equipe*.

Jacquet stepped down after the finals and handed over to assistant Roger Lemerre. The new manager proved that the World Cup triumph had been no fluke by leading France to a further international victory at the subsequent European Championships two years later with a 2-1 success over Italy.

BELOW Team-mates join Zinedine Zidane in celebrating his second goal against Brazil

THE WORLD CUP

2002

"We proved the World Cup belongs to everyone."

JAPAN'S HIDETOSHI NAKATA

Although the trophy went to hot favourites Brazil, the tournament was full of upsets. Holders France made a swift exit, while co-hosts South Korea stunned Portugal, Italy, and Spain to reach the semi-finals.

RIGHT Park Ji-sung of South Korea enjoys that winning feeling against Portugal

THE RESULT 2002

Location: Yokohama
Final: Brazil 2 Germany 0
Scorers: Ronaldo 2
Shirts: Brazil yellow, Germany white

South Korea were beaten to third place by Turkey, who had previously never progressed beyond the first round.

This was the first World Cup to be played in Asia. Japan had long been campaigning for the right to stage the finals, and one major step in their bid to impress the world authority FIFA had been the launch of the professional J-League in 1993.

Less than two years before the hosting decision, in 1996, the Japanese were challenged in the bidding race by neighbors South Korea. A major political battle within FIFA ended with a compromise that resulted in both countries being awarded the finals jointly. This decision meant that not only was the 2002 event the inaugural Asian finals but the first, and so far the only, World Cup finals to be co-hosted.

The co-hosting proved highly expensive for FIFA and highly complex in logistical terms. The match schedule for the finals had to be especially organised to ensure that each co-host played all matches in their country. In the end, the tournament organisation ran remarkably smoothly.

FRANCE FAIL TO SCORE A GOAL

Out on the pitch, the first of many shocks kicked off with the tournament's grand opening match. Defending champions France were narrowly beaten 1-0 by Senegal, who were making their debut in the finals. Midfielder Papa Bouba Diop

scored the goal for the impressive and organised Senegal side.

France may have been reigning world and European champions but, in a disastrous defence of their World Cup, they were knocked out in the first round without even scoring a goal in their three group games. It was the worst record of any defending nation in the tournament's history, although they were handicapped by the initial absence of Zinedine Zidane. The key midfielder had been injured in a warm-up friendly against South Korea on the eve of the finals. Manager Roger Lemerre, who had guided France, or 'Les Bleus,' to victory in the European Championship two years earlier, was fired on France's return home, despite having been awarded a contract extension before the finals.

The once-mighty Argentina also failed to make the second round, after finishing third in their group

behind England and table-topping Sweden. With memories of the 1998 World Cup penalty shoot-out still fresh in their memories, Argentina tackled England indoors at Tokyo's Sapporo Dome. England emerged as 1-0 winners courtesy of a penalty converted by David Beckham, who avenged his 1998 World Cup expulsion against the South Americans.

England were guided by Swede Sven-Göran Eriksson, their first foreign manager, and beat Denmark surprisingly easily 3-0 in the second round but then lost 2-1 to Brazil in the quarter-finals. The decisive goal was a long-range fluke shot from Ronaldinho that drifted over the head of helpless England keeper David Seaman. Ronaldinho was sent off in the 57th minute, but Brazil held onto their lead without the influential midfielder for both the rest of this contest and for their semi-final 1-0 victory over Turkey.

SEMI-FINAL SLOTS FILLED BY UNDERDOGS

Japan reached the second round before being eliminated 1-0 by Turkey, while South Korea made the most of their fervent home support to race into the semi-finals and finish fourth overall. South Korea were astutely organised by the Dutch coach Guus Hiddink and inspired by attacking

players such as Ahn Jung Hwan, whose extra-time goal beat Italy in a dramatic second round tie. Turkey had rarely appeared before in the finals of any major tournament, let alone the World Cup. But they made the most of this opportunity by reaching the semi-final stage. Veteran striker Hakan Sükür scored the fastest-ever goal in the World Cup by taking just 10.8 seconds to give Turkey the lead in a 3-2 win over South Korea in the third place play-off.

The final, played at the International Stadium Yokohama in Japan, belonged to Brazil's prolific striker Ronaldo. He scored twice against a competitive but uninspired German team that clearly missed their key midfielder Michael Ballack, who was suspended after collecting a second yellow card of the tournament in the semi-final.

Ronaldo finished the tournament as its eight-goal leading marksman to not only pick up the Golden Boot but to equal Pelé's Brazilian record of 12 goals overall in World Cup finals.

Oliver Kahn, Germany's captain, became the first goalkeeper to be voted as the best player of the tournament despite making a crucial error to concede the first goal in the final.

Cafu, Brazil's captain, also made history by becoming the first footballer to play in the final of three consecutive World Cups.

ABOVE Ronaldo scores Brazil's first goal after a mistake by goalkeeper Oliver Kahn

BELOW David Seaman is fooled by Ronaldinho's long shot

THE WORLD CUP

2006

Italy collected their fourth World Cup, although the final will always be associated with Zinedine Zidane's violent act. The French master was aiming for a fairytale ending to his illustrious career, but instead bowed out disgracefully.

THE RESULT 2006

Location: Berlin
Final: Italy 1 France 1 (after extra time, Italy 5-3 penalties)
Shirts: Italy blue, France white
Scorers: Materazzi; Zidane (pen)
Sent Off: Zidane

ITALY

Buffon

Grosso Cannavaro Materazzi Zambrotta

Camoranesi Gattuso Pirlo Perrotta
(Del Piero)   (De Rossi)

Totti Toni
(Iaquinta)

Henry Zidane
(Wiltord)

Malouda Vieira Makélélé Ribéry
(Diarra)   (Trezeguet)

Abidal Gallas Thuram Sagnol

Barthez

FRANCE

The final pitched France against Italy in Berlin's Olympic Stadium and saw Real Madrid midfielder Zinedine Zidane give France the lead with a cheeky penalty, in what was to be his final game before retiring from the sport.

Italy equalised through a header from rugged central defender Marco Materazzi, which sent the game into extra-time. With ten minutes of extra time and the contest still at stalemate, Zidane suddenly launched his head into Materazzi's chest and was sent off for violent conduct by the Argentinian referee Horacio Elizondo.

Subdued France had no Zidane to help them in the penalty shoot-out. Italy, coached by Marcello Lippi, became the second side to win the World Cup on penalties after the French striker David Trezeguet hit the bar with his attempt.

Despite such a disgraceful end to his career, Zidane was voted player of the tournament because of his efforts in masterminding victories over Spain, Brazil, and Portugal to reach the final.

Italy proved to be the tournament's most consistent team, largely thanks to the contributions of the outstanding goalkeeper Gianluigi Buffon, defender and captain Fabio Cannavaro, and influential midfielder Andrea Pirlo.

Their success was all the more dramatic since it occurred at the same time as a trial in Italy, in which senior figures in club football were being accused and found guilty of systemic match-fixing. Juventus official, Luciano Moggi, was the controversial central figure in the corruption scandal. Five of Italy's successful squad and seven other World Cup players returned to Italy after the tournament to find that their club had been

relegated to Serie B as punishment. The once mighty trio of Juventus, Lazio, and Fiorentina were demoted.

Italy had beaten Germany 2-0 during extra-time at the semi-final stage. The hosts had been one of the most exciting teams to watch under the guidance of former striker Jürgen Klinsmann.

KLINSMANN LEADS GERMAN REVIVAL

The German federation had appointed Klinsmann, a World Cup winner in 1990, as coach in the summer of 2004, following their nation's disappointing showing at the UEFA European Championship. Klinsmann demanded a free hand, which included the right to continue to live in California and bring in his choice of new staff – coaches, assistants, and fitness experts. His approach drew initial scepticism among other coaches and fans. By the time the World Cup finals started, it became clear that Klinsmann was winning fans with his tactics and approach to matches.

Germany made an adventurous – and, crucially, winning – start, by defeating Costa Rica 4-2 in the opening game. New heroes included young striker Lukas Podolski and defender Philipp Lahm. Ultimately, the German effort was halted in a semi-final in Dortmund by Italy in what was arguably the finest game of the tournament. Italy snatched victory through last-gasp goals in extra-time from Fabio Grosso and Alessandro Del Piero.

The Germans scored a 3-1 third place play-off win over Portugal, resulting in a far better finish to their campaign than many home fans had feared.

DULL ENGLAND SUFFER ON SPOT-KICKS

In contrast to the Germans, England's World Cup performances were dreary, in Sven-Göran Eriksson's third and last tournament as national coach. The quarter-finals were once again the end of the road as England lost on penalties for the second time in three World Cups, beaten by Portugal in a shoot-out for the second time in a row – after a similar finish in the 2004 UEFA European Championship held in Portugal.

England's hopes had been hindered by a pre-tournament foot injury to star striker Wayne Rooney, which delayed his arrival. Then fellow striker Michael Owen was seriously injured during a freak accident in a group game against Sweden.

Rooney was sent off for stamping on defender Ricardo Carvalho during the quarter-final contest. Cristiano Ronaldo, Rooney's Manchester United team-mate, endured a hate campaign on his return to English football after having been caught smiling and winking at the Portuguese bench following Rooney's expulsion.

Portugal's progress was ended by France, who inflicted a 1-0 semi-final defeat in a lacklustre match through Zidane's 33rd-minute penalty.

South America's challenge ended in the quarter-finals. In the group stage, a surprisingly adventurous Argentina had contributed the goal of the tournament against Serbia & Montenegro, a 24-pass move finished by Esteban Cambiasso. But they lost to Germany on penalties in the quarter-finals while Brazil lost their hold on the trophy at the same stage by a 1-0 reversal to France.

German striker Miroslav Klose finished top scorer with five goals, the lowest tally since 1962, for the winner of the Golden Boot.

BELOW Italy's Marco Materazzi acclaims his equaliser in the final

BOTTOM Zinedine Zidane beats Gigi Buffon to open the score for France

THE WORLD CUP

2010

Spain lifted their first World Cup at a tournament where attractive, attacking football emerged triumphant for the major European sides.

THE RESULT 2010

Location: Johannesburg
Final: Holland 0 Spain 1
Shirts: Holland orange, Spain navy blue
Scorers: Iniesta
Sent Off: Heitinga

HOLLAND

Stekelenburg

Van der Wiel Heitinga Mathijsen Van Bronckhorst

Van Bommel De Jong Sneijder

Robben Van Persie Kuyt

Pedro Villa Iniesta

Alonso Xavi Busquets

Ramos Pique Puyol Capdevila

Casillas

SPAIN

RIGHT Frank Lampard's shot clearly bounces over the German line, but the goal was not given

The final itself should have been a marvellous spectacle as the Spanish, already the European champions, came up against Holland, who had won all their matches en route to the final in Johannesburg, eliminating Brazil and surprise package Uruguay along the way. However, rather than trying to outplay the Spanish, which with stars like Wesley Sneijder and Arjen Robben in their team was not impossible, Dutch coach Bert van Marwijk sent his side out to nullify their opposition. This made for an underwhelming and at times brutal contest, with referee Howard Webb dishing out 14 yellow cards and dismissing Holland's Jonny Heitinga for a second booking.

Eventually settled by Andres Iniesta's winner four minutes from the end of extra-time, the 2010 final will not be remembered as a classic.

It confirmed Spain as worthy champions, despite a 1-0 loss in their opening game to Switzerland. They recovered well with wins over Honduras and Chile, then three consecutive 1-0 wins over Portugal, Paraguay and Germany booked them a place in their first World Cup final and allowed Iniesta to consign the Dutch to a third final defeat without ever having lifted the trophy.

Hosts South Africa had started the party with a 1-1 draw against Mexico, but would go on to become the first home team in a World Cup not to progress from the group stage. They were dumped out despite beating the troubled French, whose players had gone on strike against manager Raymond Domenech's coaching methods.

Argentina had looked like early contenders under Diego Maradona's leadership, picking up maximum points from their group, while Brazil and Portugal emerged ahead of Ivory Coast in what was regarded as the 'group of death'. The

Portuguese hit whipping boys North Korea for seven, the tournament's greatest margin of victory, but their journey would end at the last 16.

Germany were given an early scare when they lost to Serbia, but recovered to book their place in the knockout stages. They would go on to thrash an underperforming England in the first knockout round, although it could all have been different had the assistant referee seen Frank Lampard's long-range drive bounce well over the German goal-line before bouncing back into play. Germany progressed to meet Argentina in the quarter-final, where their performance in a 4-0 win led many to tip Joachim Low's enterprising young side as potential winners.

Indeed, the South American giants were not faring so well and Brazil were eliminated by the Netherlands, who came from behind to win 2-1, though they were helped on their way by an own goal and a red card to Felipe Melo. Both Maradona and Dunga, playing greats in their respective countries, would leave their coaching jobs after the tournament.

It was left to Uruguay to carry the South American flag, though their campaign will be remembered for Luis Suarez's controversial handball against Ghana in the quarter-finals. With the score tied at 1-1 in the dying moments of extra-time, the forward handled a goalbound header on the line and was subsequently sent off. Asamoah Gyan then missed the penalty for the Ghanaians, who passed up the chance to become the first African side ever to make the last four. Uruguay won the shootout, and not for the first time in his career, Suarez had won few friends.

Minus Suarez's talents, the Uruguayans were undone by two goals in three minutes from Sneijder and Robben, after Gio van Bronckhorst and the excellent Diego Forlan had set the game up for an exciting finale. Maxi Pereira pulled one back late on, but it was the Dutch who would march on to their first final since 1978.

It would be an all-European encounter, with their opponents to come from either Spain or Germany, who had also contested the Euro 2008 final two years earlier.

Once again, the Spaniards would win 1-0 and deservedly so. They controlled the game for long periods, with Low's bold side unable to get a grip on the game or create the chances they had in their earlier fixtures. As they did in 2006, the Germans would finish third thanks to a 3-2 win over Uruguay in Port Elizabeth.

That game featured the men voted the tournament's best player, Diego Forlan, and best young player, Thomas Muller, they also shared the golden boot along with David Villa and Wesley Sneijder. All four scored five goals during the course of the tournament.

ABOVE Luis Suarez handles the ball on the line, denying Ghana a goal. Ghana would then miss the crucial penalty

BELOW Spain celebrate their first World Cup triumph in Johannesburg

THE WORLD CUP

2014

A World Cup held in Brazil was always going to be a mouth-watering prospect for the fans and footballers alike. Five-time winners of the competition, Brazil had not hosted the tournament since 1950. The country and its national team had a huge legacy to live up to.

ABOVE Brazil line up and sing their national anthem at the 2014 World Cup

With 201 million expectant Brazilians watching their national team's every move, pressure was on the 'Samba Boys' to perform from the outset. But before a ball was even kicked, Brazil had to prove it could provide the necessary number of stadiums and stop social unrest in the country from boiling over.

The tournament's build-up was blighted by construction delays and subsequent accidents, as Brazil tried to ready its 12 host cities in time for the June 12 kick-off. The £4.7bn ($8bn), which officials had promised to spend on the country's stadiums, infrastructure and transport links, was seen as an extravagant waste of money by many

Brazilians. Only days before the tournament started, there were violent clashes with police, as "Our Cup is on the Street" protesters targeted the high cost of the stadiums and political corruption.

The protests continued during the competition's first match and rocks were hurled from the street at the windows of TV studios in Rio de Janeiro, as the pundits cowered inside. However, Brazilian commentators speculated that the protests would turn to celebrations if Brazil won the first match. Their predictions proved to be correct and further protests were relegated to the periphery of the tournament as the group stages got underway.

GROUP STAGES

The group stages provided goals and upsets galore. This was heralded by an unexpected 5-1 Dutch trouncing over Group B rivals and World Cup holders, Spain. After also winning Euro 2008 and the World Cup in 2012, expectations were high that Spain could recover from their loss. Instead, they suffered a 2-0 defeat to Chile, and were sent home in humiliation, as Chile and the Netherlands progressed to the last 16. Despite nearly beating the Netherlands, Australia were also sent home.

Brazil had been unconvincing in Group A, especially after their first goal of the tournament was an own goal scored by defender Marcelo. However, wonder boy Neymar proved that his billing had been worth all the hype by scoring at pivotal moments to see his side top the group. Following Brazil into the last 16 was the team that held them to a 0-0 draw, Mexico. Group A's Cameroon and Croatia were sent home.

The big story of Group C was Colombia. Thanks to striker James Rodriguez, they sailed past opposition teams Greece, Ivory Coast and Japan to become group winners. Unexpectedly taking second place was Greece, which played a largely defensive game with centre-back Konstas Manolas at its heart.

Group E played out largely as expected, with France and Switzerland coming first and second respectively, to the detriment of Ecuador and Honduras. In Group F, Lionel Messi once again showed he had the necessary talent to rescue Argentina and make them group winners. In second place was Nigeria, which didn't back down under the scrutiny of group losers, Bosnia-Herzegovina and Iran.

Another Cup upset came courtesy of the USA, which pipped Portugal to the post on goal difference to come second in the group underneath winners, Germany. Germany had started off their campaign with a 4-0 drubbing over Portugal, who seemed to have failed to show up for the tournament. Ghana had little time to feature during the melee.

Belgium were tipped to be the 'dark horses' of Group H, but Kompany, Fellaini, Hazard and co. failed to impress, while still doing enough to top the group. They were unexpectedly joined by Algeria, who showed that grit and determination could go a long way, beating favourites Russia and South Korea into the last 16.

Nobody would have predicted that rank outsiders Costa Rica would beat former World Cup champions Uruguay, Italy and England to top Group D. Led by standout players Keylor Navas and Joel Campbell, Costa Rica showed that passion and team tactics were enough to provide stunning football and the required result. England sank to a new low with two losses and one draw, in the country's worst World Cup performance since 1958. Luis Suarez managed to produce the goals needed to see Uruguay qualify for the knockout round, although a scandalous incident would ensure Suarez himself would not progress with his team.

SUAREZ SCANDAL

Suarez had twice been punished for biting opposition players during club football matches for Ajax and Liverpool, but nobody expected a return

of this behaviour on the world stage. Nevertheless, during Uruguay's last group match against Italy, Suarez ran into the six-yard box and bit centre-back Giorgio Chiellini on his shoulder.

Although Chiellini pulled down his shirt to expose Suarez's teeth marks to the referee, no action was taken against the striker at the time. However, within minutes close-up images of the teeth-marks were posted across the internet and were making international headlines across the globe.

FIFA punished Suarez retrospectively for the bite with a nine-match ban, suspension from all football related activity for four months, and a 100,000 Swiss franc fine. Despite the incident, Suarez was signed by Barcelona for £75 million ($128million) three days before the World Cup final.

ABOVE Luis Suarez holds his teeth after biting Italian centre-back, Giorgio Chiellini

2014

RIGHT USA goalkeeper, Tim Howard, makes another save against Belgium

LAST 16

The 2014 World Cup's last 16 was arguably one of the most exciting in the tournament's history. Five out of its eight matches went to extra-time, with two ending in a penalty shoot-out.

The USA put up a valiant effort against Belgium, as chants of 'USA' boomed around the stadium and President Obama watched from Air Force One. But despite goalkeeper Tim Howard's 16 record-breaking saves, he was unable to stop Lukaku's 105th minute winner and Belgium's 2-1 victory.

Colombia's James Rodriguez continued his glut of goals by netting twice to knock out Uruguay, a team in disarray following suspended Luis Suarez's biting scandal. Argentina, perhaps predictably, saw off Switzerland, although it took until the 118th minute for Angel Di Maria to find the only goal of the match.

It was the first time Algeria had reached the last 16 in a World Cup, although it was little surprise they were then knocked out by Germany. More

surprising, however, was that it took Germany until the last minute of extra-time to muster their 2-1 victory. France saw off Nigeria with a 2-0 win, although the first goal was a late 79th minute strike by Paul Pogba, and the second a 91st minute own goal by Joseph Yobo.

A ten-man Costa Rica led Greece by one goal, until Sokratis Papastathopoulos equalised in the 91st minute. Costa Rica then won 5-3 in a penalty shoot-out. Brazil and Chile also finished with a penalty decider, after Chilean Mauricio Pinilla's shot in the dying seconds of normal time was denied by the crossbar. In the end, Brazil won 3-2 on penalties.

The Round of 16's biggest upset looked likely to occur between the Netherlands and Mexico, but the Dutch snaffled the match 2-1 following a 94th minute goal, courtesy of a controversial penalty.

QUARTER-FINALS

While the competition had largely been an end-to-end goal fest, it would take a different turn at the quarter-finals. Germany beat France 1-0 in a messy and nervous game where neither side was at its best. Belgium were similarly unable to create a meaningful effort against Argentina, whose 7th minute Higuain goal saw them through to the semi-finals.

In what was tipped to be a formality for the Netherlands, they were held to a draw by Costa Rica. Then, substitute Dutch keeper Tim Krul saved two Costa Rican penalties in the shoot-out, which won the Netherlands the match 4-3.

Brazil would beat Colombia 2-1, but it was a fraught game filled with a World Cup record of 54 fouls. Ironically, only four yellow cards were shown, which led to criticism that referee Carlos Velasco Carballo had not been in control of the footballers' aggressive play. A heartbreaking example of this occurred when Colombian Juan Zúñiga leapt knee-first into Neymar's back and broke one of his vertebrae. While Zúñiga went unpunished for the foul, Neymar's injury finished his World Cup early.

SEMI-FINALS

Nobody expected a Brazilian semi-final against Germany to end in the country's worst ever defeat, but at the full-time whistle, the scoreboard told the tale: 7-1.

From the beginning, the Brazilian players were subject to a German masterclass that put the visitors 5-0 up within the first 29 minutes of play. Clearly about to suffer Brazil's first competitive home defeat in 39 years, the players came off looking shell-shocked at half time, only to suffer two more humiliating goals before the final whistle. Miroslav Klose, Toni Kroos, Sami Khedira, Thomas Muller and Andre Schurrle were the architects of the host nation's downfall. A last minute Brazilian goal by Oscar was met with sarcastic applause by those spectators at the Estadio Mineirao who had not already departed.

The margin of defeat equalled Brazil's 6-0 loss to Uruguay in the 1920 Copa America, but the day will forever be remembered alongside the 1950 World Cup final defeat by Uruguay, as the worst in its footballing history, dubbed a 'historic humiliation.'

While the Brazil/Germany semi-final provided shock and amazement, the match between Argentina and the Netherlands was an exercise in tedium. For 120 minutes neither side could create a convincing shot on target and the match went to a penalty shoot-out. The first penalty-taker and arguably the best Dutch player on the night, Ron Vlaar, could not convert his kick and Argentina went on to a 4-2 victory.

THE FINAL

A fitting end to what many pundits described as the best World Cup in memory was to have footballing titans Argentina and Germany face each other in Rio De Janeiro's Maracana Stadium.

The weight of expectation was on Lionel Messi's shoulders to produce something spectacular. Instead, he squandered his one clear goalscoring opportunity by dragging the ball wide rather than into the back of the net. Gonzalo Higuain also missed a sitter against Manuel Neuer and had a goal disallowed. It was not to be Argentina's night. As the match approached the end of extra-time, Andre Schürrle set up Mario Götze for a stunning volley into the Argentine net.

The 1-0 victory was Germany's fourth World Cup win and the first since West Germany in 1990. It also marked the first time that a European team had won the tournament in the Americas. Europe now holds 11 World Cups to South America's nine.

2014 WORLD CUP AWARDS

Golden Ball: Lionel Messi (Arg)

Golden Boot: James Rodriguez (Col)

Golden Glove: Manuel Neuer (Ger)

Best Young Player: Paul Pogba (Fra)

FIFA Fair Play Trophy: Colombia

BELOW Germany striker, Miroslav Klose, takes on Brazil defender, David Luiz

2014 STAR PLAYERS

The World Cup gives the best players on Earth the chance to shine on the greatest footballing stage. Those who overcome the weight of national expectation to perform well can expect their names to be forever etched into the history books alongside the greats of the game.

NEYMAR (BRAZIL)

Before a ball was even kicked at the 2014 World Cup, Neymar was heralded as the wonder boy who could win it for Brazil. At 22 years of age, Neymar had played nearly 50 matches for his country, was its highest paid footballer, and also given the heady honour of wearing the number 10 shirt. So when the whistle blew for Brazil's first match against Croatia, 201 million Brazilians waited expectantly for Neymar to live up to his billing.

In a World Cup where international superstars, such as Ronaldo, failed to emerge, it would have been no surprise if Neymar had turned in an sub-par performance. But instead he thrived on the world stage. He scored a pivotal two goals against Croatia to win the match 3-1, and again two goals against Cameroon to see Brazil through to the last 16. Here, the match against Chile went to a penalty shoot-out and with the score tied at 2-2, it was Neymar who took Brazil's final regulation kick. With the weight of the country again on his shoulders, Neymar's ball found the back of the net and Brazil were through once more.

Neymar's career is a tale of living up to expectations. Born Neymar da Silva Santos Jr. on February 5, 1992 to a former professional football player, Neymar joined Santos FC's youth squad at 11. By 2013, he had won four consecutive Player of the Year awards and helped Santos claim three league titles. In May 2013, Neymar signed to Barcelona FC on a five-year deal reportedly worth 87.2 million euros, with a release clause of 190 million.

While Neymar faces a bright future for his club and country, his World Cup campaign ended prematurely during the quarter-final match against Colombia. Here, Juan Zúñiga broke a vertebrae in Neymar's back during an aggressive challenge. Brazil had to face Germany in the semi-final without their talismanic striker.

ARJEN ROBBEN (NETHERLANDS)

The Netherlands' forward Arjen Robben featured in the 2014 World Cup for two reasons: one, for his skillful bursts of speed that often resulted in a goal; and two, for his diving controversies.

Robben's World Cup campaign began brightly with two goals in the Netherlands' 5-1 trouncing of Spain in their first match of the tournament. Robben struck again in the Netherlands' second group stage match by scoring the opening goal in the team's 3-2 victory over Australia. Then,

ABOVE The injured Neymar had to sit out Brazil's defeats in the semi-finals and third-place play-off matches

the Netherlands' last 16 game with Mexico was controversially won from a penalty, after Robben went down during a challenge by Rafael Marquez. Robben insisted the foul was genuine, but then admitted to a Dutch television channel that he had taken a dive.

Born on 23 January, 1984, and turning professional in 2000, Robben is no stranger to performing on the most prominent football stages. After playing for Dutch clubs Groningen and PSV, he joined Chelsea in 2004 and helped the club win two consecutive Premier League titles. In 2007, he signed for Real Madrid for £35 million, and then Bayern Munich for £25 million in 2009. Robben has won numerous national league and Champions League titles, as well as Man of the Match for games during three consecutive World Cups.

Robben's form continued in the 2014 World Cup quarter-final against Costa Rica, when his penalty kick helped secure the Netherlands eventual 4-3 win, but he was unable to stop a defeat to Argentina in the semi-finals.

LEFT Dutch forward, Arjen Robben, dribbles at speed at the 2014 World Cup

2014 STAR PLAYERS

LIONEL MESSI (ARGENTINA)

It was often said before the World Cup began that Argentina's fate rested with one man: Lionel Messi. Arguably the best footballer of the last 10 years, alongside Portugal's Ronaldo, Messi led Argentina to a 2-1 victory over Bosnia and Herzegovina in their first 2014 World Cup match. His two goals were a relief to fans, as they marked the striker's first World Cup goals since his debut at the 2006 tournament.

Messi scored his 40th international goal in Argentina's next match against Iran; a long, curling strike from 25 yards out. The striker's 4th tournament goal came in a 3-2 victory over Nigeria, which ensured Argentina came at the top of their group. Messi also assisted the only goal of Argentina's last 16 match, scored by Angel Di Maria in the 118th minute. During Argentina's 1-0 quarter-final win against Belgium, Messi was able to equal the 91 caps won by the country's most iconic footballer: Diego Maradona.

Born on 24 June 1987 and turning professional in 2003, Messi has often been compared to the great Maradona. A Barcelona FC player for the whole of his career, Messi has won more awards and broken more records than can be printed on this page. They include: 4 FIFA Ballon d'Ors; 3 European Golden Shoe Awards; the most goals scored for a single Spanish club (400); the most club goals scored in one year (91); the most international goals scored in one year (25). Messi is also one of the richest footballers in world, with his personal earnings reaching over 47 million euros for the 12 months up to May 2014 alone.

Messi' converted the first kick in a penalty shoot-out with the Netherlands in the semi-final, which helped secure Argentina's 4-2 win. Unfortunately he was not able to save his team from a 0-1 loss against Germany in the final. He did, however, win the competition's Golden Ball award.

KARIM BENZEMA (FRANCE)

Karim Benzema began France's World Cup tournament in impressive style. He scored two goals in the opening game against Honduras, and added another goal to France's 5-2 demolition of Switzerland. When played in his favoured central striker role, Benzema looked a likely candidate to

BELOW RIGHT Karim Benzema strikes the ball in a World Cup match

ABOVE Lionel Messi listens to the national anthems at the start of the 2014 World Cup final

LEFT Giancarlo Gonzalez makes a decisive sliding tackle against the Netherlands, in the quarter-finals

lead his country to success.

Born on December 19, 1987, Karim Mostafa Benzema began his professional playing career for Ligue I club Lyon in 2004. Benzema had his breakthrough season in 2007-08 when he scored 30 goals for Lyon and helped the side to its seventh consecutive league title. Benzema went on to be named the National Union of Professional Footballer Ligue I Player of the Year, and attracted the attention of La Liga's Real Madrid, which signed Benzema in for £35 million in 2009.

After a mixed first season with Real Madrid, Benzema rose to prominence at the club with 32 goals in the 2011-12 season, which helped the side win the Copa del Rey and the league title. Benzema played his first senior match for France in 2007 and has since earned over 65 caps for his country. He has represented his country at the 2008 and 2012 Euros and has twice been named French Player of the Year in, 2011 and 2012.

Benzema is known for his strength and power inside the box, which he combines with great technical ability to net a large number of goals. He is arguably at his most potent when played in a traditional centre-forward role, but is also capable of playing on either wing.

Despite being a pivotal part of France's progression through the 2014 World Cup group stages and the Round of 16, Benzema was not able to prevent a 1-0 defeat by Germany in the quarter-finals. The striker made a valiant strike in injury time that would have seen the match through to a penalty shoot-out, but he was denied by keeper Manual Neuer. France, like Brazil who were to follow in the semi-finals, were to find themselves flattened by the German juggernaut.

GIANCARLO GONZALEZ (COSTA RICA)

Costa Rica started off their 2014 World Cup as rank outsiders at best, but then surprised the world by beating off England, Italy and Uruguay to become winners of Group D. While the players were praised for their outstanding team effort, their success would not have been possible without the contribution of central defender Giancarlo Gonzalez.

Combined with fellow defenders Michael Umana and Oscar Duarte, Gonzalez managed to hold off waves of attacks from Uruguay and Italy to let through only one goal and win the matches 3-1 and 1-0 respectively. The following 0-0 shutout of England gave them complete dominance over their group rivals, and the country's progression to the last 16 was largely considered a result of Gonzalez's defensive efforts and his success in marshalling Costa Rica's back-line.

Born on February 8th 1988, Gonzalez started his professional club career with Costa Rica's L.D. Alajuelense in 2007. After helping L.D. Alajuelense to win three league titles, Gonzalez signed for Norwegian side Valerenga in 2012 and then American MLS side Columbus Crew in 2014.

Gonzalez played his first match for his national side in 2010 and has since gone on to play in 35 matches. He was named in ESPN's Best XI of the Group Stage and was one of the penalty-takers who successfully converted against Greece to beat them 5-3 in their last 16 match. However, even Gonzalez's high number of interceptions was not enough to prevent a heartbreaking exit to the Netherlands in the quarter-finals, which they lost 4-3 on penalties.

2014 STAR PLAYERS

ABOVE James Rodriguez celebrates scoring one of his six World Cup goals

JAMES RODRIGUEZ (COLOMBIA)

With their superstar striker Radamel Falcao unable to attend the World Cup due to a pre-season injury, nobody was expecting much from underdogs Colombia. Then James 'El Nino' Rodriguez stepped forward – a 22-year-old attacking-midfielder who charmed football fans everywhere with his outlandish goalscoring and boyish grin.

By the end of the group stages, Rodriguez had scored five goals and lifted his team past the Ivory Coast, Japan and Uruguay and into the quarter-finals – the first time Colombia had ever done so at a World Cup. Even at that early stage in the tournament, Rodriguez's five goals had made him Colombia's top scorer at a World Cup.

Rodriguez's stepfather took him to his first football match at five, and he often played on the pitch as a youngster with boys older than him. Even at an early age Rodriguez displayed the same precocious talent and determination that led him onto the world stage in 2014.

At 15, Rodriguez began his professional playing career for Colombian club side Envigado, before moving to Portuguese club Porto in 2010, where he played alongside countrymen Radamel Falcao and Jackson Martinez, and won three league titles. In 2013, Rodriguez was signed by Monaco for 45 million euros, making him one of the most expensive players in the world.

Rodriguez will be forever linked with one of the 2014 World Cup's most memorable goals – a stunning volley against Uruguay, described by Uruguay manager Oscar Tabarez as "One of the greatest goals the World Cup has ever seen." But despite scoring a late penalty in the quarter-finals – his 6th tournament goal – Rodriguez was unable to prevent Colombia being knocked out by host nation, Brazil. However, winning the Golden Boot award must have provided Rodriguez with some consolation.

ALEXIS SANCHEZ (CHILE)

Although Chile were knocked out on penalties by Brazil in the last 16 stage of the World Cup, Alexis Sanchez was the best example of the gallant Chilean display that could have easily won them the match. Sanchez's mesmerising trickery and pace helped lead several Chilean advances that ended in the equalising goal to take the game beyond normal playing time. Cruelly, Sanchez was one of three Chilean players that failed to convert their penalties, which ultimately lost them the match.

Despite being knocked out of the World Cup, Sanchez remained one of the most memorable and popular players of the tournament, not just for his speed and accuracy in front of goal, but also his assists and unselfish team play.

Born in 1988, Sanchez began his professional career at Chilean club Cobreloa in 2005, before being signed by Italy's Udinese Calcio in 2006. He was then loaned out to Chile's Colo-Colo for one season followed by a second loan season at Argentina's River Plate. He then retuned to play with Udinese in Serie A until he was signed by Barcelona in 2011, becoming the first Chilean in history to play for the Spanish club. The 26 million Euro fee also made the Sanchez transfer the most expensive in Chilean football history.

Sanchez's value as a player was neatly summed up by then-Barcelona manager Pep Guardiola before Sanchez even arrived:

"He can play in all three attacking positions, he shows intense defensive skills, he's direct and from what I've been told, he's a very nice kid."

In July 2014, Sanchez was signed by London club Arsenal in a deal worth around £32 million.

GUILLERMO OCHOA (MEXICO)

Guillermo Ochoa arrived at the World Cup a seemingly unlikely candidate for most memorable goalkeeper of the tournament. For one, he came to the competition unemployed after finishing his contract with club side Ajaccio and becoming a free agent. Secondly, although capped 63 times for his national side, Mexico, Ochoa was virtually unknown on the international football stage outside of the Americas. Nevertheless, the 28-year-old keeper, astounded players and fans alike by stopping some of the best shots of the tournament.

After the first three matches of the group stage, which included opponents Cameroon and Brazil, Ochoa had only let in one goal, which occurred during a 3-1 win over Croatia. His save against a Neymar header during the Brazil match drew particular attention, including praise from Brazil's manager Luiz Felipe Scolari.

Born in 1985, Ochoa made his professional debut for Mexican club side América in 2004. He made over 200 appearances for the team until being sold to French club Ajaccio in 2011. He then spent three seasons with Ajaccio before it was relegated from Ligue 1 in 2014. Ochoa has been a Mexican international since 2005, playing as the third-choice keeper in the 2006 World Cup and the second-choice keeper in the 2010 World Cup. But despite his best efforts to stop the opposition shots getting through, Ochoa was unable to stop a 2-1 Mexican defeat to the Netherlands in the knockout round. Despite losing the game and being eliminated from the competition, Ochoa was awarded man of the match for the second time in the tournament.

ABOVE Ochoa makes another vital save at the 2014 World Cup

LEFT Alexis Sanchez takes a breather after a World Cup match

2014 WINNERS AND LOSERS

The reality of every World Cup is that some countries fare better than others. Amidst the twists and turns of the tournament many teams overcome their nerves – and often the odds – to rise to the top and perform. Other teams sink straight to the bottom.

ABOVE Spain walk off the pitch and out of the 2014 World Cup

THE LOSERS

SPAIN

Before the teams arrived in Brazil, there was serious speculation that Spain – winners of the 2008 and 2012 Euros and the 2010 World Cup – might be able to do it again. After all, the country's national side had won 17 of their last 19 tournament matches, and their tiki-taka style of football was a formidable weapon when wielded by the side's extended array of talented footballers. But instead they were defeated 5-1 by the Netherlands in their first match, and then 2-0 by Chile in their second. A 3-0 win over Australia did little to soften the blow of this once great side's ignominious World Cup demise. Football fans everywhere gasped at the first great upset of the 2014 World Cup: Spain was going home in disgrace after being unable to progress past the group stage.

ENGLAND

England arrived for their first match in the sticky heat of Manaus with the nervous expectation from their fans at home that they would, at the very least, reach the last 16. Instead, the team defied the predictions of the country's greatest pessimists by losing all but one of its group matches, the other of which they drew.

The Three Lions' 2014 scoresheet was added to the pile of recent failures since the 1966 World Cup but still made for uneasy reading: 1-2 Italy, 1-2 Uruguay, 0-0 Costa Rica. Ironically, the killing blow came from Uruguayan striker Luis Suarez, who outdid his ex-Liverpool club side captain Steven Gerrard to score a second goal. Suarez, the Premier League's PFA 2014 Footballer of the Year, would be out of the World Cup himself two matches later.

RIGHT England are dejected after their 0-0 draw with Costa Rica.

England was left with a long plane journey home and hollow hopes about creating a winning side sometime in the future. "I think there is a real chance that we can develop and win in 2022 – that is the aim," said FA chairman Greg Dyke.

ITALY

Four-times winner of the World Cup, Italy, has proved a powerful adversary in the past. The national team had most recently held the cup aloft in 2006, and with international stars like Andrea Pirlo and Mario Balotelli on board, its presence could not be discounted. However, since its 2006 win, Italy had suffered from horrendous World Cup form. In 2010 and 2014 the country played six matches, won one, drew two, and lost three. Sadly the losing streak continued in Brazil. Italy beat England, but then lost 0-1 to both Costa Rica and Uruguay. The players of this once great footballing nation were also on an early flight home.

THE WINNERS

COSTA RICA

With odds of 4,000-to-1 to win the tournament, there were few bets on Costa Rica to produce their best performance in World Cup history and progress past the Group Stage. This sentiment was strengthened by the fact Group D also contained previous World Cup winners Italy, England and Uruguay. But Costa Rica's 'Los Ticos' confounded logic and popular expectation to not only win the group, but also ensure their best ever World Cup finish by beating Greece in the last 16.

Costa Rica's astounding run seemed to take nothing away from the footballers' energy levels or team spirit during their quarter-final match with the Netherlands. Keeper Keylor Navas was the hero of the night, denying the Netherlands a normal time win, but stand-out forwards Bryan Ruiz and Joel Campbell were equally unable to create a goal at the other end. Costa Rica went out 4-3 on penalties on the night, but returned home to their country of 4.5 million people to a champion's welcome.

ALGERIA

Placed in a group with Russia, Belgium and South Korea, it was widely considered that Algeria was only at the World Cup to make up the numbers. Instead, 'Les Fennecs' (the Desert Foxes) reached second place in the group and scored a higher number of goals than in their previous three World Cup tournaments combined – 6.

Algeria went on to produce a valiant effort against Germany in the last 16, but they were outdone by a goal in extra-time. However, Algeria had progressed further than any side in its World Cup history and deserved its place on the international stage.

GERMANY

Germany's 1-0 win over Argentina in the Final gave the country its fourth World Cup – placing it alongside Italy and below only Brazil, which has five. Germany's 7-1 trouncing of Brazil in the semi-final was a good indication of the country's rise to power and a portent of its likely future domination of the sport.

The country had worked for many years from grass-roots level up, to establish a new carefully thought-out footballing ideology to be played by its home-grown players. This long-term approach resulted in the 'golden generation' of young footballers that include Mesut Özil, Sami Khedira, Mario Götze and Toni Kroos. It is these now senior World Cup players combined with those rising up through the Bundesliga that will make Germany such an interesting proposition at the 2018 World Cup in Russia.

ABOVE Algeria's Faouzi Ghoulam strikes the ball in the last-16 match against Germany

BELOW Costa Rica goalkeeper, Keylor Navas, celebrates another good team performance

THE WORLD CUP
2014 RESULTS

GROUP A

Brazil

Mexico

Croatia

Cameroon

SECOND ROUND 1

Brazil 1

**WINNER A
V
RUNNER-UP B**

Chile 1

(Brazil win 3-2 on penalties)

GROUP B

Netherlands

Chile

Spain

Australia

SECOND ROUND 2

Netherlands 2

**WINNER B
V
RUNNER-UP A**

Mexico 1

GROUP C

Colombia

Greece

Ivory Coast

Japan

SECOND ROUND 3

Colombia 2

**WINNER C
V
RUNNER-UP D**

Uruguay 0

GROUP D

Costa Rica

Uruguay

Italy

England

SECOND ROUND 4

Costa Rica 1

**WINNER D
V
RUNNER-UP C**

Greece 1

(Costa Rica win 5-3 on penalties)

2014 WORLD CUP FINAL

SEMI-FINAL WINNER 1

Germany 1

(After extra-time)

QUARTER-FINAL 1

Brazil 2

**WINNER ROUND 1
V
WINNER ROUND 3**

Colombia 1

SEMI-FINAL 1

QUARTER-FINAL WINNER 1

Brazil 1

SEMI-FINAL 2

QUARTER-FINAL WINNER 3

Netherlands 0

QUARTER-FINAL 3

Netherlands 0

**WINNER ROUND 2
V
WINNER ROUND 4**

Costa Rica 0

(Netherlands win 4-3 on penalties)

THIRD PLACE PLAY-OFF

LOSER SEMI-FINAL 1

Brazil 0

SEMI-FINAL WINNER 2
Argentina 0

QUARTER-FINAL 2
France 0

**WINNER ROUND 5
V
WINNER ROUND 7**

Germany 1

QUARTER-FINAL WINNER 2
Germany 7

QUARTER-FINAL WINNER 4
Argentina 0

(Argentina win 4-2 on penalties)

QUARTER-FINAL 4
Argentina 1

**WINNER ROUND 6
V
WINNER ROUND 8**

Belgium 0

LOSER SEMI-FINAL 2
Netherlands 3

SECOND ROUND 5
France 2

**WINNER E
V
RUNNER-UP F**

Nigeria 0

GROUP E
France

Switzerland

Ecuador

Honduras

SECOND ROUND 6
Argentina 1

**WINNER F
V
RUNNER-UP E**

Switzerland 0

(After extra-time)

GROUP F
Argentina

Nigeria

Bosnia and Herzegovina

Iran

SECOND ROUND 7
Germany 2

**WINNER G
V
RUNNER-UP H**

Algeria 1

(After extra-time)

GROUP G
Germany

United States

Portugal

Ghana

SECOND ROUND 8
Belgium 2

**WINNER H
V
RUNNER-UP G**

United States 1

(After extra-time)

GROUP H
Belgium

Algeria

Russia

South Korea

INTERNATIONAL CONTINENTAL CHAMPIONSHIPS

The World Cup isn't the only international tournament. Each continent has its own regional tournament that creates a buzz and excitement each year it comes around. The nations of Europe compete every four years in the European Championships, South America holds the Copa America and the North American countries play for the Gold Cup. Africa holds the African Cup of Nations and the Asian and Oceanian associations celebrate and compete for their own continental titles.

FOUNDATION & 1960s

The idea of a rival competition to the World Cup was nothing new. Frenchman Henri Delaunay, who lent his name to the tournament, discussed the concept before World War II but never saw his dream become reality.

PAGE 48 Miroslav Klose scores for Germany against Turkey, 2008

PAGE 49 Euro 2004 winners Greece celebrate

THE RESULT 1960

Location: Paris
Final: Soviet Union 2 Yugoslavia 1 (after extra time)
Shirts: Soviets red, Yugoslavia blue
Scorers: Metreveli, Ponedelnik; Galic

FIFA feared such a tournament for the elite might undermine the status of its own World Cup but finally, in 1958, the European Championship took shape under its original name of the European Nations Cup. Sadly, Delaunay, Secretary General of the French Football Federation, died in 1954 and was unable to witness the creation of his dream. So his colleagues ensured that his name lived on by giving the tournament the alternative title of Coupe Henri Delaunay.

The inaugural competition comprised 17 countries playing on a two-leg knockout basis followed by the semi-finals, a third place play-off and then the final in one host country – appropriately enough in France.

Spain withdrew from their quarter-final against the Soviet Union because of political pressure by dictator Francisco Franco while England, Italy and West Germany failed to enter for fear of fixture congestion. The Soviets, inspired by legendary goalkeeper Lev Yashin, went on to become the first winners. They recovered from a one-goal deficit to overcome Yugoslavia 2-1 in a tense final in the old Parc des Princes in Paris.

The next competition, in 1964, was also marred by political interference. This time, Greece withdrew, after being told to face Albania in an early round though the nations were officially at war.

At least by now Cold War tension between the Soviet Union and Spain had eased, which was fortunate because the Soviets qualified for the finals that were hosted by Spain. In the semi-finals, the Soviet Union defeated Denmark 3-0 in Barcelona, while Spain scrambled past Hungary,

courtesy of a 2-1 win, in extra time, in Madrid.

Spain soon went a goal behind in the final at Real Madrid's Santiago Bernabéu Stadium, much to the distress of most of the 79,115 spectators. Fortunately for the hosts, Barcelona's Jesus María Pereda equalised and Zaragoza's Marcelino Martínez wrote himself into Spanish sporting history by heading in a late winner. England had entered for the first time, but had not progessed beyond the first round. New manager Alf Ramsey saw his men held 1-1 by France at Sheffield Wednesday's Hillsborough stadium, to then collapse 5-2 four months later in Paris.

CHALLENGE OF COMPETITION CHANGES

The tournament's name was now altered to the European Championship for the 1968 event and along with it came a change of format. For this event, eight groups of teams faced each other twice, with the top nation from each group progressing to two-legged quarter finals. Italy were hosts and for the first and only time a match was decided on the toss of a coin.

England, as the reigning World Champions, qualified for the inaugural European Championship finals with largely the same squad that had won the 1966 World Cup. So hopes were high that the Three Lions could roar to a second successive major championship. But England fell 1-0 to a late goal by Yugoslavia in a match littered with fouls and marred by Alan Müllery's sending-off one minute from the final whistle, with Dragan Dzajic scoring the decisive strike.

Italy beat the Soviets in the other semi-final on an infamous coin toss after a scoreless stalemate and no time to organise a replay.

Yugoslavia dominated in the final at Rome, but were punished for not being able to beat Dino Zoff more than once. Italy equalised nine minutes from time, made five changes for the replay and strolled past the exhausted Yugoslavs 2-0.

RIGHT The Henri Delaunay Cup

BELOW Spain vs. USSR in the 1964 final, Madrid

Location: Madrid
Final: Spain 2 Soviet Union 1
Shirts: Spain blue; Soviets red
Scorers: Pereda, Martínez; Khusainov

SPAIN

Iribar

Rivilla   Zoco   Olivella   Calleja

Pereda   Fusté   Suárez

Amaro   Martínez   Lapetra

Khusainov   Ponedelnik   Chislenko

Korneev   Ivanov   Voronin

Mudrik   Anichkine   Shesternev   Chustikov

Yashin

SOVIET UNION

Location: Rome
Final: Italy 1 Yugoslavia 1 (after extra time)
Shirts: Italy blue, Yugoslavia white
Scorers: Domenghini; Dzajic

ITALY

Zoff

Burgnich   Castano   Guarneri   Facchetti

Domenghini   Ferrini   Juliano   Lodetti

Anastasi   Prati

Dzajic   Musemic   Petkovic

Holcer   Acimovic   Trivic

Damjanovic   Paunovic   Pavlovic   Fazlagic

Pantelic

YUGOSLAVIA

1970s

THE RESULT 1972

Location: Brussels
Final: West Germany 3 Soviet Union 0
Shirts: Germany white, Soviets red
Scorers: Müller 2, Wimmer

WEST GERMANY

Maier

Höttges Beckenbauer Schwarzenbeck Breitner

Hoeness Wimmer Netzer Heynckes

Müller Kremers

Kozinkevich Banischevsky Baidachny
(Onishenko)

Konkov Kolotov Troshkine
(Dolmatov)

Kaplichny Istomine Khurtsilava Dzodzuaschvili

Rudakov

SOVIET UNION

THE RESULT 1976

Location: Belgrade
Final: Czechoslovakia 2 West
Germany 2 (Czechoslovakia 5-3 on
penalties after extra time)
Shirts: Czechs red, Germany white
Scorers: Svehlík, Dobiás; Müller,
Hölzenbein

CZECHOSLOVAKIA

Viktor

Pivarník Ondrus Capkovic Gögh

Dobiás Móder Panenka Masny
(Vesely)

Svehlík Nehoda
(Jurkemik)

Hölzenbein Müller

Hoeness Beer Bonhof Wimmer
(Bongartz) (Flohe)

Vogts Schwarzenbeck Beckenbauer Dietz

Maier

WEST GERMANY

West Germany produced the finest football yet seen in the competition en route to a 1972 victory in Belgium, seeing off the Soviet Union at the Heysel Stadium. But both Italy and England failed to reach the finals.

1972

West German manager Helmut Schön rebuilt his team after reaching the 1970 World Cup semi-finals in Mexico. Schön looked to fast-rising Bayern Munich for the foundation of his new team.

The key man was Franz Beckenbauer, who was moved back from midfield to his personally favoured role of attacking sweeper.

Striker Gerd Müller was another of the 1970 heroes alongside the new stars from Bayern Munich, namely attacking left back Paul Breitner and striker Uli Hoeness. Furthermore, Schön replaced Wolfgang Overath with the Borussia Mönchengladbach playmaker general Gunter Netzer.

Beckenbauer and Netzer commanded the first leg of the quarter-final, guiding the Germans to their a 3-1 win. They had little difficulty securing a scoreless draw in the return leg against Sir Alf Ramsey's England side in West Berlin.

Belgium hosted the four-team finals but faced favourites West Germany at the semi-final stage. The Germans edged through 2-1 with two goals from the prolific Müller. In the other semi-final, the Soviet Union overcame Hungary via Anatoli Konkov's deflected shot.

Müller, who had scored all four in a recent friendly, was on fire in the final and notched a goal in each half in the 3-0 triumph over the Soviets. Midfielder Herbert Wimmer added the third to claim Germany's first European Championship in front of 50,000 fans.

1976

Czechoslovakia emerged as surprise winners – launching their campaign in the semi-finals by stunning Holland. It was a sad occasion for Johan Cruyff because it was to become his final major

tournament in a Dutch national team shirt.

West Germany, as World Cup holders, had good reason to assume that they were well-placed to win, but they found themselves trailing 2-0 at halftime against hosts Yugoslavia. Köln forward, Dieter Muller, rescued the Germans on his international debut. He scored twice, forcing the game into extra-time. Müller went on to complete a hat-trick in a famous 4-2 victory.

In the final, Czechoslovakia took an early two-goal lead against the West Germans. Manager Helmut Schön was kept waiting until the last minute of normal time before he could celebrate an equaliser from Bernd Holzenbein. Extra-time failed to produce a winner, so penalties would decide the championships for the first time in its history. Czechoslovakia took the title after Antonin Panenka scored with a chip past Sepp Maier.

BELOW Captains Bobby Moore of England and Franz Beckenbauer of West Germany, 1972

EUROPEAN CHAMPIONSHIPS

1980s

UEFA responded to the fast-increasing popularity of the European Championship in 1980 by opting to widen out the qualifying potential and make the finals tournament itself more of a spectacle.

1980

This time, seven countries progressed out of a solely group-based qualifying system to contest the title in Italy along with the host nation. Two groups of four were contested, the winners of each progressing directly to the final in the Stadio Olimpico in Rome.

Italy scored a single goal and missed out on top spot in their group to underdogs Belgium. The decisive match in the other group was played out in Naples between West Germany and Holland. West Germany seized the initiative and carved out a 3-0 lead with a hat-trick by Klaus Allofs before a Johnny Rep penalty and Rene Van de Kerkhof's long-distance pulled it back to 3-2.

In the final, West Germany snatched an early lead, but Belgium came out fighting in the second half. Belgium equalised through a penalty converted by Rene Vandereycken. In the final minutes, Hrubesch scored his second of the game to win it for the Germans.

1984

Michel Platini dominated the finals from start to finish, captaining France to their first major international trophy. Platini scored nine goals, including two hat-tricks and the opening goal in the 2-0 final victory against Spain.

Manager Michel Hidalgo used Platini in a free attacking role at the apex of a superbly balanced midfield featuring Luis Fernandez, Jean Tigana, and Alain Giresse. They topped their group with three wins in three games.

Holders West Germany failed to progress even beyond the group stage. They finished third behind Spain and Portugal.

1988

Holland landed their one and only major prize in the 1988 finals in West Germany. Dutch star striker, Marco Van Basten had to be persuaded to play by friend and mentor Johan Cruyff. Manager Rinus Michels left Van Basten out of the line-up for Holland's opening group defeat by the Soviet Union, but Van Basten started next time out against England and hit a hat-trick.

Confident hosts West Germany topped the other group ahead of Italy, Spain and Denmark, but were knocked out in the semi-finals by Holland. Holland overcame a suspension-weakend Soviet Union in the final, with Van Basten's volleyed second goal being hailed as one of the finest of all time.

THE RESULT 1980

Location: Rome
Final: West Germany 2 Belgium 1
Shirts: Germany white, Belgium red
Scorers: Hrubesch 2; Vandereycken

WEST GERMANY

Schumacher

Kaltz   Förster   Stielike   Dietz

Briegel   Schuster   Müller   Rummenige

Hrubesch   Allofs

Ceulemans   Van der Elst

Vandereycken   Cools   Mommens   Van Moer

Renquin   Meeuws   Millecamps   Gerets

Pfaff

BELGIUM

THE RESULT 1984

Location: Paris
Final: France 2 Spain 0
Shirts: France blue, Spain red
Scorers: Platini, Bellone

FRANCE

Bats

Domergue   Battiston   Le Roux   Bossis
(Amoros)

Tigana   Fernandez   Platini   Giresse

Lacombe   Bellone
(Genghini)

Carrasco   Santillana

Casas   Manrique   Gomez   Javier
(Sarabia)

Urquiaga   Puig   Redondo   Camacho
(Bonillo)

Echarri

SPAIN

THE RESULT 1988

Location: Munich
Final: Holland 2 Soviet Union 0
Shirts: Holland orange, Soviets white
Scorers: Gullit, Van Basten

HOLLAND

Van Breukelen

Van Aerle   Rijkaard   R Koeman   Van Tiggelen

Vanenburg   E Koeman   Wouters   Muhren

Gullit   Van Basten

Protassov   Belanov
(Pasulko)

Mikhailichenko Zavarov Litovchenko Aleinikov

Rats Demanyenko Khidiyatulline Gotsmanov
(Baltacha)

Dassaev

SOVIET UNION

1990s

The dynamic Danish team surprised Europe in Sweden in 1992. This was also the first time a unified Germany took part in international competition and the first time that players' names were printed on their backs.

FAR RIGHT Paul Gascoigne volleys England's second goal against Scotland at Euro 96

1992

Denmark's remarkable feat was as unexpected as their very participation. The Danes joined the tournament only after Yugoslavia were barred for security reasons on the eve of the finals – and when the Yugoslav squad was already in Sweden – after political instability in the Balkans had erupted into armed conflict.

Richard Moller Nielsen, the Danish team's manager, was at home redecorating his kitchen when he took the call instructing him to recall his players from their family holidays in the sun.

Not surprisingly, the Danes failed initially to impress before managing to finally string their game together for the last group match against France. The French, managed by Michel Platini, disappointed despite having been unbeaten in the qualifiers and fielding an attack that featured Jean-Pierre Papin and Eric Cantona.

UEFA had changed the tournament format once more, inserting knock-out semi-finals between the group stage and the final.

Denmark, defying numerous injuries, took the lead twice in their semi-final against a complacent Holland, both goals scored by Henrik Larsen. In the resultant penalty shoot-out, Marco Van Basten – Holland's match-winner from the 1988 final – saw his penalty saved by Peter Schmeichel.

In the other semi-final, holders Germany never needed to get out of second gear on their way to a 3-2 victory over hosts Sweden. The unified German side included the likes of Karlheinz Riedle, Thomas Hässler, and Jürgen Klinsmann, and few believed Denmark could test them in the final in the Ullevi stadium in Gothenburg.

Instead, they showed skill, cunning, and determination in abundance. Schmeichel laid claim

to being the best goalkeeper in the world, while Lars Olsen was a rock in the centre of defence and Brian Laudrup – younger brother of Michael – proved a danger on the counter-attack.

Against the Germans, midfielder John Jensen put Denmark ahead and Kim Vilfort capped a fairytale fortnight with a second goal 12 minutes from the end of the game.

1996

In 1996, the number of finalists doubled to 16 for the first major tournament staged in England since the World Cup 30 years earlier. Germany clinched their third crown when Oliver Bierhoff scored the first ever 'golden goal' in the competition's history.

The golden goal was a short-lived attempt to find a better solution to deciding drawn matches. Instead of using penalties, a match was halted the moment a breakthrough goal was scored during extra-time.

England, who had lost in the semi-finals, at least had the satisfaction of seeing Germany, their competition, re-establish their position on the footballing map after their failure to qualify for the previous World Cup and a decade of disaster.

Granting hosting rights to England had been an important signal from UEFA that it considered the English game had at last got on top of the problem of hooliganism. England boasted the finest stadia in Europe because of the massive rebuilding necessitated by the imposition of all-seater requirements.

Paul Gascoigne's wonder goal against Scotland set the tournament alight, but even better was to come when England swept Holland aside 4-1 at Wembley with a display rarely matched in their modern footballing history.

THE RESULT 1992

Location: Gothenburg
Final: Denmark 2 Germany 0
Shirts: Denmark red, Germany white
Scorers: Jensen, Vilfort

DENMARK

Schmeichel

Sivebaek   Nielsen   Olsen   Piechnik
(Christiansen)

Christofte   Jensen   Vilfort   Larsen

Povlsen   Laudrup

Riedle   Klinsmann

Brehme   Hässler   Sammer   Effenberg
          (Doll)   (Thom)

Helmer   Reuter   Kohler   Buchwald

Illgner

GERMANY

In the semi-finals, however, Germany broke English hearts by holding their nerve in a penalty shoot-out. Gareth Southgate saw his penalty saved by German keeper Andy Köpke, and midfielder Andreas Möller made no mistake with his subsequent penalty shot. The Germans thus progressed to a final back at Wembley against the technically adroit Czechs, who had ousted Aimé Jacquet's France in yet another shoot-out in the other semi-final.

The Germans, under the management of former title-winner Berti Vogts, were typically well-organised, with Matthias Sammer an excellent sweeper. But they failed initially to break down a counter-attacking Czech side, who took the lead though a penalty from Patrik Berger.

The Czechs were 30 minutes from victory at that point. But then German manager Vogts sent on forward Bierhoff as a substitute. First he equalised and then, five minutes into extra-time, wrote himself into the record books with the first-ever golden goal in a major tournament.

THE RESULT 1996

Location: London
Final: Germany 2 Czech Republic 1 (Germany on golden goal in extra time)
Shirts: Germany white, Czechs red
Scorers: Bierhoff 2; Berger

GERMANY

Köpke

Babbel   Helmer   Sammer   Ziege

Hässler   Strunz   Eilts   Scholl
          (Bode)   (Bierhoff)

Klinsmann   Kuntz

Kuka

Berger   Bejbl   Nedved   Poborsky
                              (Smicer)

Nemec Suchoparek Kadlec Rada Hornak

Kouba

CZECH REPUBLIC

2000s

"At last we have proved Spain can be winners."

MANAGER LUIS ARAGONES

France, the reigning World Champions, beat Dino Zoff's Italy at the first European Championship final to be co-hosted – by Belgium and Holland – in 2000. Greece won the 2004 contest and resurgent Spain the 2008 finals.

FAR RIGHT Cristiano Ronaldo of Portugal in action during the 2004 quarter-final match between Portugal and England

RIGHT France enjoy their second title win in Rotterdam in 2000

2000

France squeezed past bitter rivals Italy in the final of the 2000 European Championship. Sylvain Wiltord equalised in the final seconds of the 90 minutes, allowing David Trezeguet to score 13 minutes into extra-time with a thunderous volley. France thus became the first reigning World Cup Champions to add the European crown to their list of achievements.

Italy had come so close to winning the title, but manager Dino Zoff resigned in anger after the defeat, upset by the public criticism of his tactics and team selection by Prime Minister Silvio Berlusconi. For England, the event proved a huge

disappointment. Under the management of former player Kevin Keegan, they failed to progress beyond the group stage.

2004

The 2004 finals produced an upset few had predicted. Greece, who had qualified previously for only one World Cup (1994) and one European championship (1980), shocked hosts Portugal by beating them 1-0 in a dramatic final.

The Greeks, who had begun the tournament as 150-1 outsiders, also eliminated holders France as well as the Czech Republic, in this case with a silver goal, a rule that replaced the previous golden goal

THE RESULT 2000

Location: Rotterdam
Final: France 2 Italy 1
(France on golden goal in extra time)
Shirts: France blue, Italy white
Scorers: Wiltord, Trezeguet; Delvecchio

FRANCE

Barthez

Thuram   Desailly   Blanc   Lizarazu
                     (Pires)

Djorkaeff Deschamps Vieira   Zidane
(Trezeguet)

        Henry   Dugarry
                   (Wiltord)

        Delvecchio   Totti
        (Montella)

Fiore   Iuliano   Di Biagio   Albertini
         (Del Piero) (Ambrosini)

Maldini Cannavaro   Nesta   Pessotto

            Toldo

            ITALY

in 2003 before being abolished shortly afterwards. The silver goal meant that teams played on to the next formal stoppage (half-time or full-time) in extra-time after a goal had been scored.

Greece's victory over Portugal in the final in Lisbon came courtesy of a solid defence, great goalkeeping, and an opportunist goal by Angelos Charisteas. The result stunned European football. However, it was not the only surprise of the tounament – Germany, Italy, and Spain had all been knocked out in the group stage.

Portugal's defeat in the final in Lisbon – in front of their own fans, denied manager Luiz Felipe Scolari a unique feat. Scolari would have become the first non-European manager to have won the continental crown.

2008

Spain ended a 44-year losing spell by winning the finals in Austria and Switzerland. Neither of the co-hosts made it through the opening group stage, but that did not affect the party atmosphere in Vienna after Spain, winners in 1964 and runners-up in 1984, defeated Germany 1-0 in the final. Fernando Torres scored the winning goal after 33 minutes.

Veteran manager Luis Aragones, a reserve to the winners of 1964, said afterwards, "At last we have proved that Spain can win the big prizes." After years of underachievement in major tournaments. Spain won all six of their matches, albeit they needed two fine saves from goalkeeper-captain Iker Casillas to defeat World Cup-holders Italy on penalties in the quarter-finals. Xavi Hernandez, the Barcelona midfielder who laid on Torres's goal in the final, was hailed as UEFA's official player of the tournament.

Portugal, Croatia, Holland, and Spain were decisive winners of the groups. All were certain of qualifying after two of their three matches and rested key players in their concluding matches. That break in competitive momentum proved fatal for all but Spain, however, since the other three all lost in the quarter-finals.

Portugal blamed their quarter-final exit to Germany partly on the distractions raised by manager Luiz Felipe Scolari's imminent move to Chelsea, and partly on a media frenzy over the uncertain future of Cristiano Ronaldo.

Germany struggled to get the better of Austria in their concluding group match before defeating Portugal and then Turkey 3-2 in a dramatic semi-final. Major disappointments were World Cup runners-up France, who were first-round failures.

THE RESULT 2004

Location: Lisbon
Final: Greece 1 Portugal 0
Shirts: Greece white, Portugal red
Scorers: Charisteas

PORTUGAL

Ricardo

Miguel   Andrade Ricardo Carvalho Nuno
(Paulo Ferreira)   Valente

Ronaldo   Maniche   Costinha   Deco
          (Rui Costa)

          Figo   Pauleta
                    (Nuno Gomes)

          Charisteas   Vryzas
                     (Papadopoulos)

Giannakopoulos Basinas Katsouranis Zagorakis
              (Venetidis)

Fyssas   Dellas   Kapsis   Seitaridis

          Nikopolidis

GREECE

THE RESULT 2008

Location: Vienna
Final: Spain 1 Germany 0
Shirts: Spain red, Germany white
Scorers: Torres

SPAIN

          Casillas

Ramos   Puyol   Marchena Capdevila

          Senna

Iniesta   Xavi   Fabregas   Silva
        (Alonso) (Cazorla)

          Torres

          Klose
          (Gomez)

Podolski   Ballack Schweinsteiger

Hitzlsperger (Kuranyi) Frings

Lahm   Metzelder Mertesacker Friedrich
(Jansen)

          Lehmann

GERMANY

EUROPEAN CHAMPIONSHIP

EURO 2012

Despite being criticised for playing a 'boring' short-passing style of football, Spain both broke records and enthralled the crowd as they thrashed Italy 4-0 in the Euro 2012 final — all without fielding a recognised striker.

THE RESULT 2012

Location: Kiev
Final: Spain 4 Italy 0
Shirts: Spain red, Italy blue
Scorers: Alba, Silva, Torres, Mata

SPAIN

Casillas

Arbeloa Pique Ramos Alba

Busquets

Xavi Alonso

Silva Fabregas Iniesta
(Pedro) (Torres) (Mata)

Balotelli Cassano
(Di Natale)

De Rossi Montolivo Marchisio
(Motta)

Pirlo

Chiellini Barzagli Bonucci Abate
(Balzaretti)

Buffon

ITALY

The victory cemented Spain's place as one of the greatest international sides of all time, as the champions of the 2008 UEFA Euro Cup and 2010 World Cup became the first team of the modern era to win three major international football tournaments in succession.

The 2012 final, however, was anything but a given result for the title holders. Four-times world champions, Italy, had played some dazzling football in the tournament's earlier matches with playmakers Mario Balotelli and Andrea Pirlo in seemingly unstoppable form.

In response to this opposition, Spanish manager Vicente Del Bosque opted to rewrite the tactical handbook by leaving strikers David Villa and Fernando Torres on the bench. Instead Del Bosque's starting side would feature his dynamic midfielders Cesc Fabregas, Andres Iniesta, David Silva, Xavi, Xabi Alonso and Sergio Busquets.

"We have strikers but we decided to play with players who went better with our style," Del Bosque said.

The gamble paid off, as Spain's pace and quick passing ensured the champions held possession for long periods of the match. In the 31st minute, Fabregas was able to outflank defender Giorgio Chiellini and deliver a sublime pass to Silva, who headed the ball into Gianluigi Buffon's net. As a portent of things to come, Chiellini limped off the field with a thigh injury only minutes later. Jordi Alba was then able to capitalise on Spain's early lead with a second goal before half-time.

Italy responded with a spirited attack by Antonio Cassano and then his replacement Antonio Di Natale, but neither man could find a way past Spanish keeper Iker Casillas. Italy made their third and final change when Riccardo Montolivo replaced Thiago Motta, but within a few minutes the

midfielder had suffered a hamstring injury. Now down to 10 men for the last 30 minutes of the match, Motta's absence signalled the final death blow for Italy. Balotelli and Pirlo, both pivotal in securing Italy's place in the final, were nowhere to be seen, while the rest of the team looked bedraggled and outdone.

Only in the last stages of the match did Del Bosque decide to bring on striker Fernando Torres. Torres sprang immediately into action by scoring himself and then setting up another for teammate Mata. With the devastation of Italy complete, all the opponents could do was try and stay on their feet and relent in the face of Spain's masterclass.

CONTROVERSY FOR THE CO-HOSTS

Poland and Ukraine were joint hosts of Euro 2012, which featured 16 teams in the finals. The pre-tournament build-up was blighted by controversy when a BBC documentary *Euro 2012: Stadiums of Hate* showed football fans in the host nations making anti-Semitic chants and Nazi salutes. The report was later criticised as being one-sided and the only visible sign of racism at the tournament came from visiting fans from Germany, Spain, Croatia and Russia, who were all fined by UEFA as a result. Despite hosting a highly successful Euro Cup, the host nations fared rather less well on the pitch, with neither Poland or Ukraine making it past the group stages.

Russia and Holland were both pegged as contenders for the final, but Russia fell victim to outsiders Greece in the group round. Despite Holland's star line-up, which included Arjen Robben and Robin Van Persie, the team seemed unable to play as a unit and also crashed out in the group round.

As with many previous international tournaments, England were knocked out of the quarter-finals during a penalty shootout, this time with Italy, who secured the win with a notable kick from Andrea Pirlo. With Spain, Portugal, and Germany following Italy into the semi-finals, the stage seemed set for a Germany and Spain final. But Germany were to be outdone by a spirited Italian team and an outstanding Mario Balotelli goal, which sent them into the final and their day of reckoning.

RECORD-SMASHING SPAIN

Spain's victory against Italy saw the country break many of football's long-standing international records, although some commentators had described their defensive, short-passing style as "negative" and "boring".

Spain's 4-0 win in the final was the largest victory margin in either a European or World Cup final, a record previously held by West Germany, which recorded a 3-0 win over the Soviet Union in 1972.

Spanish players, too, made their way into the record books, with Fernando Torres becoming the first man to score in two European Cup finals. Torres and his Chelsea teammate Juan Mata also joined a handful of players who have won both the Champions League and the European Cup in the same season.

Spanish keeper Iker Casillas played in his 100th winning match for Spain and maintained his own record of not conceding a goal in the knockout stage of a tournament for 10 successive matches. After Spain's Euro 2012 victory, the only other country to win three major tournaments in a row is Argentina, who won the Copa America in 1945, 1946 and 1947.

ABOVE Co-hosts Poland, in their match against the Czech Republic.

FAR LEFT The Spanish squad celebrate their European Championship victory.

COPA AMERICA

The Copa America boasts the unique distinction of being the world's longest-running international football tournament. It began in July 1916 as part of Argentina's centenary independence celebrations.

The competition was originally called the Campeonato Sudamericano de Selecciones (South American Championship of National Teams). Participation was limited initially to member nations of CONMEBOL, the South American football confederation. However, because the organisation comprised only ten nations, the competition was expanded in 1993 to include invited participants from the Caribbean and North and Central America.

Usually two or three teams receive such an invitation, invariably one of them being Mexico, partly because of the geographical proximity and partly because of the lucrative television rights.

The United States have also been invited regularly since 1997, but have turned down the offer several times because of scheduling conflicts with Major League Soccer. However, they did accept an invitation for the 2007 tournament, ending a 12-year absence. The tournament used to take place every two years, but in 2007, CONMEBOL decided that it should be held every four years but in an odd-numbered year so that it did not clash with the World Cup and European Championship.

The 2007 event took place in Venezuela and a second rotation began in 2011 in Argentina. Uruguay won the 2011 competition, bringing their championship tally to 15, followed by Argentina with 14, and Brazil with eight. These totals exclude earlier, unofficial competitions.

SOUTH AMERICAN CHAMPIONSHIP

In its early years, when it was known as the South American Championship, the tournament did much to popularise the game and raise playing standards across the continent.

The 1940s are regarded as its heyday, but a generation later it fell into neglect, because South America's military governments looked disparagingly at their neighbours. The national federations of major countries such as Brazil, Argentina, and Uruguay also began to question the wisdom of competing after scouts from Italy and Spain began to converge on the event and, almost before the final whistle had been blown, lured their star players away to Europe.

Most painfully hit were Argentina. They won the 1957 tournament on the inspiration of an outstanding inside-forward trio of Humberto Maschio, Antonio Valentin Angelillo, and Omar Enrique Sivori. The manner of their triumph prompted predictions of World Cup glory the following year. However, within months, all three had been spirited away to Italy. All three were even playing for Italy within three years.

The gradual return of democracy in the mid-1980s – coupled with the growing power of television – sparked a resurgence of interest in

RIGHT Argentina's midfielder Juan Roman Riquelme takes on Coloia in 2007

the competition, with the event played in a single country, rather than on a home-and-away basis.

Problems remain for South American administrators to resolve. The most important is the fact that the Copa is staged in the middle of the South American winter – which is also the close-season in Europe, where all the most glamorous players operate. Not only are European clubs reluctant to release their players, but the stars themselves are wary of the risk of burn-out. Thus Barcelona's Ronaldinho and Milan's Kaka both withdrew from the Brazilian squad heading for the 2007 event in Venezuela. As it happened, even without them, Brazil won the trophy. In the final they defeated Argentina for the second time in a row.

EXPLOSIVE FINAL

In 2004, in Lima, Brazil won on penalties following an Adriano equaliser in the third minute of stoppage-time. The goal sparked a brawl as Brazil's players celebrated in front of the Argentina bench. Argentina responded by squirting water at their opponents and referee Carlos Amarilla summoned riot-police to stop the trouble. Argentina seemed more unsettled by the incident and missed their first two penalties. Brazil converted all their penalties, just as they had in their semi-final win over Uruguay.

In 2007, Brazil found it much easier. Argentina were favourites but never justified their status and subsided to one early spectacular goal from Julio Baptista, an unfortunate own goal by their own captain Roberto Ayala, and then a superb counter-attacking strike from Dani Alves.

In 2011, Uruguay won their first Copa America since 1995 after defeating Paraguay 3–0. Interestingly, Paraguay had managed to fight their way to the final without winning a single game in normal time. Instead their victories came courtesy of penalty shoot-outs at the end of the matches.

FOOTBALL FACTS

RECENT WINNERS
1989 Host: Brazil. Winners: Brazil
1991 Host: Chile. Winners: Argentina
1993 Host: Ecuador. Winners: Argentina
1995 Host: Uruguay. Winners: Uruguay
1997 Host: Bolivia. Winners: Brazil
1999 Host: Paraguay. Winner: Brazil
2001 Host: Colombia. Winners: Colombia
2004 Host: Peru. Winners: Brazil
2007 Host: Venezuela. Winners: Brazil
2011 Host: Argentina. Winners: Uruguay

All-time winners
Uruguay 15; Argentina 14; Brazil 8; Paraguay, Peru 2 each; Bolivia, Colombia 1 each.

LEFT Brazilian players celebrate their victory against Argentina in 2007

AFRICAN CUP OF NATIONS

Africa has become a magnet for cash-rich European clubs
who are seeking an apparently unending source of talents.
The biennial tournament has been played since 1957.

Players such as Didier Drogba, Samuel Eto'o,
Michael Essien, and Jay-Jay Okocha have moved
into superstardom within the European club
system, using their experience and talents to inspire
youngsters back home to follow in their footsteps.
But it was not always the case. In the colonial era
of much of the last century, European national
teams brought African players such as Just Fontaine
and Eusébio onboard for their own use.

Fontaine, born and brought up in Morocco, set
a World Cup record of 13 goals in 1958 while
representing France. Eusébio, born and brought up
in Mozambique, finished as top scorer with nine
goals for Portugal in the 1966 World Cup finals.
But a move for change was already underway.

Ten years earlier, in 1956, the Confederation of
African Football had been organised in Lisbon and
plotted a first Cup of Nations the following year in

RIGHT Jay-Jay Okocha on the attack
for Nigeria in the 2004 finals

BELOW South Africa's "Bafana
Bafana" line up before their 2002
clash with Burkina Faso

Khartoum, the capital city of Sudan. It has since been
staged virtually every two years, which makes it
international football's African regional championship.

EGYPT CROWNED AS SIX OF THE BEST

Only three nations competed that first time.
There should have been four but South Africa
were barred because its own government, wedded
to the segregationist apartheid system, refused to
approve the selection of a multi-racial team.

Ironically, 39 years later – after the downfall of
apartheid – South Africa returned to rescue the
Confederation by staging the event after Kenya's
late withdrawal as hosts. Egypt, Ethiopia, and Sudan
became the pioneer nations of a tournament that
grew steadily down the years to encompass four, six,
eight, 12, and eventually 16 finalists. In the early days,

north African countries were the sides to beat, a trend that has also been the case half a century later, judging by the last three competitions.

Holders Egypt, the very first African champions, have a poor World Cup record. However, they have won the African title a record seven times, most recently in Angola in 2010.

THE EARLY YEARS

Eto'o and Aboutrika follow in a tournament tradition for showcasing gifted individuals including heroes of yesteryear, such as the Ghanaian dribbling wizard Osei Kofi, Ethiopian captain Luciano Vassallo, and Egypt's captain Rafaat Ateya. In that inaugural tournament he scored the very first goal in a 2-1 win over Sudan then scored all four in Egypt's 4-0 thrashing of Ethiopia in the final.

The organisation of the second tournament was granted to Egypt with the same three nations. A last-minute goal saw Egypt retain the trophy with a breathtaking 2-1 win over Sudan.

Four teams met in Addis Ababa for the third tournament with hosts Ethiopia seeing off the challenge of Egypt 4-2 in an exciting final. Ethopia's last Emperor, Haile Selassie, handed over the Cup to skipper Vassallo. Eight nations took part in Ghana in 1963, with a new format of an elimination round, semi-finals, and final. This format remained until 1976, when a second round league system was introduced.

Morocco took advantage, although the new formula proved unpopular and, in 1978, knockout semi-finals and a final were restored, along with penalty shoot-outs. Further alterations were made for the 1992 event in Senegal, when a dozen teams competed. By now the qualifying rounds were organized into mini-leagues rather than a straightforward knockout system.

A more recent expansion in 1998 raised the number of entrants in the finals to 16, which proved popular with Africa's own nations but unpopular in Western Europe, where clubs resented being forced to relinquish their key players in the middle of their own league campaigns.

As a result of this, several European clubs with African players called for the tournament's schedule to be changed in 2008 so it did not clash with the regular European season. In response, FIFA president Sepp Blatter announced his preference for the African Nations Cup to be played in June or July after the European season ends, and for these changes to take effect by 2016.

In 2010, it was announced that the African Cup of Nations would be held during odd numbered years from 2013, so it would not clash with the World Cup. This meant that two of the tournaments were played within 12 months of each other: the 2012 Cup co-hosted by Equatorial Guinea and Gabon; and the 2013 Cup, hosted by South Africa.

FOOTBALL FACTS

RECENT WINNERS
1996 Host and Winner: South Africa
1998 Host: Burkina Faso, Winner: Egypt
2000 Co-hosts: Nigeria/Ghana, Winner: Cameroon
2002 Host: Mali, Winner: Cameroon
2004 Host and Winner: Tunisia
2006 Host and Winner: Egypt
2008 Host: Ghana, Winner: Egypt
2010 Host: Angola, Winner: Egypt
2012 Co-hosts: Gabon, Equatorial Guinea, Winner: Zambia
2013 Host: South Africa, Winner Nigeria

All-time champions
Egypt (7); Cameroon, Ghana (4 each); Nigeria (3); DR Congo (2); Zambia, Algeria, Congo, Ethiopia, Ivory Coast, Morocco, South Africa, Sudan, Tunisia (1 each).

BELOW Didier Drogba enjoys Ivory Coast's progress to the 2006 semi-finals

OTHER NATIONAL TEAM COMPETITIONS

"To play for your country is the greatest possible honour."

FIFA PRESIDENT SEPP BLATTER

The history of national team competitions and their status as the ultimate peak of football achievement goes all the way back to the first official Scotland v England match in 1872. The goalless draw led to the creation of the British Home Championship.

RIGHT Ante Milicic strikes for Australia against the Solomon Islands in 2004

BELOW Harry Kewell leads the "Socceroos" to an easy win

Association football's first national team competition was staged annually until 1984, when it was killed off by dwindling crowds and the fixture congestion engendered by qualifying matches for the World Cup and European Championship.

At one stage, the British Home Championship also served as the World Cup qualifying section. That was after World War II, when the British associations – England, Scotland, Wales, and Northern Ireland – had rejoined FIFA after a 25 year absence. FIFA designated two seasons of the British championship as the qualifying group. England finished top and went to Brazil.

The British championship was put to the same use before the 1954 World Cup, but for the last time. Other nations objected that this gave the British a guaranteed place at the finals, and Wales and Northern Ireland said they would always be at a qualifying disadvantage against England and Scotland. Ironically, for the next World Cup, 'open' qualifying saw all four home nations go on to the finals.

The awkward nature of international travel in football's early years was a significant factor in the creation of regional competitions. Small federations could barely afford to send a squad to a neighbouring country for a tournament. Criss-crossing the world's oceans was also a problem. To counter this, the South Americans set up their own tournament in the early 1900s. It was not until the late 1950s, however, that Europe and Africa dared go fully international.

THE GROWTH OF COMPETITIONS

A European nations team competition, the Dr. Gerö Cup, was organised in 1927 and elsewhere around the world, the desire for national team competition saw the fledgling Central American confederation launch its own event in 1941. Further championships were staged only irregularly, even after the formal creation in 1963 of CONCACAF, which finally bonded into one

organisation the various nations who made up the football world of Central America (including some South American countries), the Caribbean and, of course, North America.

The regional competition was eventually reorganised and stabilised, in 1991, as the Gold Cup. It takes place in spring, every two years. Mexico and the United States, the two major powers of the region, have dominated the modern era with the United States winning six times and Mexico winning five. Canada have won once, while none of the other competing nations have won it at all. In 2015, Mexico and the United States – the winners of the last successive Gold Cups – will come together in a playoff. The play-off victors will then secure a place as the CONCACAF entrant to the 2017 Confederations Cup.

Oceania is FIFA's smallest region, with only 11 members. Its regional competition, the Oceania Nations Cup, began in 1973 and was played until 1980. The cup was dominated by Australia and New Zealand, which led to the tournament's demise. In its place, the Trans-Tasman Cup was played only between Australia and New Zealand. The Oceania Nations Cup returned in 1996 and was played every two years until 2004. In 2006 Australia joined the Asian Football Confederation, thus leaving the Oceanic Football Confederation and making New Zealand the main favourite for the Oceania Nations Cup. Despite this, New Zealand were beaten by

Tahiti in the 2012 competition.

The Asian Football Confederation Cup was founded in 1956 and is held every four years. The victors of the 16 competing teams become Asian champions and qualify for the FIFA Confederations Cup. Japan is the most successful team, winning the Asian Cup four times. The 2015 tournament is being hosted by newest AFC member, Australia.

ASIAN CUP

Recent winners
1980 Kuwait
1984 Saudi Arabia
1988 Saudi Arabia
1992 Japan
1996 Saudi Arabia
2000 Japan
2004 Japan
2007 Iraq
2011 Japan

All-time winners
Japan 4; Iran, Saudi Arabia 3 each; South Korea 2; Iraq 2; Israel, Kuwait 1 each

CONCACAF GOLD CUP

(North, Central American, and Caribbean Nations)

Recent winners
1998 Mexico
2000 Canada
2002 United States
2003 Mexico
2005 United States
2007 United States
2009 Mexico
2011 Mexico
2013 United States

All-time winners
Mexico 5; United States 6; Canada 1

OCEANIA NATIONS CUP

Recent winners
1996 Australia
1998 New Zealand
2000 Australia
2002 New Zealand
2004 Australia
2008 New Zealand
2012 Solomon Islands

All-time winners
Australia 4; New Zealand 4

CLUB WORLD CHAMPIONSHIPS

AC Milan have been crowned champions five times in the event's various guises. The competition has now been reformed after its early years were marred by scandal and violence.

The Intercontinental Cup kicked off in 1960 as a home and away meeting between the champions of Europe and South America. The idea had sprung from South American officials, who had launched their own Copa Libertadores for the purpose of challenging Europe at club level.

Real Madrid were crowned the first winners after drawing 0-0 with Peñarol of Uruguay at Montevideo, and then storming to a 5-1 victory back in Spain. But the competition almost ground to a halt following a string of brutal matches involving Argentinian sides. Celtic were furious at their treatment by Racing Club in 1967. A year later, Manchester United's George Best lost his temper after incessant provocation by his marker José Hugo Medina of Estudiantes de La Plata, and both were sent off.

Estudiantes were notorious for their cynical tactics. In 1969, the Estudiantes players bombarded their Milan opponents with practice balls before the game. Milan won 4-2 on aggregate, but three Estudiantes players received lengthy bans for their bad behaviour.

Several European champions, such as Bayern Munich, Liverpool, and Nottingham Forest, declined to compete because they feared losing key players to tough South American tackling. The 1975 and 1978 contests were not held.

CLUB WORLD CUP

The competition was rescued in 1980, when the Japanese Football Federation found sponsorship support from car manufacturer Toyota to host the

RIGHT Milan's Pippo Inzaghi (Number 9) scores for Milan against Boca Juniors in 2007

LEFT Skipper Paolo Maldini and his Milan teammates celebrate world domination

final as a one-off game. The inaugural showpiece was played in Tokyo until 2001, with neighbouring Yokohama hosting the 2002 and 2004 finals.

The last final in Tokyo's National Stadium saw Bayern Munich edge past Boca Juniors 1-0 in extra time. The final moved to Yokohama's new National Stadium the following year.

Meanwhile, FIFA had become directly involved in football at international club level. FIFA staged a Club World Cup Championship in 2000 at Brazil's Maracanã Stadium. Noisily impatient clubs from outside Europe and South America were invited. European champions Manchester United even withdrew from the FA Cup in England to play at the urging of the FA, who were bidding in vain to host the 2006 World Cup. Corinthians beat Vasco da Gama 4-3 on penalties after the goalless all-Brazilian affair.

FIFA set a precedent and, in 2004, it swallowed up the original match into its expanded mini-tournament. Japan remained, initially at least, as host nation. But no longer was the competition the preserve of the Europeans and South Americans.

In 2005, FIFA followed up its 2000 experiment. The competition would still be played in Japan, but now it was global. The top teams from all over the world would play off. Brazil's São Paulo won the first of the revised events, beating European champions Liverpool 1-0 in the final.

They now had rivals in hosting, which included Al-Ahly (Egypt), Al-Ittihad (Saudi Arabia), Deportivo Saprissa (Costa Rica), and Sydney (Australia). Internacional of Porto Alegre maintained Brazilian

domination in 2006, beating Barcelona 1-0. Coach Abel Braga said: "Our club's history will now come under two headings, before and after Japan 2006. We're world champions!"

Al-Ahly were there again in 2006, along with some new challengers: Auckland (New Zealand), Club America (Mexico), and Jeonbuk Hyundai (South Korea).

AC Milan's 4-2 victory over Boca Juniors in 2007 was Europe's first triumph since Porto's in 2004.

In 2008, Manchester United became Club World Cup champions after a 1-0 victory against Ecuadorian team LDU Quito. The 2009 and 2010 Club World Cups were held in United Arab Emirates, with Barcelona winning the 2009 final against Estudiantes 3-1, thanks to a late header from Lionel Messi. The 2010 Cup final featured Congo's Mazembe and Italy's Internazionale, with Internazionale seizing the day with a 3-0 win.

The 2011 and 2012 Cups were both held in Japan with Barcelona and Corinthians winning the finals respectively. Barcelona's 2011 win also made Lionel Messi the first player to score in different Club World Cup finals. The 2013 Cup final was held in Morocco and saw German superpower Bayern Munich swat aside local national team Raja Casablanca with a 2-0 victory.

GREAT NATIONS

International power in football is defined by a mixture of achievement and history. Success or failure at the World Cup finals is what counts to today's modern critic, followed by titles in the various regional championships. Brazil boast five World Cup victories, one more than mighty Italy and Germany. The gap between the 'lesser' nations and the international 'heavyweights' has shrunk in recents years, leading to some big upsets and close encounters at major tournaments.

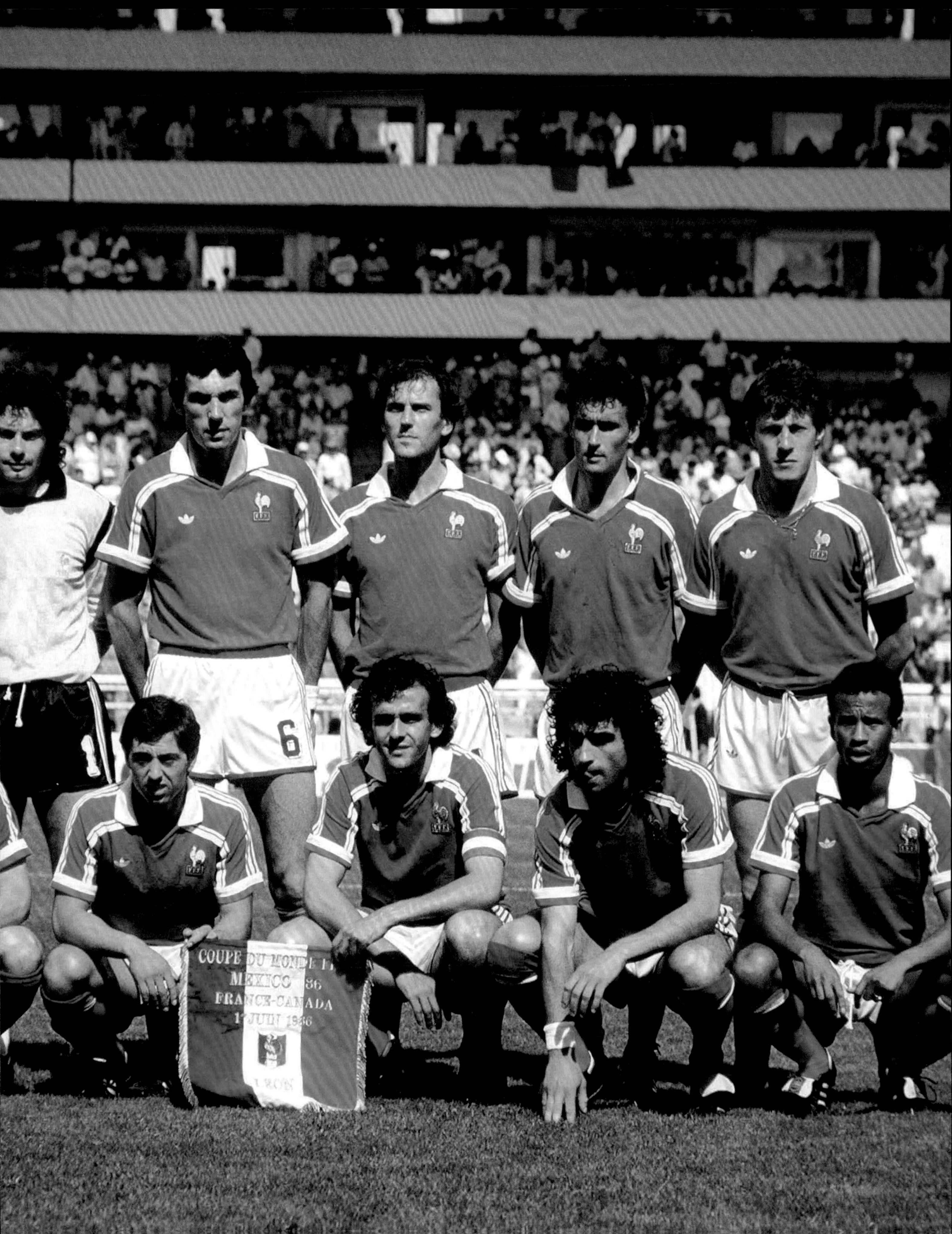
COUPE DU MONDE
MEXICO 86
FRANCE-CANADA
JUIN

BRAZIL

England may have invented the modern game, but Brazil – and Edison Pelé in particular – have perfected it to such an extent that they can now boast a record-breaking five World Cup wins.

FOOTBALL FACTS

CHAMPIONS – LAST TEN YEARS

2003 Cruzeiro

2004 Santos

2005 Corinthians

2006 São Paulo

2007 São Paulo

2008 São Paulo

2009 Flamengo

2010 Fluminense

2011 Corinthians

2012 Fluminense

2013 Cruzeiro

RIGHT A 17-year-old Pelé holds the Jules Rimet trophy

PAGE 68 Brazil star Garrincha skips past Wales defender Terry Hennessey in 1962

PAGE 69 The 1986 France team before their match against Canada

Few dare argue with the Brazilian pre-eminence in modern football – especially after watching the timeless re-runs of Garrincha and Pelé swaggering their way to Brazil's first World Cup win in 1958 or, 12 years later, witnessing the colour-soaked TV scenes from Brazil's third World Cup triumph in the Mexican sunshine.

Since then, successive new generations of Brazilians have consistently lived up to Pelé's romantic notion of 'the beautiful game.' But the original link was an English one. In 1894, Brazilian Charles Miller, whose father was originally from England, brought over the first footballs to be seen in Brazil, after a study trip in Southampton where he was taught the game. Miller envisaged a game for expatriates and their families, but its popularity swiftly spread and Brazil can now boast the proud achievement of being the only nation to have competed in every World Cup.

The country's first footballing hero was Arthur Friedenreich, who, in the early part of the 20th century, was also popularly supposed to have been the first senior player to have scored over 1,000 goals. Emulating him was Leonidas, who spearheaded Brazil's attack at the 1938 World Cup finals in France. Unwisely, the team's directors decided to rest Leonidas from the semi-final against World Cup title holders Italy in order to be fresh for the final – which, of course, they never reached.

Brazil were awarded hosting rights to the next World Cup finals, but its realisation had to wait until after World War II. It was originally due to be played in 1949, but a mixture of European uncertainty and slow preparation work put the staging back to 1950. Brazil reached the final only to suffer a shock 2-1 defeat to Uruguay in front of almost 200,000 disbelieving fans. As Brazil had lost the final while dressed in all-white, they superstitiously decided to make the switch to their current strip of yellow shirts and blue shorts – arguably today's most famous football kit. Brazil reached the quarter-final stage at the 1954 World Cup finals in Switzerland, returning to Europe to take the world title in Sweden four years later with almost an entirely new team.

Coach Vicente Feola had brought in the mercurial outside right Garrincha and a 17-year-old inside left called Pelé.

As a teenage sensation, Pelé shared top billing for Brazil with wizard dribbler Garrincha, nicknamed 'the Little Bird,' and the midfield duo of Didi and Zito. In 1970, Pelé was complemented by the likes of Gerson, Roberto Rivelino, Tostao, and explosive Jairzinho – the last of whom was the only winner to score in every match per round at the World Cup finals. When Pelé retired in 1977, he boasted over 1,000 goals in a career with Brazil, Santos and New York Cosmos.

Brazil had to wait for 24 years to claim their fourth World Cup, edging past Italy on penalty kicks at the 1994 finals in the United States. Brazil's Bebeto and Romario were the deadliest strike pairing at the tournament going into the match against Italy, yet the match finished goalless.

Ronaldo was a member of the 1994 squad without playing and, in 1998, he was hampered by injury and illness as Brazil surrendered their crown to France. Yet Ronaldo was the two-goal hero in the 2002 final victory over Germany and in 2006 became the World Cup's all-time leading scorer.

Brazil's immense size long hindered the development of a national league until 1971, and the traditional old regional championships still generate fierce rivalry. Flamengo and Fluminense insist that they are the best-supported clubs, although São Paulo have a record five league titles.

The wealth of Brazilian football has always rested on the Rio-São Paulo axis, with the South American country now the world's greatest exporter of players. Most members of Brazil's recent World Cup squads have been Europe-based, a stark contrast to 1958 and 1962, when their entire squads played for Brazilian clubs. Santos have been the most internationally acclaimed club in Brazilian football history. This is largely due to their perpetual global touring in the 1960s, when they cashed in on the fame and drawing power of Pelé. Despite the touring, Santos – even at their peak – were an extremely fine team that in 1962 and 1963 won both the Copa Libertadores and the World Club Cup.

Outstanding Brazilian coaches over the years have included World Cup-winning managers Feola, Aimoré Moreira, Mario Zagallo, Carlos Alberto

Parreira, as well as Claudio Coutinho, Sebastião Lazaroni, and Tele Santana. Last and of course not least is Luiz Felipe Scolari – the manager who led Brazil to victory in 2002 and had the hopes of the nation resting on his shoulders for the 2014 World Cup in native country Brazil.

BELOW Bebeto and Romario celebrate in 1994

GREAT NATIONS

ARGENTINA

Argentina took until 1978 to lift the World Cup despite producing legendary coaches, players, and teams. Their greatest player was the controversial Diego Maradona, who inspired them to a second world title in 1986.

Argentina has been producing great coaches, players, and teams for so long that it was remarkable that it took until 1978 before the talented men in the distinctive blue-and-white stripes won their first World Cup.

Argentina had come close to the title before, but finished as runner-up in the inaugural 1930 finals to hosts Uruguay. In 1978, it took home advantage, with brilliant goals from Mario Kempes, the midfield promptings of Ossie Ardiles, and shrewd managerial guidance by César Luis Menotti to fire them to victory.

They added a second crown at the 1986 World Cup finals in Mexico. This time they were inspired by Diego Maradona, who had failed to make the successful 1978 squad due to a lack of experience.

Argentina then finished as the runner-up to West Germany at the 1990 World Cup finals, despite Maradona's talents being restricted by his knee injury. Maradona's slide from glory continued at the 1994 World Cup finals in the United States, when he failed a dope test and was immediately sent home in disgrace. In his absence, Argentina bowed out to Romania in the second round. They also crashed out of the quarter-final stage four years later, as well as in the 2006 and 2010 World Cups.

Despite a controversial career, Maradona remains an idol for his outrageous talent and the sheer nerve with which he scored a remarkable two goals against England in the 1986 World Cup

RIGHT Three generations of greats: Di Stefano, Messi and Maradona

finals. These goals are legendary. One was helped in with his hand, the other one after a solo run from the halfway line.

Argentina's Boca Juniors and River Plate are among the world's greatest clubs, with the majority of the country's finest players having used them as a springboard to lucrative careers in Europe. Boca Juniors' uniform is blue and yellow, River Plate famously play in white shirts with a red sash.

In the late 1940s, River carried all before them with a forward line nicknamed 'The Machine' for its goal-scoring efficiency. They fielded two inside forwards, Juan Manuel Moreno and Angel Labruna, while in reserve was a young Alfredo Di Stefano. The side broke up in the early 1950s, when Argentinian league players went on strike in a demand for improved contracts and wages. Many players, including Di Stefano, were lured away to a "pirate" league in Colombia and never returned.

Boca became the first Argentinian club to reach a South American club final in 1962, but narrowly lost to Pelé's Santos in the Copa Libertadores. Independiente, from neighbouring city Avellaneda, became Argentina's first Continental champions in 1964 and Racing Club were crowned as the country's first Intercontinental Cup champions in 1967.

Argentina have won the Copa America 11 times, most notably in 1957 when the inspirational performances of inside forward Humberto Maschio, Antonio Valentín Angelillo, and Omar Sivori established them as early favourites to win the following year's World Cup. By the 1958 World Cup finals, the trio had been sold to Italian clubs and Argentina's hopes went with them.

From then on there was a steady stream of Argentinian players heading for the riches on offer in Europe. By the mid-1990s, as most Western European countries eased their restrictions on foreign players, a minor industry grew up in "finding" European forebears – and European Union passports – for many Argentinian players.

The national game has been split down the years between a clash of styles. In the 1960s and 1970s, coaches such as Juan Carlos Lorenzo (Boca), Manuel Giudice (Independiente) and Osvaldo Zubeldía (Estudiantes de La Plata), ruthlessly put the achievement of results above the quality of play and entertainment. Yet the country's

football federation deserved enormous credit for appointing the more positive Menotti as coach. Under Menotti, Argentina's triumph and style of play at the 1978 World Cup finals inspired a significant shift in opinion.

There has, however, been a failure to deal with hooligan violence in domestic Argentinian football. In fact, many club directors have preferred to provide complimentary match tickets and transport for the more notorious hooligans, known as 'Barras Bravas,' to avoid major disruption in the stadiums and around the grounds.

Argentina have played a major role in the history of the Copa Libertadores, the South American equivalent of Europe's Champions League, which has been dominated by six clubs – Argentinos Juniors, Boca Juniors, Estudiantes, Independiente, Racing Club, and River Plate.

ABOVE Daniel Passarella holds the World Cup trophy aloft in 1978

ITALY

Italy has tasted glory on the world stage with four World Cup crowns. A dramatic penalty shoot-out won them the final against France in 2006 – 12 years after they lost the World Cup to Brazil on penalties.

FOOTBALL FACTS

CHAMPIONS – LAST TEN YEARS

2004 AC Milan

2005 (not awarded: Juventus title revoked)

2006 Internazionale

2007 Internazionale

2008 Internazionale

2009 Internazionale

2010 Internazionale

2011 Milan

2012 Juventus

2013 Juventus

2014 Juventus

Italy is second only to Brazil in terms of World Cup wins, having lifted the Jules Rimet trophy four times. Known as 'the Azzurri,' or 'Blues,' the national side also triumphed at the 1968 European Championship, but this has been their lone triumph at confederation level. They came close, however, in 2000. Under the management of former World Cup-winning goalkeeper Dino Zoff, they had a 2-1 defeat to France on the 'golden goal' rule in Rotterdam, Holland.

A combination of English and Swiss students and teachers introduced the sport to Italy in the second half of the 19th century, with the English influence still evident in the anglicised style of club names such as AC Milan and Genoa (rather than Milano and Genova).

Their national league was founded in the late 1920s, and top Italian clubs took part with limited success in the Mitropa Cup – an inter-war predecessor of the modern-day competition known as the Champions League.

Turin-based Juventus proved to be the outstanding side of the 1930s, winning the league title five years in a row and providing the backbone of the national team that won the World Cup in 1934.

Italy had refused to play in the 1930 World Cup finals in Uruguay, but won the next two world crowns thanks to the managerial wisdom of Vittorio Pozzo and the genius of inside forward Giuseppe Meazza. Pozzo played three Argentinians in the team that beat Czechoslovakia in the 1934 final. Pozzo responded to criticism by pointing out their eligibility to national service, saying: "If they can die for Italy, then I'm sure they can play football for Italy!"

Torino also won five consecutive titles in the 1940s with an outstanding squad that was so strong the national team used 10 of their players in one match. However, the Torino squad was destroyed by a 1949 plane crash returning from playing a testimonial match in Lisbon.

RIGHT Fabio Grosso hits the winning penalty at the 2006 World Cup

The Torino disaster wrecked the national team's prospects ahead of their World Cup defence in Brazil in 1950. Also, many clubs invested financial strength in foreign players, which did nothing to help rebuild the national team. In 1958, Italy failed for the first time to progress through the qualifying rounds and into the World Cup finals.

During the early 1960s, clubs such as AC Milan and their bitter rivals Inter Milan ruled the European scene, even though the national team were unable to follow suit. Italy's participation in the 1966 World Cup finals remains notorious for their 1-0 defeat at the hands of North Korea, one of football's biggest upsets.

Adversity turned to glory when Italy captured the 1968 European Nations Cup after a replay. And two years later, inspired by the legendary figures of Giacinto Faccheti, Sandro Mazzola, Gigi Riva, and Gianni Rivera, Italy took part in one of the greatest games ever played. They edged past West Germany 4-3 in extra time to secure a place in the final of the World Cup. But they were so exhausted after the victory in the altitude of Mexico that they surrendered 4-1 to Brazil.

Italy arrived at the 1982 World Cup finals in the wake of a match-fixing scandal. Coach Enzo Bearzot and veteran captain Dino Zoff imposed a press blackout. Paolo Rossi had just returned from a two-year ban for his alleged role in the scandal and proved to be their inspiration, with six goals – including a hat-trick against Brazil – guiding his nation to overall victory.

For the next 24 years, the leading league clubs kept the Italian flag flying at international level with a string of European trophies. Pride was finally restored at national team level in 2006 when, Italy became world champions again by beating France in a penalty shoot-out in Berlin. In the 2010 World Cup Italy was knocked out in the first round. Italy's football had been partially overshadowed by another match-fixing scandal that saw a number of teams, including Juventus, relegated as punishment to Serie B. Juventus had been under investigation for the illegal administration of unspecified stimulants to their players when telephone-tap investigators uncovered a match manipulation system created by Juventus' 'transfer king' Luciano Moggi.

Evidence produced at a variety of hearings suggested that Moggi had used his influence with referees to generate yellow and red cards and suspensions for opposing players before they were due to play against Juventus and that he had also put pressure on players and coaches over transfers and even national team selection.

ABOVE The great Roberto Baggio stands dejected after missing his penalty in the 1994 final

NETHERLANDS

Dutch football is synonymous with 'total football' – the all-action strategy pioneered by Ajax Amsterdam under the inspiration of centre forward Johan Cruyff in the early 1970s.

FOOTBALL FACTS

CHAMPIONS – LAST TEN YEARS

2004 Ajax

2005 PSV Eindhoven

2006 PSV Eindhoven

2007 PSV Eindhoven

2008 PSV Eindhoven

2009 AZ Alkmaar

2010 Twente

2011 Ajax

2012 Ajax

2013 Ajax

2014 Ajax

Yet while Cruyff provided the brains and leadership out on the pitch, it was Ajax Amsterdam's coach Rinus Michels who masterminded the strategy. With two fabulous feet and mesmeric ball skills, Cruyff was at the heart of the Holland team – all of their goals in the 1974 World Cup finals either started or ended with a contribution by their captain.

Cruyff was supported by Johan Neeskens out of midfield, Ruud Krol from full back, and the duo of Johnny Rep and Rob Rensenbrink in attack. At the peak of their success, the team were nicknamed 'Clockwork Orange,' after the colour of their shirts

RIGHT Rinus Michels, the figurehead behind Total Football

as well as their precision passing. They again finished as runner-up at the World Cup finals, even without Cruyff at the helm in 1978.

Yet in terms of international status, Holland had been late developers. A crucial reason was the fact that it was not until the mid-1950s that domestic clubs such as Feyenoord, Sparta and Excelsior – notably all from Rotterdam – forced the recognition of professionalism, even initially part-time. The amateur status that ruled the Dutch game previously meant that star players, such as Faas Wilkes, had been forced abroad to the likes of Italy and Spain to earn a living from their talent.

Feyenoord became the first Dutch club to reach the semi-final stage of the European Champions' Cup in 1963, when they lost narrowly to Benfica. This was the start of a remarkable era, during which Feyenoord won the domestic double – league and cup – in both 1965 and 1969.

They then became the first Dutch club to win a European crown in 1970, edging past Celtic in extra time with a team that included outside left Coen Moulijn – one of the finest of Dutch players before the Ajax era.

Later Feyenoord, while largely playing second fiddle to Amsterdam Ajax at home, won the UEFA Cup twice. In the early 2000s, PSV Eindhoven were also regular group stage contenders in the Champions League.

Holland's national team had not qualified for the World Cup finals since the inter-war period but this, and the entire international status of Dutch football, was about to change with the explosive eruption of Amsterdam Ajax, which had reached the 1969 Champions' Cup final and then won it in

1971, 1972, and 1973, before Cruyff was sold to Barcelona.

Cruyff stepped out of national team football at the end of 1977 but Dutch football continued to produce an apparently endless stream of talented players and coaches.

PSV Eindhoven won the 1988 European Champions' Cup under the wily management of Guus Hiddink, while Holland won the European Championship in West Germany six weeks later. The Dutch national hero at that time was AC Milan – and former Amsterdam Ajax – striker Marco van Basten, who scored a group stage hat-trick against England, a semi-final winner against West Germany and a magnificent volleyed winning goal against the Soviet Union in the final at Munich's Olympic Stadium.

Controversy was never far away whenever the Dutch faced their German arch rivals. A spitting incident involving Holland midfielder Frank Rijkaard and German striker Rudi Völler marred a dramatic clash in the second round of the 1990 World Cup finals in Italy, which Holland lost 2-1.

At major tournaments, including the 2006 and 2010 World Cups, Holland's potential has been undermined by squabbling between players and coaching staff. Inspirational forward Ruud Gullit, a former World and European Player of the Year, refused to put on the shirt and play for Holland at the 1990 World Cup finals. Manager Hiddink sent midfielder Edgar Davids home during Holland's continued involvement in the 1996 European Championship after internal squabbling among the squad.

The unpredictability of the Dutch game's biggest names was evident up to the spring of 2008. Van Basten, by now manager of Holland, agreed to return as coach to Amsterdam Ajax after the European Championship in Austria and Switzerland, with Cruyff as a senior consultant. However, Cruyff had barely been confirmed in the role before he withdrew in an apparent disagreement with Van Basten – his one-time protégé – over youth strategy.

This is a sector that has become more crucial than ever to the Dutch game. The Ajax youth set-up is famed worldwide, with its players coached in a style and tactical system imposed on all the teams right through to the senior professionals. The club raises significant income selling players to the big leagues in England, Italy, and Spain to supplement its income from regular annual participation in European competitions.

ABOVE Marco van Basten fires home spectacularly in the 1988 European Championship final

GREAT NATIONS

ENGLAND

England lays justifiable claim to be the home and birthplace of football – the game itself is thought to originate in the Middle Ages, but its rules weren't formalised until the mid-19th century.

FOOTBALL FACTS

CHAMPIONS – LAST TEN YEARS

2004 Arsenal

2005 Chelsea

2006 Chelsea

2007 Manchester United

2008 Manchester United

2009 Manchester United

2010 Chelsea

2011 Manchester United

2012 Manchester City

2013 Manchester United

2014 Manchester City

The formation of the Football League in 1863, the first FA Cup Final in 1872, and the introduction of a revolutionary league system in 1888 were major events in the game's development in England.

But the country has only one World Cup triumph to date; the 1966 glory at London's Wembley Stadium. This victory was founded upon Alf Ramsey's coaching, Bobby Moore's captaincy, Bobby Charlton's long-range shooting, and Geoff Hurst's famous hat-trick. Bobby Robson's team, inspired by Paul Gascoigne and Gary Lineker, came close to tasting success by reaching the 1990 World Cup semi-final in Italy.

Despite international disappointment, England has some of the world's richest and most watched domestic teams. The national game's image was marred by hooliganism and tragedy in the 1980s and only booming television revenues and the lucrative FA Premier League's 1992 launch have helped tempt over some of the world's top talents. Manchester United, the world's best supported club, have dominated this in recent years, with big- spending Chelsea and Manchester City now wanting a slice of glory.

Manchester United claimed England's first European Champions' Cup by beating Lisbon's Benfica in 1968, some five years after Bill Nicholson's Tottenham had become the first English winners of a European trophy in the Cup Winners' Cup. Under the management of Sir Alex Ferguson, Manchester United won an unique hat-trick for an English club in 1999, with victory in the Premier League, FA Cup, and the Champions League to complete a unique hat-trick for an English club.

A third Champions League triumph followed in 2008, when United defeated Chelsea in a penalty shoot-out in Moscow in the first all-English final in the competition's history.

English clubs dominated Europe, with the European Cup won by an English side for five successive years in the late 1970s and early 1980s. The dark side of the English passion for football has been a long history of hooliganism. Trouble began to be noted in English League grounds in the early 1970s, but English fans' passion for travelling to away matches meant that hooliganism was exported and earned clubs a bad name. Leeds

RIGHT Paul Gascoigne is inconsolable after defeat to West Germany in 1990

United were barred from European football in the mid-1970s after their fans, angered by controversial refereeing in the 1975 Champions' Cup final against Bayern Munich, ripped out seats in the Parc des Princes in Paris.

A string of incidents occurred over the next decade and it was only after the Heysel disaster of 1985, when 39 Juventus fans died in Brussels after being charged by Liverpool fans, that both football and the law took action. After a crowd crush disaster at Hillsborough, Sheffield, in 1989, all-seater stadiums were imposed on all major sports venues, leading to the building of new grounds and total redevelopment of others. The pace of the stadia and security revolution persuaded UEFA to grant England hosting rights to the European Championship finals in 1996, which proved to be a huge success on and off the pitch.

English football has led the world game in many ways. In the late 1920s and early 1930s it was Arsenal, thanks to manager Herbert Chapman and forward Charlie Buchan, that conceived the 'WM's system, a formation, that dominated the sport for four decades. In the early 1990s, England opened the way for foreign investors and owners, also creating the FA Premier League at a crucial time

when satellite television was booming and clubs were turning to the London Stock Exchange.

Enormous controversy was generated by the purchase of Manchester United by the American Glazer family. Concerns about the club's debt were overshadowed by their continuing success on the pitch, until their devastating 2013-2014 season which followed Alex Ferguson's retirement.

Manchester City and Chelsea emerged as United's major rivals after being purchased by the Abu Dhabi United Group and Roman Abramovich, respectively. The two clubs now appear to have limitless sums in paying off the club's debts and buying in some of the world's finest players. But in an attempt to stop clubs buying their way to success in football, UEFA fined Manchester City in 2014 for breaching its Financial Fair Play Regulations. UEFA said the club had spent more money on wages and transfers than it had earned.

ABOVE Bobby Moore receives the Jules Rimet trophy from the Queen in 1966

FRANCE

France's contribution to football goes far beyond its national team's significant achievements on the pitch. French administrator Jules Rimet was the brains behind the creation of the World Cup finals.

FOOTBALL FACTS

CHAMPIONS – LAST TEN YEARS

2004 Lyon

2005 Lyon

2006 Lyon

2007 Lyon

2008 Lyon

2009 Bordeaux

2010 Marseille

2011 Lille

2012 Montpellier

2013 Paris Saint-Germain

2014 Paris Saint-Germain

Another French administrator, Henri Delaunay, paved the way for the European Championship. Gabriel Hanot, editor of the daily sports newspaper *L'Equipe*, was the creative force behind the European Champions Clubs' Cup.

France's greatest achievement on the field was their World Cup victory, on home soil, in 1998. Inspired by midfielder Zinedine Zidane, they saw off Paraguay, Italy and Croatia in the knock-out stage before crushing Brazil 3-0 in the final.

Two years later, David Trezeguet scored the 'golden goal' that beat Italy 2-1 in the 2000 European Championship final.

Zidane, who retired from international football after the 2004 European Championship, made an impressive comeback as France reached the final of the 2006 World Cup, but was sent off for head butting an opponent during defeat by Italy. In the 2010 World Cup, France were knocked out in the first round.

One of the greatest personalities in the modern French game has been Michel Platini. In 1984, he towered over the Euro finals – in France – scoring nine goals as the home team went on to beat Spain 2-0 in the final. Later, Platini progressed to become the country's national manager, President of the Organizing Committee of the 1998 World Cup and then a Counsellor to the FIFA President before being elected UEFA President in 2007.

French club football is often overshadowed by the national team, as so many home-grown players have moved abroad. One of the persisting problems for the league had been the lack of a successful club in the French capital, until the resurgence of Paris Saint-Germain in the 1990s. The club hit a slump in the early 2000s until they were bought by the Qatar Investment Authority in 2011, and won the league in 2013. In 2014, PSG was fined by for breaching its Financial Fair Play Regulations.

RIGHT The French team before the 1998 World Cup final

The first French club to make an international impression were Reims. Prompted by creative centre forward Raymond Kopa, they reached the first European Champions' Cup final in 1956 and were losing finalists again three years later. Kopa was the playmaker for the France side that finished third in the 1958 World Cup finals and helped set up most of Just Fontaine's record tally of 13 goals. Fontaine had been brought into the team only at the last minute because of injury to Reims team-mate René Bliard.

No French club managed to reach the European Champions' Cup final again until the eruption of Olympique Marseille in the late 1980s and early 1990s. The team were bankrolled by the flamboyant businessman-turned-politician Bernard Tapie.

A team starring top-scoring French player Jean-Pierre Papin and England winger Chris Waddle finished as runner-up in the 1991 European Champions' Cup, losing on penalties to Red Star Belgrade. Two years later, Olympique Marseille defeated AC Milan 1-0 with Papin playing for the Italian club. But that triumph was tarnished almost immediately as Marseilles were thrown out of European competition over a domestic match-fixing scandal that saw Tapie imprisoned.

Other French football clubs and their directors were punished, with sentences ranging from suspensions to fines for financial irregularities.

Lyon President Jean-Michel Aulas said: "What we need in the French game is greater financial freedom to run our own affairs. Then maybe we wouldn't have these other problems. Fans demand success and directors want to give that to them, for their own reasons."

Software millionaire Aulas knew his subject well. He had taken over Lyon when the club were in the second division, and supplied both financial and administrative resources to secure promotion and then a record run of seven successive league titles from 2002 to 2008.

Aulas even pressed successfully for a relaxation of laws barring sports clubs from obtaining outside, foreign investment. He claimed that, without new revenue streams, French clubs could not afford to buy the best players nor could they develop stadia to such an extent that the country could ever hope to host the finals of the World Cup or European Championship.

The factor that has continued to elude Aulas has been success in European competitions. Lyon have regularly reached the knock-out stage of the European Champions League without ever reaching even the semi-finals. Saint-Etienne (1976) and AS Monaco (2004) remain the only other French clubs aside from Reims and Marseille to have reached a European Champions League final. Saint-Etienne lost narrowly to Bayern Munich while AS Monaco crashed 3-0 to Porto.

BELOW Raymond Kopa trains in 1958

GERMANY

Germany has long been one of the most powerful countries in international football with four World Cup victories to their name – only Brazil has more.

FOOTBALL FACTS

CHAMPIONS – LAST TEN YEARS

2004 Werder Bremen
2005 Bayern Munich
2006 Bayern Munich
2007 Stuttgart
2008 Bayern Munich
2009 VfL Wolfsburg
2010 Bayern Munich
2011 Borussia Dortmund
2012 Borussia Dortmund
2013 Bayern Munich
2014 Bayern Munich

Football had difficulty establishing itself initially in Germany because of the social strength of the gymnastic movement. Attitudes changed gradually partly because of football's popularity among young people and, partly because toward the end of World War I, the Kaiser ascribed British strength of character on the battlefield to the morale and physical qualities developed through the team sports played at schools and universities.

Football clubs thrived in the inter-war years even though the domestic game was riven with tension over the issue of professionalism. Even under Hitler's National Socialist government in the 1930s, football was considered a recreation with payments to players prohibited. This did not prevent many clubs from bending the rules.

The leading club in the 1930s were FC Schalke, which came from the mining town of Gelsenkirchen in the Ruhr. All their players were paid as miners. Their star winger Ernst Kuzorra

revealed years later: "The nearest we saw of a mine was the pithead in the distance."

The German game was organised in a regional championship, topped off by a play-off series to decide the national champions. The play-off final regularly drew crowds of 70,000–80,000. FC Schalke were crowned champions six times and won the domestic cup once in the 1930s. Their inside forward, Fritz Szepan, led Germany to third place in the 1934 World Cup. Kuzorra and Szepan both have roads named in their honour around the present FC Schalke stadium.

After the war, political reality saw Germany divided into west and east sectors. Ultimately, Soviet-supported East Germany, known as the German Democratic Republic, developed its own football federation and league. Although East Germany became a force in international swimming and athletics, it did not replicate this success in football. East Germany only ever

RIGHT Jurgen Klinsmann and Bastian Schweinsteiger in 2006

qualified for the World Cup finals in 1974, and in the same year, Magdeburg won the nation's only European club trophy by taking the Cup Winners' Cup.

In contrast, football in West Germany went from strength to strength. Wily coach Sepp Herberger and captain Fritz Walter guided the West German team to a shock victory over hot favourites Hungary in the final of the 1954 World Cup. The victory was known as the "miracle of Berne." Hungary – as Olympic champions – had not been beaten for four years. Further World Cup triumphs followed in 1974, 1990 and 2014.

In 1990, the collapse of the Berlin Wall led to the reunification of Germany and the integration of East German football into the German football federation, which had always styled itself as the "overall" Deutscher Fussball Bund. Germany, whether West or unified, have also finished as World Cup runner-up four times (1966, 1982, 1986, and 2002) and third three times (1976, 1992, and 2008). They have also won the European Championship three times (1972, 1980, and 1996) and three times finished as runner-up (1976, 1992, and 2008).

A significant factor in the national team's success was the creation of the unified, fully professional Bundesliga in 1963. Bayern Munich, who have won 24 modern championships to add to their success in 1932, hold the record for the greatest number of domestic titles. The greatest personality to emerge from within Bayern Munich was Franz Beckenbauer, known as 'Der Kaiser,' who netted 68 goals in 62 games for his country, including the winning goal in the 1974 World Cup final against Holland.

As captain and sweeper, Beckenbauer led Bayern Munich to a European Champions' League hat-trick (1974, 1975, and 1976). He was ably supported by a host of stars that included goalkeeper 'Sepp' Maier, full-back Paul Breitner, midfielder Uli Hoeness, and the greatest goalscorer of the modern era, Gerd Müller.

Beckenbauer later coached West Germany to 1990 World Cup victory over Argentina in Italy, having guided them to the final four years earlier. In the meantime, he coached Bayern Munich to UEFA Cup success in 1996 and became their club president in time to oversee their fourth European

Champions' League victory in 2001.

Moving on up the political ladder, Beckenbauer led the German bid to win hosting rights to the 2006 World Cup finals for Germany and was then president of the FIFA Organizing Committee. As a vice-president of the German Football Federation he was also voted onto the executive committees of both FIFA and UEFA.

ABOVE Franz Beckenbauer challenges Johan Neeskens in the 1974 World Cup final

GREAT NATIONS

PORTUGAL

FOOTBALL FACTS

CHAMPIONS – LAST TEN YEARS

2004	Porto
2005	Benfica
2006	Porto
2007	Porto
2008	Porto
2009	Benfica
2010	Porto
2011	Porto
2012	Porto
2013	Porto
2014	Benfica

The Portuguese team are often known as the 'Brazilians of Europe,' thanks to the flamboyance of Eusébio in the 1960s, the 'golden generation' of Luis Figo, João Pinto, and Rui Costa in the 1990s, and the country's latest idol, Cristiano Ronaldo.

Traditionally the power of the Portuguese game has been dominated by the three leading clubs of Benfica, Porto, and Sporting Lisbon. Only Belenenses in 1948 and Boavista in 2001 have broken their monopoly of the league since its formation in 1934. Benfica lead the way with 31 championships, with Porto picking up 16 of their 23 titles in the past 24 years.

Football was introduced to Portugal through the ports in the 19th century, but the relatively small size of the country meant the national team had little or no impact internationally.

However, Portugal had a source of playing talent in their African territories, such as Angola and Mozambique. An increasing number of African players were imported by the clubs and, from the late 1950s, also selected for the national team. Such players included Benfica's goalkeeper Jose Alberto Costa Pereira, striker Jose Aguas, and the two inside forwards Joaquin Santana and Mario Coluna.

All four were members of Benfica's Champions' Cup-winning side that, in 1961, defeated favourites Barcelona 3-2 in Berne, Switzerland. Simultaneously, Benfica had also acquired the greatest African

RIGHT Luis Figo at the 2006 World Cup

discovery of all in young striker Eusébio da Silva Ferreira. One year later he scored two thundering goals as Benfica defeated Real Madrid 5-3 to win their second Champions' Cup. Eusébio would also lead Benfica to three more finals, albeit finishing on the losers' side against AC Milan (1963), Inter Milan (1965), and Manchester United (1968).

A mixture of Sporting Lisbon's defence, along with Benfica's midfield and attack, provided the backbone for the Portuguese national side that finished third in their first ever World Cup finals, Eusébio a nine-goal top scorer in England.

Like the country itself, Portuguese football suffered from economic decline in the following decades but a new era dawned with triumphs in the 1989 and 1991 World Youth Cups. Ever since the emergence of the so-called 'golden generation,' Portugal became a potential threat at major tournaments.

Porto emerged as the dominant club under the controversial presidency of Jorge Nuno Pinto da Costa. He hired an equally controversial coach in Jose Mourinho and was rewarded with victory in the 2003 UEFA Cup and then, more impressively, in the European Champions League a year later – before Mourinho was lured away to Chelsea.

Portugal reached the semi-final stage of the 2000 European Championship in Belgium and Holland. The inability to compete in wages with the giants of England, Italy, and Spain meant the departure of stars such as Figo (Barcelona, Real Madrid, and Inter Milan), Simao Sabrosa (Barcelona and Atletico Madrid), Deco (Barcelona), and Cristiano Ronaldo (Manchester United and Real Madrid). The national team gained from these players competing in better-quality leagues.

From 2003–08, the Portuguese Football Federation hired Luiz Felipe Scolari, Brazil's 2002 World Cup-winning coach, to bring the competitive best out of the country's depth of talent. Scolari succeeded to a qualified degree. Portugal finished as runner-up on home territory in the 2004 European Championship – losing to outsiders Greece in the final – and were fourth at the 2006 World Cup finals in Germany. Scolari conceded on leaving in 2008 to return to club football with Chelsea: "I did not win something big which is what I came to do."

Scolari's final game with Portugal was at the 2008 European Championship finals, when Portugal fell 3-2 to Germany in the quarter-finals. Scolari's replacements, Carlos Queiroz and then Paulo Bento fared little better in the 2010 World Cup and Euro 2012 respectively. In both competitions, Portugal failed to reach the final.

ABOVE Eusebio is consoled after England beat Portugal in the 1966 semi-final

GREAT NATIONS

SPAIN

Spain's dominance of world football began in 2008, with the country's European Championship win. In 2010, Spain won the World Cup which was followed by another European Championship victory in 2012.

FOOTBALL FACTS

CHAMPIONS – LAST TEN YEARS

2003 Real Madrid
2004 Valencia
2005 Barcelona
2006 Barcelona
2007 Real Madrid
2008 Real Madrid
2009 Barcelona
2010 Barcelona
2011 Barcelona
2012 Real Madrid
2013 Barcelona
2014 Atletico Madrid

Spain have a history rich in great players and their 2008 European Championship victory meant that their best players – goalkeeper and captain Iker Casillas, the midfielder trio of Cesc Fabregas, Xavi Hernandez and Andres Iniesta, and the strikeforce of Fernando Torres and David Villa – could claim equality of star billing in the hall of fame with older heroes. These include legends of the 1920s and 1930s, when goalkeeper Ricardo Zamora, defender

Jacinto Quincoces, and inside forward Luis Regueiro helped Spain become the first foreign nation to beat England 4-3 in Madrid in 1929.

At the end of the 1950s, a team packed with stars such as Alfredo Di Stefano, Ladislav Kubala, and Luis Suarez Miramontes saw Spain ranked as favourites to win the inaugural Nations Cup. However, when the 1960 quarter-final draw matched Spain against the Soviet Union, dictator

RIGHT Emilio Butragueno in action in Mexico in 1986

Francisco Franco ordered the team to withdraw on political grounds.

Even so long after the Spanish Civil War, Spain still had no diplomatic relations with countries from the Communist Block. In 1964, on home soil, Spain won its first title success. Relations with the East had thawed significantly enough for the USSR squad to be allowed entry into Spain for the European Championship finals. Strikers Jesus Pereda and Marcelino each scored in Spain's 2-1 victory over the Soviets.

Spain's failure to achieve national team success in the succeeding four decades remains one of football's mysteries. The football federation has long run one of the most successful international youth sections and Juan Santisteban, once a European Cup-winning halfback with Real Madrid, has been perhaps the most respected age level coach in the world. But the best the seniors could point to was a runner-up spot at the 1984 European Championship finals and a stunning 5-1 win over Denmark in the second round of the 1986 World Cup finals, when Emilio Butragueno, nicknamed 'the vulture,' scored four goals.

However, at club level the story could not be more different. Real Madrid were Europe's first club champions in 1956 and retained the trophy for the next four years, during a period of total domination in which the team enthralled with their victories in an entertaining manner. With nine European Champions' Cups, two UEFA Cups, and 32 domestic league titles, Real Madrid have their own special place in the history books.

They also led the way in European stadium development, which they owed to the vision of Santiago Bernabeu – a former player and coach, who became president in 1943. Bernabeu issued bonds to finance the building of a new stadium that was opened in 1947, and named the Bernabeu Stadium. Its capacity was increased in the late 1950s to 125,000, as fans flocked to watch their heroes and superstars at work.

Standing toe to toe with Real Madrid is Barcelona, a team that has dominated club football alongside Real in Spain for the last decade. With its motto of "More than a Club," Barcelona claims a unique loyalty on and off the field. The current team has some of the brightest stars of world

football including Lionel Messi, Neymar and Andres Iniesta. However, in the 2013-14 season Atletico Madrid led an outstanding campaign to usurp the authority of both Barcelona and Real Madrid and win the La Liga crown.

Spain crashed out of the 2014 World Cup in the group stages. They failed to recover after an opening game 5-1 thrashing against Holland.

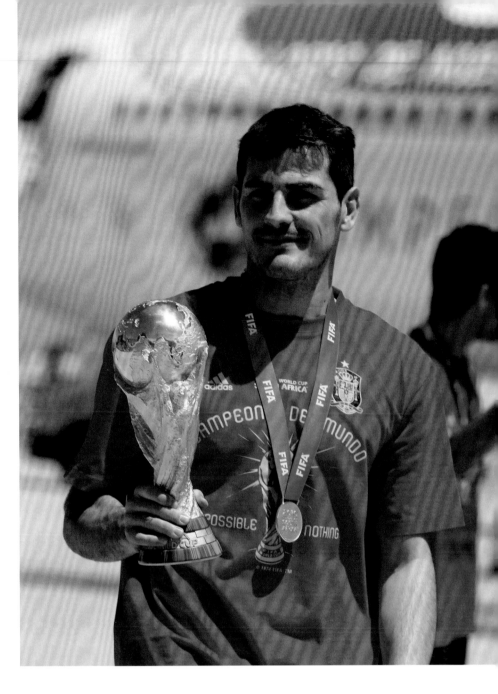

ABOVE Captain Iker Casillas after winning the 2010 World Cup

RUSSIA

Europe's most populous nation has rarely punched its weight in international football. So far, its greatest days came in the early 1960s, while it was a part of the Soviet Union.

FOOTBALL FACTS

CHAMPIONS – LAST TEN YEARS

2003 CSKA Moscow

2004 Lokomotiv Moscow

2005 CSKA Moscow

2006 CSKA Moscow

2007 Zenit St. Petersburg

2008 Rubin Kazan

2009 Rubin Kazan

2010 Zenit St. Petersburg

2011-12 Zenit St. Petersburg

2012-13 CSKA Moscow

2013-14 CSKA Moscow

Note: The Russian league switched to an autumn-spring schedule for the 2011-12 season.

Moscow, the capital of the USSR, was the central force in its national football. It boasted all the major clubs – Dynamo, Spartak, Torpedo, Lokomotiv, and CSKA – and had all the finest players. The size of the country made it difficult for any other clubs to compete effectively until air travel was possible. Even that was a risk, with the entire first team squad of Pakhtakor Tashkent killed when their plane crashed in 1979.

By the mid-1960s, however, major powers were emerging in the club game in Georgia and Ukraine especially, and also in Armenia and Belarus. Dynamo Tbilisi, Dynamo Kiev, Dynamo Minsk, and Ararat Yerevan may have owed their creation to the Soviet model but all developed a style of football very different to the physical Moscow style. Tbilisi and Kiev played football with a Latin-style touch of flair. Kiev twice won in the European Cup Winners' Cup and Tbilisi won it once but their officials and coaches and players never co-existed happily with the Moscow factions.

The Soviet Communist attitude to sport brought other complications. The USSR ignored FIFA and would not compete internationally until after World War II. A tour of Britain by Moscow Dynamo in the winter of 1945 marked a slight

RIGHT Soviet Union's Valreiy Parkoujan scores against Chile in 1966

thaw. Two years later the Soviet Union joined FIFA on condition that it could have a permanent vice-president.

By definition, Soviet footballers were amateurs, not paid for playing football though they were paid for their nominal roles in the armed services or other professions. The Soviet Union felt free to send its strongest possible team to the Olympics, while Western European rivals were weakened by the transparency of their own players' professional status. The Soviet national team competed internationally for the first time at the 1952 Olympic Games, which they duly won four years later in Melbourne, Australia. Their heroes were world-class footballers, goalkeeper Lev Yashin, and left-half skipper Igor Netto.

Yashin was a hero again when the Soviets won the inaugural 1960 European Championship. Milan Galic had given Yugoslavia the lead, right winger Slava Metreveli levelled, and journalist turned-centre forward Viktor Ponedelnik wrote his own page in history by scoring the extra time winner. The Soviet Union lost the 1964 final 2-1 to Spain and finished fourth in the 1966 World Cup finals.

The change in the balance of power is reflected in the league honours list when the Soviet Union was finally wiped off the map after perestroika led to the break-up of the former Soviet Union. From that point on a Russian national team was formed. Kiev won 13 league titles in the Soviet era, Spartak Moscow 12, Dynamo Moscow 11, CSKA Moscow seven, and Lokomotiv Moscow three.

Yet not once in the Soviet era did a club from the Russian Republic win a European cup. That feat had to wait until 2005 when CSKA Moscow beat Sporting Lisbon 3-1 in the UEFA Cup final. Zenit St. Petersburg followed their example in 2008, when they also won the UEFA Cup, beating Glasgow's Rangers. Those achievements demonstrated how far Russian clubs have come since the break up of the Soviet Union and the formation of a Russian league – then virtually bankrupt – in 1992.

The collapse of central funding for football clubs from the various state organisations threw the domestic game into turmoil. Within a decade, only Lokomotiv were still in the controlling, supporting hands of the railway unions. All the other clubs

had long since been cast adrift by (Dynamo), army (CSKA), and farms (Spartak).

The domestic game was rescued by the oligarchs who had taken massive financial advantage of the collapse of Communism and the bargain-basement sell-offs of the major utilities. Roman Abramovich's oil company Sibneft originally supported CSKA and the Russian energy giant Gazprom funded the 2007 champions Zenit. The outcome has been that Russian clubs now import star players from all over the world.

ABOVE Oleg Salenko scored five in the 6-1 win over Cameroon at USA 1994

GREAT NATIONS MOMENTS

RIGHT Pelé celebrates Brazil's first in the 1970 World Cup final victory

BELOW Fabio Capello (front, left) lines up for Italy against England in 1973

ABOVE North Korea and Portugal emerge for their sensational 1966 World Cup tie

BELOW The Soviet Union greet their English host fans in 1966

RIGHT Franz Beckenbauer betters rival captain Johan Cruyff in the 1974 World Cup final

ABOVE Argentina poised to win their first World Cup, in 1978

RIGHT England line up, optimistically, ahead of their 1982 World Cup assault

BELOW Holland in 1978 – about to finish World Cup runners-up once more

ABOVE Didier Six opens up for France against Czechoslovakia in 1982

ABOVE Mexico head for a 2-1 defeat by Portugal in Germany in 2006

LEFT Gary Lineker's penalty goal against West Germany in 1990 is not enough for England

GREAT NATIONS

REST OF THE WORLD

From small nations such as Luxembourg and San Marino to the array of African sides and former Soviet states, the status and power of world football is forever changing.

BELOW Bulgaria's Hristo Stoichkov (left) celebrates another goal for Barcelona

ALBANIA (Europe): Despite being among UEFA's founder members in 1954, Albanian football has been hampered by the country's poverty and isolation. They beat newly-crowned European champions Greece in the 2006 World Cup qualifiers, but are still waiting to reach their first tournament.

ALGERIA (Africa): Having broken away from France in 1958, Algeria's footballers beat eventual finalists West Germany at the 1982 World Cup thanks to Lakhdar Belloumi's goal, but were eliminated in a convenient draw between the West Germans and Austria. Their finest moment came when Moussa Saïb captained the hosts to success at the 1990 African Cup of Nations. JS Kabylie have dominated at home, having won 14 league titles, but ES Setif are the current team to beat.

ANDORRA (Europe): Not too much can be expected of a country with a population of 72,000, squeezed between Spain and France. Andorra's team, largely made up of part-timers, only began playing international football in 1997.

ANGOLA (Africa): On the rise after years of being constrained by civil war and having their finest players poached by Portugal, Angola made an encouraging World Cup finals debut in 2006. Petro Atlético have been crowned as Angolan champions 15 times.

AUSTRALIA (Asia): After achieving nothing at the 1974 World Cup, the 'Socceroos' did not return until 2006, when Dutch manager Guus

Hiddink made effective use of such talents as Tim Cahill, Harry Kewell, and Mark Viduka. Australia left the uncompetitive Oceania Football Federation for Asia later that year, and have since qualified for the 2010 and 2014 World Cups. The national A-League kicked off in 2005–06, and has attracted big name Europeans like Alessandro Del Piero to the region.

AUSTRIA (Europe): The so-called 'Wunderteam' of the 1930s, inspired by playmaker Matthias Sindelar and coach Hugo Meisl, finished fourth at the 1934 World Cup. Austrian coach Ernst Happel took Holland to the 1978 World Cup final; the Ernst Happel Stadium in Vienna is named after him. The stadium was also the venue for the Euro 2008 final. Rapid Vienna lead the way in home games, with an astonishing 32 league titles, yet in recent years Red Bull Salzburg have won four of the past seven.

AZERBAIJAN (Europe): This former Soviet state has struggled since independence despite a spell in charge by World Cup-winning Brazil captain Carlos Alberto. The main stadium in Baku is named after linesman Tofik Bakhmarov, who decided England's third goal in the 1966 World Cup final really did cross the line.

BELARUS (Europe): Midfielder Alexander Hleb put Belarus on the map with his club displays in Germany, England and Spain, but the former Soviet state narrowly missed out on a place at the 2002 World Cup finals after a last-gasp defeat to Wales. BATE Borisov have won the past seven titles, and became the first Belorussian club to qualify for the Champions League group stages.

BELGIUM (Europe): Despite its small size, Belgium reached the 1980 European Championship final, beat holders Argentina in the opening game of the 1982 World Cup, and finished fourth in 1986 under Guy Thys. Goalkeeper Jean-Marie Pfaff, defender Eric Gerets, midfielder Jan Ceulemans, and forward Enzo Scifo formed the side's spine. Anderlecht have won not only a record 32 league titles but one UEFA Cup, a pair of European Super Cups, twice been crowned European Champions, and twice won the Cup Winners' Cup.

BOLIVIA (South America): The Hernando Siles Stadium in La Paz is one of the world's highest playing surfaces, at 3,637 metres above sea level. The national side have struggled, although they did win the 1963 Copa America courtesy of a 5-4 win over Brazil, and famously beat Argentina 6-1 in a 2009 World Cup qualifying game. Bolívar FC have won the domestic league 18 times.

BOSNIA-HERZEGOVINA (Europe): This former Yugoslav republic was accepted by UEFA in 1991, but, despite a wealth of talent, had been unable to reach a major tournament until they qualified for the 2014 World Cup. Željezničar have won five Premier League titles.

BULGARIA (Europe): This is one of Eastern Europe's most consistent producers of quality players. The national team's finest achievement was in reaching the World Cup semi-finals in 1994 with a team starring the legendary Hristo Stoichkov and Emil Kostadinov, while Dimitar Berbatov and Stiliyan Petrov have been the outstanding performers of the last decade. The record domestic champions are CSKA Sofia with 31 league titles to their credit, while city rivals Levski have 26.

BURKINA FASO (Africa): Burkina Faso lost to Algeria in qualifying play-offs ahead of the 2014 World Cup, which meant 2013 will be remembered with disappointment despite reaching the final of the African Cup of Nations for the first time. They have never appeared at a World Cup finals.

CAMEROON (Africa): Known as the 'Indomitable Lions', Cameroon were the surprise package at the 1990 World Cup. They upset holders Argentina and pushed England hard in the quarter-finals, spearheaded by veteran striker Roger Milla. Samuel Eto'o holds the scoring record for the African Cup of Nations, a competition that Cameroon have won four times. Canon Yaoundé have won the African Championship three times to go with their 10 domestic league titles.

CANADA (Central and North America): Often overshadowed by CONCACAF rivals such as Mexico and the US, Canada still await their second World Cup qualification, having lost all three group games in 1986.

CHILE (South America): Strike duo Marcelo Salas and Iván Zamorano helped guide Chile to the 1998 World Cup quarter-finals. But Chile's best run came when hosting the 1962 tournament, eventually losing to Brazil in a fiery semi-final. Colo-Colo have won 31 Chilean league titles, more than double the tally of their main rivals.

ABOVE Samuel Eto'o acknowledges the cheers greeting another of his goals for Cameroon

GREAT NATIONS

REST OF THE WORLD

CHINA (Asia): The national team faced Manila in Asia's first international match in 1913, but only made their World Cup finals debut in 2002 when they lost all three matches under Serb Bora Milutinovic. Versatile midfielder Zheng Zhi captained the side that hosted but lost the 2004 Asian Cup final to Japan.

COLOMBIA (South America): Carlos Valderrama, Faustino Asprilla and goalkeeper Rene Higuita (famous for his 'scorpion kick') made Colombia one of the world's most entertaining yet underachieving sides in the 1990s. Iván Córdoba's goal beat Mexico in the 2001 Copa America final. Club Deportivo Los Millonarios, whose riches lured stars such as Alfredo Di Stefano to a breakaway league in the 1940s and 1950s, have picked up 14 league titles.

CONGO (DR) (Africa): Under their former name of Zaire, they became the first black African side to reach the World Cup finals. But at the 1974 competition they were humiliated by eventual champions West Germany. They were crowned African champions in 1968 and 1974, and have produced several excellent players for other countries, such as France's Claude Makelele. Lomana Tresor Lua Lua was a Premier League regular at Newcastle United and Portsmouth. Étoile du Congo, of Brazzaville, have won 12 league titles.

COSTA RICA (Central and North America): Consistent performers who reached their first World Cup in 1990 under charismatic coach Bora Milutinovic. They also appeared at the 2002 and 2006 tournaments, with striker Paolo Wanchope as the figurehead. They have won nine CONCACAF championships, though surprisingly none since 1989. Former CONCACAF club champions Deportivo Saprissa have a record 29 domestic league titles.

CROATIA (Europe): This Balkan country taught England a footballing lesson in qualifiers for the

2008 European Championship – just as they did to Germany on their way to third place at the 1998 World Cup. Back then they were inspired by the likes of Robert Prosinecki, Golden Boot winner Davor Šuker, and future national coach Slaven Bilic. More recently, Brazilian-born striker Eduardo and nimble midfielders Luka Modric and Ivan Rakitic have caught the eye. Dinamo Zagreb have won the league 15 times since Croatia achieved independence from the former Yugoslavia in 1992.

CYPRUS (Europe): Cyprus have pulled off some unlikely results down the years, but have never appeared in a major finals, missing out on a European Championship play-off spot in 2000 by a single point. APOEL Nicosia, who have featured in the Champions League, have won the Cypriot league 22 times and are its pre-eminent club.

CZECH REPUBLIC (Europe): The Czechs formed the larger part of the old Czechoslovakia, which reached the World Cup Final in 1934 and 1962 – when Czech wing-half Josef Masopust was voted European Footballer of the Year. Czechoslovakia won the European Championship in 1976 thanks to a penalty shootout victory against West Germany. The 'new' Czech Republic side lost the Euro 1996 final to the Germans on a golden goal. Sparta Prague have dominated domestic football, winning 11 championships since the Czechs and Slovaks split in 1993. The best Czech players inevitably move to the big clubs in the West. Pavel Nedved of Juventus was voted European Footballer of the Year in 2003, while Petr Cech was a Champions League winner with Chelsea in 2012.

DENMARK (Europe): The Danes' greatest triumph came in 1992, when they beat Germany 2-0 to win the European Championships. The Danes also reached the semi-finals of Euro 1984 and the last 16 of the 1986 World Cup. Denmark has produced many stars for rich Western clubs, such as the Laudrup brothers

ABOVE Colombia's Carlos Valderrama has earned more than 100 caps playing for his country

(Michael and Brian), Morten Olsen, and Manchester United great Peter Schmeichel. FC Copenhagen have won nine titles since 2001.

ECUADOR (South America): Qualified for the last three World Cup finals tournaments and reached the last 16 in 2006, losing to England. Domestically, Sporting Club Barcelona have won 14 titles, one more than El Nacional.

EGYPT (Africa): Won the African Cup of Nations for a record seventh time in 2010, but have struggled on the world stage with only two World Cup appearances, the last in 1990, and the troubled Egyptians missed out on 2014 with defeat to Ghana. At home, Al-Ahly have dominated.

EL SALVADOR (Central and North America): Reached the 1970 World Cup finals by beating local rivals Honduras. This stoked up an already tense situation between the two countries, culminating in a six-day conflict that became known as 'the football war'. They also qualified in 1982, but have lost all six games they've played.

ESTONIA (Europe): Estonia are yet to make their mark internationally, though goalkeeper Mart Poom was a Premier League regular at several sides. Flora Tallinn have dominated the domestic championship since Estonia became a republic in 1992, taking nine titles.

FAROE ISLANDS (Europe): Minnows of European football, the Faroes beat Lithuania in 2009 to record their first competitive win in seven years, the same year they beat neighbours Iceland in a friendly.

FINLAND (Europe): Noted for producing players for Europe's big clubs, such as Jari Litmanen (Ajax) and Sami Hyypia (Liverpool), Finland have nonetheless struggled on the international stage and still await a major tournament appearance. The domestic championship has been dominated by HJK Helsinki, United Tampere, and Haka Valkeakoski.

GEORGIA (Europe): Their greatest moment came in 1981, when Dinamo Tbilisi, inspired by midfielder David Kipiani, beat Carl Zeiss Jena 2-1 in the European Cup Winners' Cup final. The national side is currently coached by one of Georgia's greatest players, Temuri Ketsbaia.

GHANA (Africa): Ghana reached the quarter-finals of the 2010 World Cup, and were within a penalty kick of becoming the first Africans ever to make the last four, only for Asamoah Gyan to miss his spot kick before Uruguay won the shootout. Featuring stars such as Michael Essien and Kevin-Prince Boateng, Ghana failed to make it out of the group stages in Brazil 2014. Ghana have won the African Cup of Nations four times. Asante Kotoko have won 22 domestic titles.

GREECE (Europe): Shock winners of the 2004 European Championship when Otto Rehhagel's side beat hosts Portugal 1-0 in the final with a goal from Angelos Charisteas. They then failed to qualify for the 2006 World Cup finals. Panathinaikos reached the 1971 European Cup final, losing to Ajax at Wembley. Olympiakos have dominated the domestic game, winning 15 of the last 17 championships. In 2008, they became the first Greek side to play in the last 16 of the Champions League.

ABOVE Theo Zagorakis, a European title-winning hero for Greece

GREAT NATIONS

REST OF THE WORLD

HAITI (Central and North America): Haiti reached the World Cup finals in 1974 when Emmanuel Sanon scored a historic goal against Italy but have not been back since. They were CONCACAF champions in 1957 and 1973.

HONDURAS (Central and North America): Reaching the World Cup finals for the first time in 1982, they had been CONCACAF champions the previous year. Their team, now driven by Wilson Palacios, is probably as good as it ever has been.

HUNGARY (Europe): The 'Magnificent Magyars' were the finest team in the world in the early 1950s. Led by Ferenc Puskas, they included greats such as striker Sandor Kocsis, playmaker Nandor Hidegkuti, flying winger Zoltan Czibor, goalkeeper Gyula Grocis, and wing half Jozsef Boszik. But they were shocked by West Germany in the 1954 World Cup final and the team broke up two years later after the Budapest uprising against Soviet control. A new side finished third in the 1964 European Championship and reached the 1966 World Cup quarter-finals after beating Brazil 3-1. Hungary have struggled at international level ever since. Ferencvaros have 27 titles, but Debrecen have won six of the last 10.

ICELAND (Europe): Yet to make an impact in major competitions, they are, however, well known for exporting star players, such as former Chelsea and Barcelona forward Eidur Gudjohnsen. They were beaten in a play-off for the 2014 World Cup by Croatia.

INDIA (Asia): The team reached the World Cup finals once, in 1950, but withdrew after FIFA barred them from playing in bare feet.

IRAN (Asia): Although they have reached the World Cup finals three times, they have yet to reach the last 16. They have won the Asian Cup

three times. Iran's greatest player Ali Daei won 149 caps, and scored a record 35 World Cup qualifying goals.

IRAQ (Asia): Iraq won the 2007 Asian Cup, after a 1-0 win over Saudi Arabia in the final, appearing in the Confederations Cup final two years later. They have had one World Cup appearance, in 1986.

ISRAEL (Europe): Israeli clubs dominated the early years of the Asian Club Championship, before political problems forced the country out into the cold and then into UEFA. The national team reached the World Cup finals in 1970.

IVORY COAST (Africa): Winners of the African Cup of Nations in 1992, the national team reached the World Cup finals for the first time in 2006 with a golden generation of players expected to perform in 2010, where they were unfortunate to be drawn alongside Brazil and Portugal. The country is most famous for exporting star players such as Didier Drogba, Salomon Kalou and the Toure brothers, Kolo and Yaya.

JAMAICA (Central and North America): Their best performance was reaching the 1998 World Cup finals with a team that included many England-based players, beating Japan in their final group game.

JAPAN (Asia): Reaching the World Cup finals in 1998, Japan advanced to a best-yet place in the last 16 on home soil in 2002, which they matched in 2010. They have won the Asian Cup four times, and are the current holders after a 1-0 win over Australia in the 2011 final. The J-League continues to develop since its formation in 1992, though most of Japan's top talents move to Europe.

KAZAKHSTAN (Europe): After gaining independence from the Soviet Union, the country

BELOW Haiti's Sanon runs with the ball in a 1974 World Cup match against Italy

ABOVE The Ivory Coast team before their game against Ghana in the 2008 African Cup of Nations

switched from the Asian Confederation to UEFA in 2002. Arguably their greatest player was Oleg Litvinenko, who died tragically in November 2007, just four days short of his 34th birthday.

KUWAIT (Asia): The national team had one appearance in the World Cup finals in 1982. They managed a draw with Czechoslovakia but lost to both England and France. During the last of these, France famously 'scored' while some of the Kuwaiti players had stopped playing, having heard a whistle. They walked off the pitch in protest and resumed only after the goal was disallowed. They have previously been coached by both Carlos Alberto Parreira and Luiz Felipe Scolari.

LATVIA (Europe): Having regained their independence in 1992, they are the only Baltic team to have qualified for the European Championship finals when they upset Turkey in the qualifiers for the 2004 tournament in Portugal. At home, Skonto Riga were the dominant side during the 1990s, but have won the league just once in the last nine years, with FK Ventspils winning five of those.

LIECHTENSTEIN (Europe): One of the whipping boys of European football, comprising mainly part-timers, the tiny principality improved in the Euro 2008 qualifiers when they upset Latvia 1-0 and followed that up with a 3-0 win over Iceland. Tournament qualification remains a distant dream.

LITHUANIA (Europe): They came third in their group in both the Euro 96 and 1998 World Cup qualifying campaigns. Since then they have managed away draws with both Germany and Italy but, like many former Soviet states, they lack depth of quality as yet.

LUXEMBOURG (Europe): Historically one of Europe's minor teams, they once went 12 years without winning a competitive fixture, but beat Switzerland in 2008. They are almost exclusively part-timers, though record appearance maker Jeff Strasser had a solid Bundesliga career in Germany.

MACEDONIA (Europe): Only since the break-up of Yugoslavia have they had their own officially recognised team. The inaugural Macedonian side featured Darko Pancev, who won the European Cup with Red Star Belgrade in 1991. Away draws with England and Holland represent two of the country's modest high spots.

MALTA (Europe): With one of the oldest national associations in Europe, Malta owes much of its football fanaticism to the island's former British occupation. With a population of under 400,000, however, the national team draws from one of the smallest populations on the European continent. Sliema Wanderers, Floriana and Valletta have dominated the domestic league.

MEXICO (Central and North America): World Cup regulars Mexico relied on a play-off win over New Zealand to seal a place at 2014. They reached the quarter-finals in 1970 and 1986, both times on home soil. Their 2-1 defeat by Argentina in the 2006 World Cup was regarded as one of the finest technical matches of recent tournaments. Chivas Guadalajara and Club America have 11 titles each, with many top players remaining on home soil.

MOLDOVA (Europe): Their two best-ever results came within a month of each other in the mid-1990s during the qualifiers for Euro 96, beating Georgia and Wales. Sheriff Tiraspol have won 12 of the last 13 league titles, overtaking Zimbru Chisinau as Moldova's top club.

REST OF THE WORLD

ABOVE Mexico's Rafael Marquez and keeper Oswaldo Sanchez clear their lines at the 2006 World Cup

MONTENEGRO (Europe): Came into existence only after the 2006 World Cup after being politically tied to Serbia. The 2010 tournament was their first competitive opportunity, and although they did not qualify they impressed with some excellent attacking play, and pushed England and Ukraine all the way in qualifying for 2014. It is felt the future is bright.

MOROCCO (Africa): The first African team to win a group at the World Cup (1986), finishing ahead of Portugal, Poland, and England, and also appeared in the 1994 and 1998 tournaments. Nourredine Naybet, the former Deportivo La Coruna and Tottenham defender, is their record appearance maker of all time.

NEW ZEALAND (Oceania): In a country where rugby union is king, the New Zealand football league is semi-professional. They reached the World Cup in South Africa in 2010, and drew all three games, including against Italy, making them the only unbeaten side at the tournament. They had previously qualified only once, in 1982, but lost all three games. They are now the most powerful Oceanic nation after Australia's switch to the Asian confederation.

NIGERIA (Africa): With a rich footballing pedigree, Nigeria has exported a string of exceptional players to Europe, such as Jay-Jay Okocha, Nwankwo Kanu and John Mikel Obi. The current African champions, Nigeria have been at every World Cup, bar 2006, since 1994. Enyimba have been the most successful domestic club in recent years.

NORTHERN IRELAND (Europe): Fans still talk nostalgically about their heyday when they qualified for the 1982 World Cup, reaching the quarter-finals, having beaten hosts Spain. Norman Whiteside became the youngest-ever player in the

finals, at 17 years 41 days. Billy Bingham, a player in the team who had also reached the quarter-finals in 1958, was the manager and led his country to the finals again in 1986, the smallest European nation to qualify twice. Still capable of a shock, they beat England in 2005 and Spain in 2006.

NORTH KOREA (Asia): The North Koreans' shining moment came in the 1966 World Cup when they upset Italy 1-0 to gain a spot in the quarter-finals. There, they went 3-0 up against Portugal, but the brilliance of Eusébio and his four goals stopped the fairytale and the match ended with the Koreans down 5-3. Political isolation has cost their football dear, but they did qualify for the 2010 finals, where they were beaten by Brazil, Portugal and Ivory Coast.

NORWAY (Europe): The greatest moment in Norwegian football, a 2-1 win over Brazil in the 1998 World Cup, sparked wild scenes back home, four years after they had been a well-respected side at USA '94, where they were harshly eliminated at the group stage on goals scored. Rosenborg, the country's leading club, have perennially competed in the Champions League and famously beat AC Milan in 1996, but almost all of Norway's top players move abroad.

PARAGUAY (South America): Although they reached the second round of the World Cup in 1986, 1998, and 2002, they have never advanced beyond that stage. They appeared in four consecutive World Cups between 1998 and 2010, and won the Copa América in 1953 and 1979, and finished runner-ups to Uruguay in 2011.

PERU (South America): Peru's 'golden generation' in the 1970s and early 1980s was highlighted by the skills of Teofilo Cubillas, who scored five goals in two different World Cup finals. Defender Hector Chumputaz was one of the first South American players to have 100 international appearances. Universitario and Alianza Lima are the top two clubs at home.

POLAND (Europe): They have twice finished third in the World Cup in 1974 and 1982, thanks to talents of outstanding players such as Zbigniew Boniek and Grzegorz Lato. Goalkeeper Jan Tomaszewski, whose performance at Wembley in 1973 prevented England reaching the World Cup finals in West Germany, remains an icon. More recently, they appeared in the 2002 and 2006 World Cups, but were eliminated at the group stage, where they also exited Euro 2012, which they joint-hosted with Ukraine.

QATAR (Asia): Opening up the domestic league to foreign players turned Qatar into an attractive and lucrative new destination for veteran stars over the last decade. Qatar's wealth has also been invested in a sports academy to help develop home-grown talent, and the country was awarded the 2022 World Cup, though there are concerns about playing football in the heat of the Qatari summer.

REPUBLIC OF IRELAND (Europe): The Irish enjoyed their most euphoric era under the guidance of Jack Charlton and his successor Mick McCarthy. They qualified for Euro 88, reached the quarter-finals of the 1990 World Cup and made the last 16 at both the 1994 and 2002 World Cups. The side gets its strength from the fact that most of the squad feature regularly in the English Premier League. They recently qualified for Euro 2012, while record goalscorer Robbie Keane is now one of the standout performers in the American MLS.

ROMANIA (Europe): The national side contested the first World Cup in 1930, and their golden generation, led by Gheorghe Hagi, reached the 1994 World Cup quarter-finals and the 1998 last 16. They were beaten by Greece in 2014 qualification play-offs. Steaua Bucharest became the first Eastern European side to win the European Champions Cup in 1985. The domestic scene is dominated by the clubs from Bucharest, with Steaua and Dinamo holding 42 titles between

them, though CFR Cluj were champions three times between 2008 and 2012.

SAUDI ARABIA (Asia): Three-time Asian Cup champions, their former goalkeeper Mohamed Al-Deayea is the most capped international male footballer, with 181 appearances. Al-Hilal have won the league title 13 times since it began in 1972.

SCOTLAND (Europe): The first-ever international game took place between Scotland and England in 1872. The fixture remains one of football's fiercest rivalries. Scotland have never reached the second stage of an international tournament, despite a famous victory over Holland in 1978. The 'Old Firm', Celtic and Rangers, have long enjoyed a near-monopoly on the Scottish Premier League, though Rangers were relegated due to financial irregularities in 2012. In 1967, Celtic became the first British team to win the European Cup. Scottish players and managers have contributed enormously to the English League, including Kenny Dalglish and Graeme Souness at Liverpool and Sir Alex Ferguson at Manchester United.

SENEGAL (Africa): Senegal stunned the world by beating defending title-holders France in the 2002 World Cup on their way to becoming only the second African team to reach the tournament's quarter-finals, but have not qualified before or since. Most members of the Senegalese squad play in Europe's top leagues.

SERBIA (Europe): They became a single footballing nation in 2006 after Montenegro gained independence, and reached the World Cup in 2010. Serbia's most powerful clubs remain the ones that dominated within the original Yugoslavia – Partizan and Red Star, both from Belgrade.

SLOVAKIA (Europe): Originally a member of FIFA in 1907, Slovakia rejoined in 1994 after the break-up of Czechoslovakia. They qualified for their first World Cup in 2010, and a memorable 3-2 victory over Italy put them into the knockout rounds.

BELOW Kenny Dalglish, hero of Scotland and Celtic

REST OF THE WORLD

SLOVENIA (Europe): A decade after gaining independence from Yugoslavia, Slovenia reached its first finals in the 2000 European Championship and the 2002 World Cup. NK Maribor, which beat Villarreal to win the 2006 Intertoto Cup, hold the most Slovenian league titles, with 11.

SOUTH AFRICA (Africa): They became the first African nation to host the World Cup finals in 2010, and also the first home side to be eliminated in the group stage, despite a win over France. Re-admitted to world footballing bodies in 1990 after the end of apartheid, the national team won the African Cup of Nations in 1996 after stepping in at the last minute as hosts. South African players Benni McCarthy, Mark Fish, Lucas Radebe, and Quinton Fortune were all successful at European club level.

SOUTH KOREA (Asia): With their semi-final appearance in 2002, South Korea recorded the best-ever performance by an Asian team in the World Cup. Traditionally strong in Asia, they won the first two Asian Cups. Park Ji-Sung is the most famous South Korean player in the world, but has now retired from international football. Seongnam Ilhwa Chunma are the K-League's most successful team with seven championship trophies.

SWEDEN (Europe): World Cup runners-up as hosts in 1958, Sweden have also reached three other semi-finals, the most recent being third place in 1994. Swedish players have been successful across Europe, and Swede Sven-Göran Eriksson won the Italian title at Lazio before managing England to three successive tournament quarter-finals. Malmö are the leading domestic title-winners with 20 and once appeared in the European Cup final. IFK are the only Swedish club to have won a European trophy, however, twice landing the UEFA Cup.

SWITZERLAND (Europe): One of Switzerland's major roles in the world game is off the pitch – hosting FIFA headquarters in Zurich and UEFA's headquarters near Geneva. Switzerland holds the dubious honour of being the only team to be eliminated from the World Cup (in 2006) in a penalty shoot-out without netting a single spot-kick. The domestic league is dominated by Grasshoppers (27 titles) and the recently resurgent FC Zurich and Basel.

TOGO (Africa): Togo's first-ever appearance in the World Cup in 2006 was blighted by a dispute over player bonuses. The federation was subsequently fined by FIFA for "behaviour unworthy of a participant in the World Cup." Tragedy struck in 2007, when 20 members of their delegation to the African Cup of Nations qualifier, including the Sports Minister but not any players, were killed in a helicopter crash. Then, in 2010, their team coach was ambushed on the way to the African Cup of Nations tournament, killing three and injuring several others. Star player Emmanuel Adebayor retired from the international game afterwards, but has since returned.

TRINIDAD AND TOBAGO (Central and North America): Ex-Manchester United striker Dwight Yorke is such a hero in Tobago that the national stadium bears his name. Other notable players to have succeeded in England include goalkeeper Shaka Hislop, Stern John, and Kenwyne Jones. Trinidad and Tobago qualified for their first World Cup in 2006 under Leo Beenhakker, where they were eliminated without scoring a goal.

TURKEY (Europe): Turkey's biggest footballing success came in the 2002 World Cup, where they finished third. Turkish teams have proved fearsome opposition in the Champions League, especially in their home legs, where an intimidating atmosphere is guaranteed. Hakan Sukur, scorer of the fastest-

BELOW Trinidad's Dwight Yorke strikes for goal against Paraguay

ever World Cup goal in 11 seconds in 2006, is Turkish football's top scorer. Galatasary, Fenerbahce and Besiktas are the traditional superpowers, though Bursaspor won their first title in 2010.

TUNISIA (Africa): Tunisia were the first African team to win a World Cup finals match, beating Mexico 3-1. They won the African Cup of Nations as host in 2004. Esperance de Tunis have won the domestic league 25 times, while Etoile du Sahel have performed well in African tournaments.

UKRAINE (Europe): Having provided some of the finest players to the Soviet Union national team for years, Ukraine reached the quarter-finals in their first World Cup as an independent nation, in 2006. Dynamo Kiev, the most successful Ukrainian team with 12 championships, were often the only challenger to Moscow clubs' domination during the Soviet era. Andriy Shevchenko and Sergei Rebrov spearheaded their European campaigns in the mid–late 1990s before the latter moved on to great success in Italy with AC Milan.

UNITED ARAB EMIRATES (Asia): The UAE has a lively and popular domestic league, dominated by Al-Ain FC, the first UAE winners of the Asian Champions Cup, in 2003. The national team's only appearance at a World Cup in 1990 ended in three defeats. Their major international successes have come recently, with the 2007 and 2011 Gulf Cup of Nations titles.

UNITED STATES OF AMERICA (Central and North America): Though football struggles to compete with other American sports, the game is hugely popular with both young men and women, and the MLS continues to grow after the arrival of stars like David Beckham and Thierry Henry. The US women's team are one of the most successful in the world, having won the inaugural Women's World Cup in 1991 and repeated the feat in 1999, thanks to key players such as Brandi Chastain and Mia Hamm. Historically, the US shocked England in 1950 at the Brazil World Cup, and did well as hosts in 1994.

URUGUAY (South America): The first hosts and first winners of the World Cup in 1930, Uruguay won the tournament again in 1950, and have recently enjoyed a resurgence, reaching the last four in South Africa thanks to the brilliance of Diego Forlan and Luis Suarez. Peñarol (38) and Nacional (33) have won the most national championships.

VENEZUELA (South America): Venezuela are the only member of the South American federation never to have qualified for the World Cup finals. Their best performance in the Copa America came in 2011, when they reached the semi-finals after drawing with Brazil and Paraguay, and beating both Ecuador and Chile before losing to Paraguay on penalties.

WALES (Europe): Welsh club football is enjoying a fine time, with both Swansea and Cardiff City seeing action in the English Premier League. Cardiff are the only non-English side to ever win the English FA Cup (in 1927) and they were runners-up to Portsmouth in 2008, while Swansea lifted the League Cup in 2013. Wales reached their only World Cup finals in 1958, with 'Gentle Giant' John Carles, leading them to a quarter-final defeat against Brazil. Despite producing world-famous players in the 1980s and 1990s, as well as the world's most expensive player, Gareth Bale, in the current era, Wales have not qualified for a major tournament in over half a century.

ABOVE David Beckham turns on the style in the US for LA Galaxy

CONTINENTAL CLUB COMPETITIONS

The UEFA Champions League is the most lucrative international club competition ever to be played. It has evolved over the last 80 years, and there are further exciting changes planned for the future that will make matches more entertaining for fans. The original tournament was the Mitropa Cup – also known as La Coupe de l'Europe Centrale. This was held among the leading clubs of central Europe during the late 1920s and 1930s. South America holds the Copa Libertadores, North American clubs compete in the CONCACAF Champions League and there are similar major tournaments in Africa, Asia and Oceania.

COUPE
CHAMPIONS
EUROPÉENS
Finale
1956

FOUNDATION & 1950s

"The Champions League is where every player wants to be."

KAKA OF MILAN

UEFA has come a long way since it was founded in Basel on 15 June 1954. It currently stands as the richest and most important of the six continental confederations of world governing body FIFA. UEFA oversees the numerous competitions from its headquarters in Nyon, a town on the shores of Lake Geneva in Switzerland.

EUROPEAN CUP

1950s FINALS

1956 Real Madrid 4 Reims 3

1957 Real Madrid 2 Fiorentina 0

1958 Real Madrid 3 Milan 2 (after extra time)

1959 Real Madrid 2 Reims 0

All the world's greatest players have a strong desire to play for European clubs, tempted by both the lucrative contracts and the chance of winning high-profile titles and medals.

UEFA was formed as a result of talks between the respective Football Federations of Belgium France and Italy, and was set up during the 1954 World Cup.

France's Henri Delaunay was the driving force. and immediately tackled the role of general secretary; Denmark's Ebbe Schwartz was voted in as the inaugural president.

UEFA grew hand in hand with the European Champions' Club Cup. This tournament was dreamed up by the then editor of the French sports daily newspaper L'Equipe, Gabriel Hanot, who became irritated by the claims of a national English newspaper that Wolverhampton Wanderers – after beating Hungary's Kispest Honvéd in a friendly – were the champions of the world.

In April 1955, UEFA agreed to take over the running of the European Champions' Club Cup. Later that month, three leading officials – Ernst Thommen (Switzerland), Dr Ottorino Barassi (Italy) and Sir Stanley Rous (England) – conceived the idea of the International Inter-Cities' Industrial Fairs Cup, the forerunner to today's UEFA Cup.

The Champions' Club Cup, based on a two-leg knock-out system, grew from strength to strength. Lennart Johansson, the UEFA president between 1990 and 2007, was the man responsible for converting the Champions' Club Cup into the Champions League.

Real Madrid dominated the early European Champions' Club Cup, crowned winners at the first five successive finals. Santiago Bernabéu was the president who oversaw their phenomenal rise. He had the vision to change Madrid's 20,000-capacity Chamartín ground and create a giant stadium that would house a great team. Bernabeu and his secretary Raimundo Saporta built that team.

ABOVE Sir Stanley Rous

RIGHT Red Star goalkeeper Beara foils a Manchester United attack

CONTINENTAL COMPETITIONS

EUROPE 1960s

Real Madrid launched a new European competitive decade in glory. Their 7-3 thrashing of Eintracht Frankfurt – West Germany's first finalists – in Glasgow in 1960 was hailed by experts as the greatest match of all time.

The inspirational Alfredo Di Stefano hit a hat-trick but was out-scored by Hungarian Ferenc Puskas who scored four goals. Madrid's five-year reign ended the next season, when they were beaten by Spanish rivals Barcelona. .

Barcelona signed some of the world's finest players and coaches and believed their hour had come when, with the help of refereeing errors, they defeated Madrid in the opening rounds of the 1960–61 Champions' Cup.

Barcelona were then clear favourites to win the final, but they were surprisingly beaten by Benfica. Two of Barcelona's stars, the Hungarian forwards Sandor Kocsis and Zoltan Czibor, had finished on the favourites' losing side at the same stadium in Bern, Switzerland, seven years earlier in the World Cup final against West Germany. Then, as now, the score was 3-2.

Benfica, unlike cosmopolitan Barcelona, relied solely on Portuguese players but this gave them the option of plucking many outstanding players from Portugal's African colonies. The most important was Eusebio da Silva Ferreira, from Mozambique, who scored two goals the following year when Benfica thrashed the ageing maestros of Real Madrid 5-3 in Amsterdam. The Hungarian veteran Puskas ended up on the losing side despite scoring another Champions' final hat-trick.

A hat-trick of titles proved beyond Benfica, however, as the balance of power in Europe swung towards Italy and the city of Milan.

AC Milan overthrew Benfica in 1963, in the first European final at Wembley. Eusebio struck early for Benfica, but was then played out of the game by Milan wing-half Giovanni Trapattoni as the Italians hit back twice through their Brazilian forward Jose Altafini.

Milan's reign lasted only one season, however. They fell in the quarter-finals the next term to Real Madrid, who were, in turn, beaten 3-1 in the final in Vienna by Internazionale.

Inter were managed by master coach Helenio Herrera. In the spring of 1960 Herrera had been sacked by Barcelona after a European defeat at Madrid's hands. Now, he enjoyed taking his belated revenge. Herrera was born in Morocco, but brought up in Argentina. He became a professional footballer in France and had worked hard on the tactics, science, and psychology of football.

Inter secured two cups – against Real Madrid in 1964 and Benfica in 1965 – before Celtic and Manchester United struck the first blows for British football. In 1967 Scotland's Celtic, under the shrewd management of Jock Stein. Their brand of thrilling football swept aside even ironclad Inter in the final in Lisbon.

One year later, Manchester United marked the tenth anniversary of the Munich air disaster by seizing the trophy for the first time themselves. Matt Busby had built a remarkable new team. Charlton was partnered in attack by George Best and Denis Law. Injury meant Law missed the final in which United beat Benfica 4-1 in extra-time at Wembley, thanks to two goals from Charlton.

Their reign, however, lasted only one year. United were dethroned in the 1969 semi-finals by Milan, who then beat Holland's emerging Ajax Amsterdam in the final in Madrid's Estadio Bernabeu. Ajax were the first Dutch club to have reached the Champions' final. Their coach Rinus Michels was building a team and a style, which would earn worldwide admiration.

FOOTBALL FACTS

THE FINALS

1960 Real Madrid 7 Eintracht Frankfurt 3

1961 Benfica 3 Barcelona 2

1962 Benfica 5 Real Madrid 3

1963 Milan 2 Benfica 1

1964 Internazionale 3 Real Madrid 1

1965 Internazionale 1 Benfica 0

1966 Real Madrid 2 Partizan Belgrade 1

1967 Celtic 2 Internazionale 1

1968 Manchester Utd 4 Benfica 1, after extra time

1969 Milan 4 Ajax Amsterdam 1

RIGHT Celtic's Billy McNeill takes delivery of the European Cup in 1967

EUROPE 1970s

ABOVE Ajax Amsterdam, hat-trick winners in the early 1970s

The 1970s was a European Cup decade which could be split into three reigns – those of Ajax Amsterdam, Bayern Munich, then the English. First though, in 1970, came Feyenoord of Rotterdam, Ajax's long-time rivals.

Feyenoord became the first Dutch team to win the trophy, beating 1967 winners Celtic 2-1. Sweden striker Ove Kindvall scored the winner four minutes from the end of extra-time.

Ajax followed, with a vengeance. Their forward Johan Cruyff was one of the all-time greats. His touch and vision inspired Ajax to three European titles and Holland to reach the 1974 World Cup Final.

Ajax coach Rinus Michels, had players that could switch positions in bewildering style in the system known as 'total football.' They won three finals, all comfortably. They defeated Panathinaikos of Greece 2-0 at Wembley, put together their best performance of the three to defeat Internazionale 2-0 in Rotterdam, and then finished off with a 1-0 win over Juventus in Belgrade.

Cruyff left Ajax for Barcelona and they became vulnerable to a challenge from German champions Bayern Munich, that featured legends Franz Beckenbauer, Sepp Maier and Gerd Muller.

But Bayern had to battle for their three successive final wins. First opponents were Atletico Madrid in Brussels in 1974. Only a last-minute goal at the end of extra-time earned a replay – the only one in the history of the competition – which Bayern won easily by 4-0. Leeds had a seemingly good goal disallowed before Franz Roth and Muller netted in the 1975 final; then Dominque Rocheteau hit the woodwork for Saint-Etienne ahead of Roth's winner a year later at Hampden Park, Glasgow.

Bayern grew old together – and the English succeeded them. Liverpool's revival had been masterminded by Scottish manager Bill Shankly and Paisley, his assistant, was comparatively unknown when he took over in the summer of 1975.

Very soon, however, it became clear that Paisley was a managerial giant. It was under his guidance that Liverpool won their first European Champions' Cup by defeating Borussia Monchengladbach 3-1 in the 1977 final in Rome.

At the time, Borussia were one of Europe's outstanding football teams. In Rome, however, Borussia proved no match for a Liverpool side, who had found a style pitched midway between the demands of the frenetic English league and the more thoughtful version demanded by European competition.

The match was a personal triumph for Liverpool's right-winger Kevin Keegan. However, it was Keegan's last game for Liverpool. Within weeks he had been sold to Hamburg and Liverpool replaced him with an even more outstanding player, Kenny Dalglish.

A year later, Dalglish scored the lone winning goal for Liverpool in their second Champions' final victory over Brugge. Liverpool's reign ended early the next season with the success of Nottingham Forest. Under the idiosyncratic management of the controversial Brian Clough, Forest went all the way to defeat Sweden's Malmo in the 1979 final. The decisive goal was scored by the England forward Trevor Francis.

Months earlier Francis had become Britain's first £1 million footballer when Clough bought him from Birmingham City. The Malmo game was his Champions' Cup debut.

FOOTBALL FACTS

THE FINALS

1970 Feyenoord 2 Celtic 1 (after extra time)

1971 Ajax Amsterdam 2 Panathinaikos 0

1972 Ajax 2 Internazionale 0

1973 Ajax 1 Juventus 0

1974 Bayern Munich 4 Atletico Madrid 0 (replay after 1-1 extra time draw)

1975 Bayern Munich 2 Leeds United 0

1976 Bayern Munich 1 Saint-Etienne 0

1977 Liverpool 3 Borussia Monchengladbach 1

1978 Liverpool 1 Club Brugge 0

1979 Nottingham Forest 1 Malmo 0

CONTINENTAL COMPETITIONS

EUROPE 1980s

One event overshadowed the European Cup in the 1980s: the Heysel disaster of 1985. Thirty-nine fans, Italian and Belgian, were crushed to death as Liverpool fans attacked Juventus fans before a European Cup final in Brussels.

It was Juventus' first Champions' Cup victory, but that went almost unnoticed amid the carnage. Michel Platini, now UEFA president, and their star forward, said: "I'm physically and emotionally incapable of going back to Heysel. It's a wound that cannot be healed."

UEFA blamed Liverpool and their supporters. UEFA banned all English teams indefinitely. That was later reduced to a five-year ban with an extra year for Liverpool. UEFA and other officials were also punished by the Belgian legal system for a series of blunders, which extended from choosing an inadequate venue in the first place, to failure to ensure sufficient security controls.

In due course the Heysel – which had hosted previous Champions' Cup finals in 1958, 1966, and 1974 – was razed. The King Baudouin Stadium was built in its place.

The tragedy was all the more shocking for English football since it took place only 18 days after 56 people had died in a fire at the Bradford City stadium. Not until after the 1989 Hillsborough disaster, however, were measures finally put in place to improve security and safety at British sports stadia.

English clubs had extended their domination of the European Champions' Cup throughout the early 1980s, in a series of low-key finals. First Nottingham Forest extended their successful run to two years by defeating Kevin Keegan's Hamburg on a lone goal from Scotland winger Jimmy Robertson in 1980. Then Liverpool were equally cautious in beating Real Madrid the following year on a late goal. In 1982, Aston Villa pipped Bayern Munich also by 1-0.

The only interruption to English command came from Hamburg who, inspired now by midfielder

Felix Magath, beat Juventus 1-0 in 1983. It was a second win with a different club for Hamburg's Austrian coach, Ernst Happel. He had previously guided Feyenoord to victory in 1970.

The expulsion of English clubs from European competition in the second half of the 1980s left a gap which no one other European club could fill. Romania's Steaua Bucharest became the first eastern European winners on penalties against favourites Barcelona – coached by Englishman Terry Venables – in 1986. Porto beat Bayern 2-1 the following season. Holland's PSV Eindhoven shaded Benfica on penalties again in 1988.

Soon afterwards, real champions soon emerged in Italy's revived club, AC Milan. The club had been refinanced in the mid-1980s by media magnate and future prime minister Silvo Berlusconi. He paid off the club's debts and invested heavily in Dutch stars such as Ruud Gullit, Frank Rijkaard, and Marco Van Basten.

Milan won the Italian league in 1988, then thrashed Steaua Bucharest in the following season's Champions' Cup final. The final was staged in Barcelona amid a TV blackout after local technicians went on strike. Berlusconi flew in staff from his own Italian TV channels to ensure that no one in Europe should miss his team's achievement.

Already, however, the talismanic Van Basten was starting to become more vulnerable to a series of ever-more damaging injuries which would ultimately force him into premature retirement – he played his last game in 1993.

RIGHT The wrecked terracing at Heysel in 1985

FOOTBALL FACTS
THE FINALS
1980 Nottingham Forest 1 Hamburg 0
1981 Liverpool 1 Real Madrid 0
1982 Aston Villa 1 Bayern Munich 0
1983 Hamburg 1 Juventus 0
1984 Liverpool 1 Roma 1 (Liverpool 4-2 on penalties)
1985 Juventus 1 Liverpool 0
1986 Steaua Bucharest 0 Barcelona 0 (Steaua 3-0 on penalties)
1987 FC Porto 2 Bayern Munich 1
1988 PSV Elindhoven 0 Benfica 0 (PSV 6-5 on penalties)
1989 Milan 4 Steaua Bucharest 0

CONTINENTAL COMPETITIONS

EUROPE 1990s

FOOTBALL FACTS

The finals

1990 Milan 1 Benfica 0

1991 Red Star Belgrade 0
Marseille 0 (Red Star 5-3 on
penalties after extra time)

1992 Barcelona 1 Sampdoria
Genoa 0 (after extra time)

1993 Marseille 1 Milan 0

1994 Milan 4 Barcelona 0

1995 Ajax Amsterdam 1 Milan
0

1996 Juventus 1 Ajax 1
(Juventus 4-2 on penalties after
extra time)

1997 Borussia Dortmund 3
Juventus 1

1998 Real Madrid 1 Juventus 0

1999 Manchester United 2
Bayern Munich 1

BELOW Ole Gunnar Solskjaer wins the
1999 final for Manchester United

The late 1990s marked the biggest change in the format of the European Cup since the competition was established more than 40 years earlier. No longer would it be a knockout competition for league champions.

From 1956 onward, the structure had been simple. The holders and the champions of each European county had met in a series of two-leg ties, leading to a one-match final. The team who scored most goals in the matches, home and away, progressed. It was a copy of the formula devised for the Mitropa Cup, which had proved hugely popular in central Europe in the 1930s.

Initially, if scores were level after two matches, a replay on neutral territory was organised. When it became more difficult to find neutral zones the clubs tossed to decide who would stage the replay. Eventually, however, the pressures of time led to the play-offs being scrapped – with the second leg of a balanced tie being extended into 30 minutes of extra-time and then, if necessary, to a penalty shoot-out.

In 1991–92 this format was radically altered. Extra clubs were admitted from the major nations and experiments began with a mini-league formula, until the present system – eight groups, then three knockout rounds before the final – was perfected.

These changes, which also raised the clubs' income through TV and sponsorship, were matched by another crucial development – the Bosman Judgement which, in December 1995, ruled that restrictions on the number of foreign players in any team and playing squad were illegal. The world's best players inevitably gravitated to a handful of rich European clubs.

The drama of the European finals continued. One of the most dramatic moments came in 1999, when Teddy Sheringham and Ole Gunnar Solskjaer scored in the last seconds of stoppage time to lead Manchester United to an astonishing victory over Bayern Munich in Barcelona. Bayern had led by a single goal from Mario Basler for most of the match.

United's victory secured them a historic treble of European Cup, plus domestic league and FA Cup success.

Johan Cruyff's 'Dream Team' earned Barcelona's first Champions' Cup in 1992, when Ronald Koeman's rocket settled the contest against Sampdoria in extra-time at Wembley. Fabio Capello's Milan then produced the finest performance of the decade's finals when they unexpectedly came out in attack to rout Cruyff's Barcelona in 1994.

Surprisingly, Milan were beaten themselves a year later by a revived Ajax Amsterdam. Coincidentally, Ajax were guided to victory out on the pitch by the experienced string-pulling in midfield of Frank Rijkaard, a European Cup-winning hero with the Italian club in 1989 and 1990.

Ottmar Hitzfeld oversaw Dortmund's 3-1 success against Juventus in 1997. Then fellow German Jupp Heynckes guided Real Madrid to victory in 1998. Pedja Mijatovic scored Madrid's winner to secure their seventh Champions' Cup at the expense of favourites Juventus.

Surprisingly, Heynckes was sacked by Madrid's impatient president Lorenzo Sanz on the grounds that the team had not, in addition, won the Spanish league. Sanz's unpredictable direction of the club backfired when impatient fans voted him out of a job and voted in millionaire builder Florentino Perez.

Olympique de Marseille became the first French champions of Europe in 1993. They beat Milan 1-0 in what would prove the last final in Munich's Olympic stadium.

EUROPE 2000s

By 2000, the European Cup had become the Champions League. Oddly though, it was often not the teams which had towered over their domestic leagues that lifted the Champions' Cup.

Only three teams – Bayern Munich in 2001 and 2013, Barcelona in 2006 and 2009, and Manchester United in 2008 – also won their domestic championships in the same season.

It was as if chasing a domestic championship and the Champions League was a task too far. But a few clubs adapted ideally to the last 16 knockout system. Liverpool, under Rafa Benitez, were the prime example. They won the Champions' Cup in 2005, despite finishing 37 points behind Chelsea in the Premiership.

In 2007, when they lost to Milan, they ended up 21 points behind Manchester United. English critics claimed that Benitez knew Liverpool could not match the consistency of Chelsea or Manchester United; his season's strategy revolved around the latter stages of the Champions League.

Chelsea twice fell to Liverpool in Champions League semi-finals, much to coach Jose Mourinho's disgust. Milan, meanwhile, also put all their eggs in the Champions League basket. The 2007 winners finished 36 points behind Serie A champions and local rivals Internazionale. Both Liverpool and Milan rested and rotated players with the European Cup in mind, a pragmatic possibility often denied to their championship-chasing rivals.

A dramatic final was staged in 2005 in Istanbul. Milan led Liverpool 3-0 at half time before Steven Gerrard inspired Liverpool's fight back as he, Vladimir Smicer, and Xabi Alonso scored within seven minutes of each other to force extra-time. The tie was settled on penalties.

Madrid, playing with pace and power, had swarmed over Valencia in the all-Spanish final of 2000. Fernando Morientes, Steve McManaman, and Raul swept aside Hector Cuper's team. Caretaker boss Vicente Del Bosque had quelled the competing

egos in the Madrid dressing room. He guided them to victory again in 2002, when Zinedine Zidane volleyed a magical winner against Bayer Leverkusen at Hampden Park, Glasgow. Leverkusen thus finished the season as runners-up not only in the Champions League but also in the German league and cup.

Barcelona won again for Spain in 2006 in the Stade de France after teetering on the verge of defeat against Arsenal who went ahead through centre-back Sol Campbell and held out until an unlucky 13 minutes from time. One factor in this decade had been a demonstration of the power of the big leagues. After an all-Spanish final in 2000 (Real Madrid beating Valencia) came an all-Italian final in 2003 (Milan beating Juventus) and then an all-English final in 2008.

The latter saw Manchester United win the crown for the third time after defeating Chelsea, also runners-up to United in the Premier League, on penalties. Just to prove that football is no respecter of personalities, the three misses in the shoot-out were committed by United's Cristiano Ronaldo and by Chelsea's John Terry and Nicolas Anelka.

While 2008 had been an all-English affair, so was 2013 for Germany. The two great powers of the Bundesliga, Bayern Munich and Borrusia Dortmund, came together for the final at Wembley Stadium. In the end, the superior Bayern squad proved too strong for fond underdogs Dortmund.

The 2014 final saw the two clubs of Madrid clash in Lisbon, Portugal. Real Madrid were were chasing 'La Decima', the club's self-determined, destiny of 10 European Cup victories. Real defender, Sergio Ramos, scored a last-minute equaliser to crush Atletico Madrid fans' hearts. Real then went on and scored three extra-time goals to win 4-1.

FOOTBALL FACTS

THE FINALS–LAST 10 YEARS
2004 Porto 3 Monaco 0
2005 Liverpool 3 Milan 3 (Liverpool 3-2 on penalties after extra time)
2006 Barcelona 2 Arsenal 1
2007 Milan 2 Liverpool 1
2008 Manchester United 1 Chelsea 1 (Manchester United 6-5 on penalties after extra time)
2009 Barcelona 2 Manchester United 0
2010 Internazionale 2 Bayern Munich 0
2011 Barcelona 3 Manchester United 1
2012 Chelsea 1 Bayern Munich 1 (Chelsea 4-3 on penalties)
2013 Bayern Munich 2 Borussia Dortmund 1
2014 Real Madrid 4 Atletico Madrid 1 (After extra-time)

RIGHT Delight for Milan's Kaka means despair for Liverpool

OTHER CLUB COMPETITIONS

UEFA CUP & CUP WINNERS' CUP

The UEFA Cup and the now-defunct Cup Winners' Cup have always been poor relations of the Champions League.

ABOVE Tottenham's John White, Bill Brown, Cliff Jones, Ron Henry, and Terry Dyson enjoy a happy homecoming to the UK in 1963

These were competitions for the 'nearly' clubs who had fallen short of winning the major domestic trophy. Originally, the UEFA Cup was known as the Fairs Cup. It was founded in 1955 – a fortnight after the Champions' Cup – by future FIFA president Sir Stanley Rous and vice-presidents Ottorino Barrasi of Italy and Ernst Thommen of Switzerland.

With one eye on post-war rapprochement between Europe's former enemy nations, it was originally confined to representative teams whose cities staged trade fairs. Since the games were organised to coincide with the trade fairs, the first tournament lasted three years. The final was held in 1958, when a team made up entirely of FC Barcelona players beat a London representative side 8-2 on aggregate over two legs.

Club teams were admitted to the next competition, and Barcelona beat Birmingham City 2-0 on aggregate in the 1960 final. Barcelona's heroes were the Hungarian Ladislav Kubala and Spain's own Luis Suarez. The competition was played annually after that. Initially, southern European clubs dominated, but Leeds' win in 1968 heralded a change. English teams (Newcastle, Arsenal, Leeds, Tottenham, and Liverpool) won the trophy for the next five years.

In 1971, the tournament was re-named after the European federation took formal control. The Fairs label was scrapped and the competition was called the UEFA Cup. Initially it continued as a two-leg knockout competition and the closing stages sometimes boasted a more glamorous mixture of clubs than the Champions' Cup. Winners down succeeding years included the likes of Real Madrid, Internazionale, Juventus, and Roma.

Everything changed, however, with the development of the Champions League. The quality threshold dropped significantly with the departure from the UEFA Cup of the bigger second, third, and fourth-placed clubs and the massive influx of clubs from the newly independent nations thrown up by the fragmentation of the Soviet Union and Yugoslavia.

UEFA also bowed to pressure from the clubs to produce a group stage which guaranteed three home matches for each club, while then allowing some teams that were knocked out of the Champions League entry into the UEFA Cup at the halfway stage for the knockout rounds. However, the system of five-team groups was unsatisfactory for fans and fixture patterns and was reorganised again in 2009.

Sevilla, under coach Juande Ramos, proved masters of the competition in 2006 and 2007, though they had to thank a spectacular shoot-out performance from goalkeeper Andres Palop for the second of their two victories, over fellow Spanish opposition in Espanyol.

An intriguing factor in the UEFA Cup has been evidence of the revival of Russian club football after the chaos that followed the collapse of the Soviet Union. CSKA Moscow won the UEFA Cup in 2005, beating Sporting Libson in front of their own fans, and then Zenit St Petersburg beat Rangers in 2008. Zenit also provided the nucleus of the Russian national side which proved outstanding six weeks later in reaching the semi-finals of the European Championship.

From 1999 onwards, entrance into the UEFA Cup was also the formal reward for clubs who had won their national cups. This followed UEFA's decision to scrap the Cup Winners' Cup which had been running since 1960. The Cup Winners' Cup was always a poor relation because, while popular in Britain, the domestic knockout event had barely caught on in many other countries.

Italy's Fiorentina won the first final, beating Rangers of Scotland. Tottenham became the first British winners of a European competition when they defeated Atletico Madrid 5-1 in the final in 1963. The last final, in 1999, saw Italy's Lazio, coached by Sven-Goran Eriksson, beat Mallorca at Villa Park, Birmingham.

In the 2009–10 season the UEFA Cup was renamed and restructed, and became the Europa League. Since 2000, six of the 15 winners have been teams that qualified through losing in the Champions League. Only four of those finals were solely contested by teams who originally qualified for the Europa League.

BELOW Andres Palop wins the 2007 UEFA Cup for Sevilla by saving Marc Torrejon's penalty

UEFA CUP (EUROPA LEAGUE)

RECENT FINALS

1999 Parma 3 Marseille 0

2000 Galatasaray 0 Arsenal 0 (Galatasaray 4-1 on penalties after extra time)

2001 Liverpool 4 Alaves 4 (golden goal after extra time)

2002 Feyenoord 3 Borussia Dortmund 2

2003 Porto 3 Celtic 2 (silver goal after extra time)

2004 Valencia 2 Marseille 0

2005 CSKA Moscow 3 Sporting Lisbon 1

2006 Sevilla 4 Middlesbrough 0

2007 Sevilla 2 Espanyol 2 (Sevilla 3-1 on penalties after extra time)

2008 Zenit St Petersburg 2, Rangers 0

2009 Shakhtar Donetsk 2, Werder Bremen 1 (After extra time)

Europa League Finals

2010 Atletico Madrid 2, Fulham 1 (After extra time)

2011 Porto 1, Braga 0

2012 Atletico Madrid 3, Atletico Bilbao 0

2013 Chelsea 2, Benfica 1

2014 Sevilla 0, Benfica 0 (Sevilla won 4-2 on penalties after extra time)

CONTINENTAL COMPETITIONS

SOUTH AMERICA

"For me, penalties are a lottery."

COACH RENATO GAUTO

The Copa Libertadores is the South American equivalent of the European Champions' Cup. The winners tackle their European counterparts for the prestigious honour of becoming the world's greatest club.

ABOVE Boca captain Diego Cagna strikes a cup-winning pose in 2003

The Copa Libertadores grew out of a tournament of seven South American champions, played in Santiago de Chile in 1948 and won by the Brazilian club Vasco da Gama – a side that were named after the great Portuguese explorer.

A dozen years later the Copa Libertadores was launched as an annual tournament. The reasoning was that South American club directors, notably those of Peñarol from Uruguay, had seen the success of the European Champions' Cup and wanted a version of their own.

Once the Copa Libertadores was established, then the vision was to eventually introduce an annual series matching the champions from Europe and South America to tackle each other for the coveted world club crown.

The Copa Libertadores kicked off in 1960 with the participation of the champions from Argentina, Bolivia, Brazil, Chile, Colombia, Ecuador, Paraguay, Peru, and Uruguay.

Much to the delight of many South American club directors, Peñarol from Uruguay were crowned champions after defeating Paraguay's Olimpia 2-1 on aggregate.

Pedro Spencer, the free-scoring Ecuadorian striker, was Peñarol's inspiration and went on to become the most prolific marksman in the history of the Copa Libertadores.

Peñarol, happily fulfilling their original ambition, went on to arrange a world club showdown with their European counterparts Real Madrid. However, the Spanish side steamrollered past Peñarol to the tune of 5-0.

Peñarol bounced back to be crowned South American champions the following season, but then they were toppled by Brazilian outfit Santos.

The legendary Pelé proved to be the inspiration for Santos, who also won two years in a row and saw off the first serious Argentinian challenge from Boca Juniors.

Although Peñarol and Montevideo rivals Nacional would both win the Copa Libertadores again, Uruguay's pre-eminence faded and the tournament is currently dominated by clubs from Argentina and Brazil. Their supremacy has been interrupted only by a trio of wins for Olimpia, two successes apiece from Colombia's Atlético Nacional and Once Caldas, and a single triumph by Chile's Colo Colo.

Over the years, the Copa Libertadores has featured a string of dramas – from crowd pitch invasions to 20-plus penalty shoot-outs and some of the most cynical football imaginable. Culprits for the latter were the Argentinian club Estudiantes de La Plata in the late 1960s. Under influential coach Osvaldo Zubeldía, they took anti-football to a vicious new art and a new low for the sport.

Originally the competition involved only the champions from each country. Since the knockout formula failed to grip the imagination of the fans, most countries stage two league championships in a single year. Opening up the Copa Libertadores to two teams proved a successful solution. The simultaneous introduction of a first-round group stage also assisted with travel costs, as the two clubs from whichever country would be drawn in the same group as the two clubs from another country. This meant teams could travel together and, for convenience, play their matches on successive days.

The tournament expanded in the 1970s, allowing Argentina and Brazil five clubs each along with three teams each from other countries – including new participants, Venezuela and Mexico. Mexico does

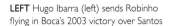
LEFT Hugo Ibarra (left) sends Robinho flying in Boca's 2003 victory over Santos

not belong to the South American confederation and are guests in the competition, their best ever showing was Cruz Azul losing to Boca Juniors in the 2001 final.

Boca Juniors, winners of the Copa Libertadores in 2000, 2001, 2003, and 2007, can lay claim to being the dominant club of South American soccer's new century. Brazilian clubs are their only real challenge, often led by three-time winners São Paulo. However, Liga de Quito pulled off a major surprise in the 2008 final after they became the first Ecuadorian winners and earned a place in FIFA's 2008 Club World Cup in Japan.

Liga de Quito's 2008 opponents, Brazil's Fluminense, were also in the final for the first time. Despite Fluminense' defeat, Brazilian teams have dominated the competition ever since. In 2010, SC Internaciaonal defeated Mexican side Guadalajara 6-0; in 2011, Santos overcame Uruguay's Peñarol 2-1; and in 2012, Corinthians beat Argentina's Boca Juniors 2-0 after winning every previous match in

the competition. In 2013, Atletico Mineiro won their first ever title after needing a 2-0 victory to take Olimpia to penalties, which they then won thanks to some outstanding saves by keeper Victor.

COPA LIBERTADORES

RECENT FINALS (OVER TWO LEGS)

2004 Once Caldas (Col) 1 Boca Juniors (Arg) 1 (on agg, Once Caldas 2-0 on penalties)

2005 Sao Paulo (Brz) 5 Atletico Paranense (Brz) 1 (on agg)

2006 Internacional (Brz) 4 Sao Paulo (Brz) 3 (on agg)

2007 Boca Juniors (Arg) 5 Gremio (Brz) 0 (on agg)

2008 LDU Quito (Ec) 5 Fluminense (Brz) 5

2009 Estudiantes (Arg) 4 Cruzeiro (Brz) 1 (on points)

2010 Internaciaonal (Brz) 6 Guadalajara (Mex) 0 (on points)

2011 Santos (Brz) 4 Peñarol (Uru) 1 (on points)

2012 Corinthians (Brz) 4 Boca Juniors (Arg) 1 (on points)

2013 Atletico Mineiro (Braz) 2 Olimpia (Par) 2 (3–3 on points, 2–2 on agg, Atletico Mineiro 4-3 on penalties)

ALL-TIME WINNERS

Independiente (Arg) 7; Boca Juniors (Arg) 6; Penarol (Uru) 5; Estudiantes de La Plata (Arg) 4; Nacional (Uru), Olimpia (Par), Sao Paulo (Brz), Santos (Brz) 3 each; Cruzeiro (Brz), Gremio (Brz), River Plate (Arg), Internacional (Brz), 2 each; Argentinos Juniors (Arg), Colo (Chi), Flamengo (Brz), LDU (Ec), Liga de Quito (Ec), Once Caldas (Col), Racing (Arg), Vasco da Gama (Brz), Velez Sarsfield (Arg), Colo-Colo (Chi) 1 each

REST OF THE WORLD

The contest between national champions is not confined to Europe and South America. Central and North America started its own championship in 1962. Africa followed two years later. Asia began its continent-wide challenge in 1967.

AFRICAN CHAMPIONS LEAGUE

RECENT WINNERS

2009 TP Mazembe (Congo)

2010 TP Mazembe (Congo)

2011 Es Tunis (Tunisia)

2012 Al Ahly (Egypt)

2013 Al Ahly (Egypt)

2014 ES Sétif (Algeria)

LEADING ALL-TIME WINNERS

Al-Ahly (Egypt) 8; Zamalek (Egypt) 5; TP Mazembe (Congo) 4; Raja Casablanca (Morocco), Canon (Cameroon), Hafia FC (Guinea) 3 each

ASIAN CHAMPIONS LEAGUE

RECENT WINNERS

2009 Pohang Steelers (S Korea)

2010 Seongnam Iihwa Chunma (S Korea)

2011 Al-Sadd SC (Qatar)

2012 Ulsan Hyundai (S Korea)

2013 Guangzhou Evergrande (China)

2014 Western Sydney Wanderers (Australia)

LEADING ALL-TIME WINNERS

Pohang Steelers (S Korea) 3; Esteghlal (Iran), Seongnam (S Korea), Al-Hilal (S Arabia), Al-Ittihad (S Arabia), Al-Sadd SC (Qatar), Suwon Samsung Bluewings (S Korea), Maccabi Tel-Aviv (Israel), Thai Farmers Bank (Thailand) 2 each

Only the Oceania confederation held back, until 2004–05. But the 2006 defection of Australia to the Asian confederation has robbed the tournament of its strongest teams.

The central American competition has long been dominated by Mexican clubs. Teams from North America are yet to win the CONCACAF Champions League, although LA Galaxy and the Seattle Sounders have both threatened in recent years. Other challengers to Mexican supremacy have included Costa Rica's LD Alajualense and Canada's Toronto FC.

Interest in the CONCACAF club competitions was enhanced by the creation first of the Copa Interamericana and then by the expansion of the Club World Championship. The Copa Interamericana pitched the winners of the CONCACAF Champions' Cup – now the CONCACAF Champions League – against the champions of South America, the winners of the Copa Libertadores.

Today, the Club World Championship is known as the FIFA Club World Cup and is contested by the winners of the Asian Football Confederation Champions League, the CONCACAF Champions League, the Copa Libertadores, the Oceania Football Confederation Champions League, the UEFA Champions League and the Confederation of African Football Champions League.

Clubs from the Arab north have historically dominated the African Club Championship, now known as the CAF Champions League. Egypt's Al-Ahly and ES Tunis from Tunisia have proven particularly difficult opponents. One African team to break the dominance of Al-Ahly and ES Tunis is the Congolese TP Mazembe, which won the league in 2009 and 2010.

Other rival African clubs have been a proven recruiting ground for Western European clubs. Perhaps this is one reason for the North African clubs' success: they do not lose as many players to Europe as their southern neighbours.

Southern Africa has yet to make its mark, despite the success of the 2010 World Cup. South Africa's Orlando Pirates have come the closest to bucking this losing trend by proving worthy rivals to 2013 league winners Al-Ahley.

Israeli teams dominated the opening days of the Asian competition. Maccabi Tel-Aviv won twice and Hapoel once, before the Israelis were forced out for political reasons. The Arab-dominated Asian confederation expelled Israel, whose clubs remained absent from international competition for almost 30 years. Israel joined UEFA in the 1990s after which its clubs entered the European competitions.

In the meantime, middle-eastern sides had taken command of the Asian club tournaments until the development of the ambitious, rich new leagues in both Japan and South Korea. The Urawa Red Diamonds underlined the power of the J. League when they became Asian champions in 2007 after beating Sepahan from Iran. In 2013, China flexed its new footballing muscles when its team Guangzhou Evergrande overcame South Korean opponents, FC Seoul, to become AFC Champions.

South Korea and Japan have both benefited from importing European and South American coaches but also from the experience the best of their players gain playing in Europe. The Middle East countries have not capitalized on the same international exchange, partly because their clubs could pay the players so well there was no financial incentive for them to seek a move to Europe.

Africa, Asia – strengthened by Australia in 2006

– and Central/North America have already shown they can challenge the traditional powers. While Oceania is considered less competitive – especially after the departure of Australia to join the Asian confederation – the OFC Champions League remains a widely followed competition in the Southern Hemisphere.

The FIFA president, Sepp Blatter, has said: "We want everyone to take their place in the greatest competitions but we also have to protect the status and value of those competitions."

ABOVE Etoile de Sahel guard the African Super Cup

BELOW LEFT Pachuca players celebrate after beating Los Angeles Galaxy in a shoot-out in 2007

DOMESTIC LEAGUES

A country's football clubs compete against each other
in its domestic league. Each nation sets its own league
rules, tournament formats, season durations, and the
number of teams which participate. Clubs compete
in several divisions and the best teams are often
promoted to a higher division at the end of the season,
or relegated to a lower one. It is the ambition of every
team to play in, and win, the league's top division.

DOMESTIC LEAGUES

EUROPEAN DOMESTIC LEAGUES

THE ENGLISH PREMIER LEAGUE

The Premier League, also known as the Premiership, was formed by first division football clubs that split away from England's Football League after the 1991-92 season. The reason for the move away from the existing league was to tap into the economic potential of English football. This resulted in lucrative broadcasting rights, sponsorship deals and multi-million pound investment into domestic clubs. It also led to larger, more comfortable stadiums, increased safety for fans, and an influx of expensive, high-profile players and managers into English football. Aside from the Premier League, the English Football League comprises three divisions: the Championship, League One and League Two. In 1998, Scotland also created its own Premier League.

The English Premier League is made up of 20 clubs, the bottom three of which are relegated and replaced by the top three teams from the Championship. The top four teams of the Premier League qualify for Europe's Champions League, and as such, each spot is highly desired and hotly contested. Manchester United have traditionally dominated the top of the Premier League table, winning five titles in the last ten years alone. But recent investment from foreign interests into Chelsea and Manchester City football clubs has tipped the balance of power in their favour. Chelsea was bought by Russian billionaire Roman Abramovich in 2003 and is today ranked the 7th most valuable football club in the world, at £588 million. Manchester City was purchased by the oil-rich Abu Dhabi United Group in 2008 and

RIGHT Manchester United striker, Wayne Rooney, celebrates scoring against Liverpool at Old Trafford.

today is the sixth wealthiest club in the world. With seemingly unlimited funds to buy the world's most expensive players, it is not surprising Chelsea has won the Premier League three times in the last 10 years, and Manchester City twice. But despite winning the Premier League crown in 2014, Manchester City also fell foul of UEFA's Financial Fair Play Regulations, which dictate that a club cannot spend more money on player transfers and wages than it made in revenue. The subsequent £49 million fine coupled with transfer market restrictions was not limited to English Football Clubs, with French Ligue 1 Paris Saint-Germain also being penalised in 2014.

Although teams such as Chelsea and 2013-14 title winners Manchester City are widely considered by fans from other clubs to have an unfair financial advantage, the 2013-14 season showed that money is not always a guarantee of success. Although Tottenham Hotspur invested over £100 million into players for the new season, the club was unable to achieve a top four place in the league table. Arsenal and Liverpool, by comparison, were able to achieve top four places in the Premier League after spending substantially less on transfers. The 2013-14 season also provided the greatest upset in the Premier League in a decade, following the retirement of long-serving manager Alex Ferguson from Manchester United and the club's subsequent fall from grace. David Moyes was sacked as Ferguson's replacement only 10 months after taking over, leaving the club with its worst ever Premier League finish, at 7th in the table.

SPAIN'S LA LIGA

The Primera Division, commonly known in English as La Liga, is the top professional division of the Spanish football league. Like the English Premier League, La Liga is contested by 20 teams, with three lower teams relegated to the second division, or the Segunda Division, and replaced by the two top teams from that division and a third which is decided by a play-off. According to UEFA, La Liga is the strongest league in Europe of the last five years, and has the third highest average attendance of any professional football league in the world behind only the Premier League and the Bundesliga.

La Liga was founded in 1929 and originally featured the 10 teams which had won the Copa

ABOVE Former Atletico Madrid forward, David Villa, challenges Barcelona star, Lionel Messi in a league match at the Camp Nou.

del Rey, including Barcelona, Real Madrid, Atletico Madrid, Real Sociedad and Real Union. Barcelona won the first La Liga in 1929, followed by Real Madrid in 1932 and 1933, with Atletico Madrid the champions in 1950 and 1951. After these early 1950s wins, Barcelona and Real Madrid began their dominance of La Liga,- which still remains today. Real won the championship 14 times between 1961 and 1980 and continued holding onto a regular La Liga top spot until ex-player Johan Cruyff returned to Barcelona as the manager and put together the legendary dream team which won the La Liga crown four times in the early 1990s.

In the new century, Valencia, under manager Rafael Benitez, won a La Liga title in 2002 and the double of a league title and the UEFA Cup in 2004. But the real story of La Liga in the new century has been the hotly contested rivalry between Real Madrid, which has won three titles in the last 10 years, and Barcelona, which has won six. Real won

the 2006-07 and 2007-08 seasons of La Liga under Fabio Capello and Bernd Schuster respectively, while Barcelona won the 2008-09 season as part of the season under manager Pep Guardiola. During this time a great rivalry also grew between Barcelona's Lionel Messi and Real Madrid's Cristiano Ronaldo, with both strikers battling to score more goals and win more individual awards than the other.

The 2013-14 season shook up the Real Madrid/Barcelona monopoly over La Liga, when an outstanding Atletico Madrid side threatened both clubs on all trophy fronts. In the end, an inspired Atletico Madrid was able to beat Barcelona in the final game of the season and put together the points to win the club its first La Liga crown since 1996.

THE GERMAN BUNDESLIGA

Founded in 1962, The Bundesliga is the top tier of domestic German football. It is contested by 18 teams and works on a system of promotion and relegation, similar to La Liga and the Premier League. The winner of the Bundesliga qualifies for the DFL-Supercup. The Bundesliga boasts the highest average match attendance of any sports league in the world, with an average of 45,000 fans attending every game. Most Bundesliga games are played on a Saturday or Sunday.

The Bundesliga has enjoyed high attendance levels ever since its 1960s beginnings, although the money this generated was also responsible for match-fixing in the early 1970s. Despite a number of high-level suspensions, German football did not lose its popular appeal after the World Cup win of 1974 injected a fresh round of enthusiasm for the sport. The 1970s also introduced the Bundesliga's first great rivalry, between Bayern Munich and Monchengladbach, with both clubs winning three titles in that decade.

By the 1980s, Bayern Munich had become the powerhouse of German football. During this decade, Bayern would win around half of the Bundesliga titles, with various other teams coming away the other half. After the Berlin Wall fell in 1989 and Germany won the 1990 World Cup, German football was once again rejuvenated.

In the 1990s, Bayern Munich's dominance of the Bundesliga was challenged by Borussia Dortmund,

and the club won the title in both 1995 and 1996. Dortmund's squad, which featured Portuguese midfielder Paolo Sousa and Swiss striker Stephane Chapuisat, proved that German domestic football was becoming more international in its choice of players. While the rivalry between Bayern Munich and Borussia Dortmund continues to the present day, the Bundesliga hit a slump at the turn of the century when inflated transfer fees and player salaries drove many of its clubs to near bankruptcy.

German football was reinvigorated by the emergence of a number of native youth players coming of age, including Philipp Lahm, Mario Gotze, Marco Reus and Thomas Müller. These players emerged alongside a new style of fast, high-pressing German football being practised by Bundesliga teams in the 2000s. Borussia Dortmund used this style to deadly effect to win the Bundesliga in 2010 and 2011. However, the side would be outdone by Bayern Munich in the following two seasons, under manager Pep Guardiola's tried and tested tiki-taka football.

ITALY'S SERIE A

Serie A is the top division of the Italian football league, which was formed in 1929. UEFA considers Serie A to be Europe's 4th best league, behind the Bundesliga, the Premier League and La Liga. Serie A became a major proving ground for players from South America and Asia in the 1990s, which in turn led to financial difficulties for clubs which had spent too heavily on foreign talent.

The three most famous Serie A clubs are Juventus, AC Milan and Internazionale. Juventus is Serie A's most successful club, which has won the league 30 times including the 2013-14 season. Milan is the most successful club in world football along with Brazil's Boca Juniors, and has 18 UEFA and FIFA titles to its name, as well as 18 Serie A wins. Milan has also spent the whole of its history in the top tier of Italian football, except for two seasons in the 1980s. Internazionale is the first Italian side to win the Treble of the Serie A, Coppa Italia and UEFA Champions League, which they achieved during the 2009-10 season.

In 2004 Serie A expanded from 18 teams to 20, but in 2006 Italian football was rocked by news of match-fixing. This led to Juventus being stripped of its 2005 and 2006 Serie A titles. Serie A has faced further trouble in recent years with clubs such as Inter Milan being fined for their fans hurling racist abuse at black players during matches. During the 2014 Coppa Italia final, Napoli fans created mayhem at the stadium in Rome after throwing flares and chanting at the opposing Fiorentina fans. Napoli was fined 60,000 Euros as a result of the fans' behaviour. Fiorentina won the match 3-1.

THE FRENCH LIGUE I

Also known as Le Championnat, Ligue I is the top division of football in France. It works on a system of relegation and promotion with second division Ligue 2. Ligue I is contested by 20 clubs, which play 38 games each during the season, with most of the matches taking place on a Saturday or Sunday.

Ligue I was created in 1932 under the names National and Division I before becoming Ligue I in 2002. After facing three corruption scandals in 1933, 1950 and 1993, Ligue I has stayed free of controversy and is considered by UEFA to be the 6th-ranked league in Europe.

Despite producing some of the world's greatest football players, including Thierry Henry and Zinedine Zidane, Ligue I clubs have historically not had the adequate funds or resources to keep these players in France. Only two French clubs have ever won European competitions: Marseille, winners of the 1993 Champions League; and Paris Saint-Germain, winners of the 1996 Cup Winners Cup.

Paris Saint-Germain, winners of Ligue I's 2013-14 season, look to be France's best hope of competing for club trophies in Europe. The team was purchased by the oil-rich Qatar Investment Authority in 2011, making it the wealthiest team in France. This has allowed the club to buy high profile names such as Zlatan Ibrahimovic and Edison Cavani, and reach the quarter-finals of the Champions League in 2014. But Paris Saint-Germain was also fined in the same year for contravening UEFA's Financial Fair Play Regulations, which stipulate that a football club is not allowed to spend more on players and wages than it earned through revenue.

THE NETHERLANDS' EREDIVISIE

Founded in 1956, the Eredivisie is the top division of football in the Netherlands. It features 18 clubs, with three teams being relegated to the lower

Eerste Divisie at the end of each season, and three teams being promoted to the Eredivisie. A play-off round is used to decide the fate of four of those teams.

AFC Ajax has won the most Eredivisie titles, with 24, followed by PSV Eindhoven with 18, and Feyenoord with nine. These three teams have also won all but three of the Eredivisie titles from 1965 until the present day. Ajax is one of the world's most successful clubs which won the continental treble in 1972 by winning the Eredivisie, the KNVB Cup and the European Cup. Some of the best players in the world have also played for Ajax, including Dennis Bergkamp, Edwin van der Sar, Klaas-Jan Huntelaar, Luis Suarez, Wesley Sneijder and Zlatan Ibrahimovic. Ajax is the current champion of the 2013-14 Eredivisie.

In 2012, it was announced that Australian tycoon Rupert Murdoch had taken over the sponsorship rights to the Eredivisie for the next 12 years, at a reported price of one billion Euros. It is thought the deal will bring increased revenue of four million Euros to each club for the duration of the Murdoch contract.

BELOW Montpellier midfielder, Remy Cabella, is tackled by Paris Saint-Germain defender, Christophe Jallet.

SOUTH AMERICA

THE CAMPEONATO BRASILEIRO SERIE A

Because of Brazil's enormous size and its geographical and political division of territories, the history of its domestic footballing league is relatively short compared to that of other countries. It wasn't until 1959, when air travel had become a common and accessible mode of transport, that a national league was established. Its formation was also, in part, due to the need to send a Brazilian team to the first Copa Libertadores in 1960. The result was the Campeonato Brasileiro, the Brazilian domestic football league, which is today considered one of the strongest leagues in the world.

The Campeonato Brasileiro is broken up into four divisions – Serie A, B, C and D. Serie A is made up of 20 teams that play each other twice a season, which runs from May to December. The Campeonato Brasileiro works on a system of relegation and promotion, whereby the four lowest teams in Serie A are relegated to Serie B, and replaced by the four highest teams in Serie B. Most games in the league are played during the weekend.

The Campeonato Brasileiro Serie A boasts four Club World Cup titles – the highest number of any national league – and 17 Copa Libertadores. In the 1993 and 2012 seasons, Brazilian Serie A teams won every club competition open to them. The Campeonato Brasileiro is ranked the 6th most powerful league in the world and has an annual turnover of over $1.2 billion USD. It is also the most watched football league in the Americas. The Campeonato Brasileiro's television rights were valued at $610 billion USD in 2013, the highest of any league in the Western Hemisphere. The clubs themselves are also wealthy by international standards. Corinthians, Brazil's richest club, was estimated to be worth over $358 million USD in 2012.

Since the Campeonato Brasileiro Serie A's inception, 17 clubs have won the league and 12 clubs have won it more than once. The most successful clubs are Palmeiras and Santos, both of which have been crowned champions eight times. Santos is considered the best club in Brazil, and it has fielded such outstanding international players as Gilmar, Menalvio, Coutinho, Pepe and Pelé. In 1962, Santos became the first club in the world to complete a quadruple, which consisted of the Campeonato Paulista, the Intercontinental Cup, the Copa Libertadores and the Campeonato Brasileiro Serie A title.

Santos has a historic rivalry with clubs Sao Paulo, Corinthians and Palmeiras, all of which hail from Sao Paulo. Derbies between Palmeiras and Santos are known as 'Classico da Saudade' and are hotly contested. Palmeiras has won a record 11 Brazilian trophies, which include eight league titles and one Copa Libertadores.

RIGHT Geuvanio and Lucas Lima challenge for the ball in a match between Santos and Palmeiras.

Cruzeiro has won the Campeonato Brasileiro Serie A three times and is the 10th wealthiest club in Brazil. Cruzeiro's players have often featured in Brazil's World Cup squads, including Tostao, Nelinho and Piazza. In modern times, however, most of Brazil's stars played their club football abroad. Of the 23 players in the Brazilian 2014 World Cup squad only four play in the Campeonato Brasileiro: Jefferson (Botafogo), Victor and Jô (Atlético Mineiro) and Fred (Fluminense).

ARGENTINA'S PRIMERA DIVISION

The Primera Division is the top division of Argentina's football league, and it is contested by 20 clubs. The league works on a system of promotion and relegation whereby three of the worst-performing teams are relegated to the lower Primera B Nacional division and the three best teams from Primera B are promoted to the Primera Division. A system that calculates a club's average performances over its last three years helps determine which teams are relegated.

The Primera Division season runs from August until June and consists of two tournaments: the Torneo Inicial, which is played from August to December; and the Torneo Final, which is played from February to June. The winners of the tournaments then play in a final match to decide who is the champion. The top five teams of the Primera Division also get a chance to play in the Copa Libertadores.

Argentina's football league was founded in 1891, making it the only country apart from the United Kingdom to have one at that time. In 1931, the league gained professional status, although the duration of its season and its overall format have been changed four times since. The league's current format has been in use since 1992. Altogether, 108 teams have played in the Primeria Division since its inaugural 1931 season and 16 clubs have won it. Those clubs with the most league titles are: River Plate, with 35 wins; Boca Juniors, with 30 wins, and Independiente, with 16 wins. Boca Juniors is the only club to have played in every season without being relegated.

Boca Juniors and River Plate are also the teams with the fiercest rivalry in the league, and their matches are the eagerly anticipated 'Superclasicos'. River Plate is considered the most successful club in Argentina. On top of its 35 league titles,

ABOVE Flamengo players Hernane, Nixon and Carlos Eduardo celebrate a goal in a league game against Cruzeiro.

RIGHT River Plate's Gabriel Mercado takes on Claudio Riano of Boca Juniors.

River Plate has won two Copa Libertadores, one Intercontinental Cup, one Supercopa Sudamericana and one Copa Interamericana.

Argentina has a long history of high-profile international players, including Diego Maradona. However, within the current national team, the country's three brightest stars – Lionel Messi, Sergio Aguero and Gonzalo Higuain – play their club football outside of the Primera Division.

COLOMBIA'S CATEGORIA PRIMERA A

Founded in 1948, Colombia's football league ranks 9th in the world and third in South America, according to the International Federation of Football History & Statistics. Its top division is the Categoria Primera A, which is contested by 18 clubs and works on a system of promotion and relegation with the lower division, Categoria Primera B.

The league's most successful club is Millonarios, which has won 14 titles, followed by traditional rivals Atletico Nacional, which has won 13 titles. Millonarios, Atletico Nacional and Independiente are also the only three teams to have played in every Categoria Primera A tournament since the league's creation. On top of its league wins, Bogota-based Millonarios has won five Copa Colombias

and one international Copa Merconorte in 2001. The club won its last Categoria Primera A title in 2012, after a gap of 24 years.

CHILE'S PRIMERA DIVISION

The Primera Division del Futbol Profesional Chileno is Chile's top football division, which was rebranded the Campeonato Nacional Scotiabank in 2014. Like many South American domestic clubs, the Primera Division has two tournaments per season – the Apertura and Clausura – which are contested by 18 teams.

The story of Chile's football league has been one of its ever-changing format, occurring mainly to accommodate the varying number of professional clubs involved in its domestic tournaments. The league was most recently reorganised in 2013 so its Apertura tournament would be played in the second half of the year and its Clausura tournament played in the first half of 2014.

Fourteen clubs have won the Primera Divison and 11 have won the championship more than once. The most successful clubs are Colo-Colo, with 30 titles; Universidad de Chile, with 15 titles; and Universidad Catolica, with 10 titles.

CENTRAL AND NORTH AMERICA

MEXICO'S LIGA MX

The Liga MX is Mexico's top division of football, officially called Liga Bancomer MX, after its sponsor's name. The league is comprised of 18 teams, which play in two tournaments every season: the Apertura, which runs from July to December; and the Clausura, which runs from January to May. In each tournament, the teams accrue points over 17 matches. The top eight teams then go onto the La Liguilla, or play-off round, where the champion is decided. This means there are two domestic champions every year, one from each tournament. At the end of the season one team from Liga MX is relegated down to lower division Ascenso MX, while one Ascenso MX team is promoted up to Liga MX.

The league has changed its domestic formats several times, including after Mexico's World Cup hosting success in 1970, when a play-off stage was introduced. The two most successful clubs in the league are Club America and its arch-rival Guadalajara. Both clubs have a total of 11 national titles.

AMERICA'S MAJOR LEAGUE SOCCER

Major League Soccer represents the top tier of football in the United States and Canada. The MLS is made up of 16 teams from the United States and three from Canada. Its season runs from March to October, with 34 games played by every team. Halfway through the regular season, the teams – which are geographically divided into Eastern and Western Conferences – meet for the annual All-Star Game. At the end of the regular season the MLS team with the most number of points wins the Supporters' Shield. In November and December, the post-season MLS Cup Play-offs are contested by 10 teams to decide the championship winner.

The formation of the MLS was first announced in 1993 to coincide with the United States' bid for the 1994 World Cup. A FIFA requirement for awarding the World Cup to the United States was that the country had a professional first division football league in place.

The first MLS season generated higher-than-expected average attendances of 17,000 per game, with the MLS Cup play-off final attracting 34,000 fans to watch D.C. United beat LA Galaxy 3-2.

In 2007, David Beckham signed for LA Galaxy which gave the sport a major boost in attendance numbers. The introduction of David Beckham into US football, alongside other European football stars such as Thierry Henry, is thought to have raised the sport's popularity in American schools. After retiring from playing football, David Beckham announced his intentions to stay a part of America's growing domestic football league in 2014 by setting up a Major League Soccer franchise in Miami.

BELOW Puma's Efrain Velarde celebrates a goal against Toluca.

DOMESTIC LEAGUES

REST OF THE WORLD

RIGHT Seongnam Ilhwa's Dzenan Radoncic celebrates scoring a goal.

BELOW Urawa Red Diamonds' Tomoaki Makino talks to his teammates in a J-League match.

AUSTRALIA'S A LEAGUE

The A League is Australia's premier football division, made up of nine Australian clubs and one from New Zealand. The league's tournament is played over the Southern Hemisphere summer, from October until April, and consists of a regular season followed by play-offs and then a grand final.

During the regular season, the teams play each other three times and accumulate points: three for a win and one for a draw. The club with the most points at the end of the season becomes the A League Premiers, and is awarded the Premier's Plate, and given an AFC Champions League spot. After the regular season ends, the top six teams on the table go on to play the finals series, which according to its most recent format, is a knockout competition. The finals culminate in a Grand Final, and the winner becomes the A League Champion, and is awarded the A league Trophy, and a spot in the AFC Champions League. Unlike many football leagues in the rest of the world, there is no system of promotion and relegation in the A League.

The A League was created in 2004 to replace the country's National Soccer League. Of the 10 clubs currently in the A League, only four – Adelaide United, Brisbane Roar, Newcastle Jets and Perth Glory – existed under the National Soccer League. New Zealand's most recent club, Wellington Phoenix, replaced the New Zealand Knights for the 2007-08 season. Brisbane Roar has the most number of wins in the finals series, with three, and is the top equal winner of the regular season alongside Central Coast Mariners and Melbourne Victory, all with two wins.

JAPAN'S J LEAGUE

The J League is the top tier of professional football in Japan and is contested by 18 teams. The teams play a total of 34 games in a season that runs from March until December, although in 2014 a break of several weeks was introduced so players could travel to the World Cup.

During the league's season, teams accumulate points to decide the winning club, which receives prize money of 200 million yen. If two clubs are tied on points, then they are declared co-winners. The top three clubs on the table qualify for the AFC Champions League, while the three teams with the least points are relegated to the J League Division 2, and replaced with its three best teams. In 2015, the league format will change to follow the South American Apertura and Clausura system, whereby a regular tournament is followed by a play-off 'super stage' tournament.

The J League began in 1993 to replace the Japan Soccer League, which was contested by amateur clubs. After an initial boom in its first three years, attendance figures hit a rapid decline from 1996 onwards. To boost the sport's popularity, the league encouraged clubs to become more involved in their local communities and it also announced its

'J-League Hundred Year Vision' which promised the creation of 100 professional Japanese clubs by 2092. The country's successes in the AFC Champions League helped raise its domestic league profile and boost supporter numbers within Japan. The J League is the only Asian league successful enough to be given the AFC's top ranking of 'A'.

SOUTH KOREA'S K LEAGUE CLASSIC

The K League Classic is South Korea's premier footballing division, which is contested by 12 clubs. Beneath it is the second division K League Challenge, which promotes three teams to the K League Classic at the end of every season and receives three relegated teams in turn. The fate of two of the teams about to be relegated/promoted are decided by a play-off match. The top three teams in the K League Classic qualify for the AFC Champions League.

The K League was created in 1998, and was made up of the reformed Korean Super League which had been running since 1983. Today the K League is well known for its success in the AFC Champions League, with its Pohang Steelers the current all-time highest winner, with three victories; followed by Seongnam FC, with two.

THE SAUDI PROFESSIONAL LEAGUE

The Saudi Professional League is Saudi Arabia's top tier of football, which was founded in 1976. The league features 14 teams that play each other in two tournaments: a round-robin regular season and a club competition called 'The Custodian of The Two Holy Mosques Champions Cup'. The cup is contested by the six best teams from the regular season, who are joined by the winners of the Crown Prince Cup and the Prince Faisal Cup. The winning club is awarded prize money of 2.5 million Riyals. The top four teams in the league also qualify for the AFC Champions League. Saudi teams Al-Hilal Saudi Football Club and Ittihad FC have featured regularly at the AFC Champions League, and each club has won the championship twice.

THE EGYPTIAN PREMIER LEAGUE

The Egyptian Premier League is the country's top tier of football which uses a similar format to that used in the English Premier League. In the Egyptian Premier League, 18 teams play each other twice in a season that runs from August to May, with a six-week break for winter from December to February. Teams accrue points during the season and then the club with the most points is crowned the champion. The three teams with the lowest points are relegated into the lower Division II league and replaced with the division's three best teams. The only rule that stands in stark contrast to the English Premier League is one that dictates only a maximum of three foreign players are allowed on any Egyptian Premier League side.

SOUTH AFRICAN PREMIER DIVISION

The South African Premier Division is the top tier of the country's Premier Soccer League, which was founded in 1996. Beneath it is the National First Division, also organised by the PSL. There are 16 teams in the Premier Division who play eachother twice in a season, which runs from August to May. Teams receive three points for a win, and one point for a draw. At the end of the season, the team with the most points qualifies for the CAF Champions League, and the winners of the Nedbank Cup qualify for the CAF Confederation Cup – the equivalent of the UEFA Europa League. The team with the least points on the table is relegated to the First Division and replaced by its best team. The team at 15th place on the Premier Division table enters a play-off with the 2nd and 3rd team from the First Division for a last Premier Division spot.

BELOW Egyptian Premier League side Al Ahly pose for a team photograph.

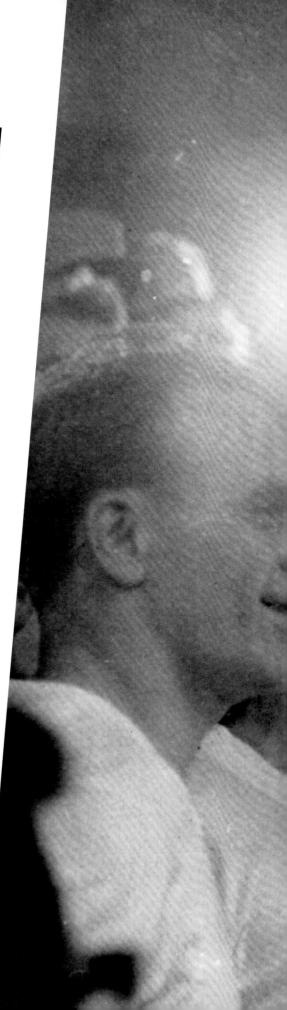

GREAT CLUBS

Club football provides the power base that keeps supporters
mesmerised across the world, week-in and week-out.
Initially, domestic leagues and cup competitions provided the
staple diet for fans, but then the glamour of international
competition provided the icing on the cake from the 1950s
onwards. Nowadays, international competition is crucial to
the financial health of many clubs, and provides the funds
that keep fans entertained with high-profile new signings.

EUROPE

ABOVE Johan Cruyff, three times a European champion with Ajax

PAGE 128 Liverpool celebrate a goal in 2005

PAGE 129 Zarrago, Real Madrid's captain, holds aloft the European cup

AJAX AMSTERDAM (Holland)
Ajax reached their peak in the early 1970s, when they pioneered the style known as 'total football' and won the European cup three times in a row. Coach Rinus Michels painstakingly built the side, led by the legendary Johann Cruyff, for five years before their victories from 1971 to 1973. Cruyff was the coach when Ajax lifted their next European trophy, the cup winners' cup, in 1987. The club's renowned youth system created another European cup-winning side in 1995, which finished as runner-up the following season. But the effects of the 'Bosman rule' have diminished Ajax's power, and now their stars inevitably move to richer clubs abroad.
Titles: European cup/champions league 1971, 1972, 1973, 1995; UEFA Cup 1992; Cup Winners' Cup 1987; Dutch champions 33 times; Dutch Cup 18

ARSENAL (England)
Arsenal became the dominant force in England in the 1930s. Manager Herbert Chapman created their first truly great side, which won four league titles in five seasons, including three in a row between 1933 and 1935. After two post-war titles, Arsenal went through a barren spell. Victory over Anderlecht in the 1970 Fairs Cup Final brought their first trophy for 17 years. They won the domestic 'double' the following season and star player George Graham later delivered two more titles as coach with a host of home-grown players. Long-serving manager Arsène Wenger imported a host of foreign players with a French connection. His rewards include two league and cup 'doubles.'
Titles: UEFA/Fairs cup 1970; cup winners' cup: 1994; English champions 13 times; FA Cup 11; League Cup 2

ASTON VILLA (England)
Aston Villa were one of the 12 founding members of the Football league in 1888. They were a major force in its early years, winning five championships between 1894 and 1900 and the 'double' in 1897. But after lifting the FA cup in 1920, they went 37 years before gaining another major crown, beating Manchester United in the FA Cup Final. Their most remarkable success was winning the European Cup in 1982. A quarter-final defeat by Juventus in 1983 signalled the start of a decline, and they were relegated in 1987. Aston Villa regained their elite status a season later. They finished league runner-up in both 1989 and 1993.
Titles: European Cup 1982; English champions 7 times; FA Cup 7; League Cup 5

ATLETICO MADRID (Spain)
Atletico Madrid have spent years playing second fiddle to neighbours Real Madrid, until the 2013-14 season when they gave both Real and Barcelona a run for their money. Spanish champions in 1973, they came within a minute of winning the European Cup a year later, but were denied glory by a late equaliser that forced a replay, which Bayern Munich won 4-0. Atletico won the 1974 World Club Cup after Bayern Munich declined to compete. The club became unstable during the reign of president Jesus Gil, who hired and fired 23 different coaches between 1987 and 2003. In 2008, they secured entry into the Champions League for the first time in over a decade, lifted the Europa League in 2012, and won La Liga in 2014.
Titles: Cup Winner's Cup 1962; UEFA Cup/Europa League 2010, 2012, Spanish champions 10 times; Spanish Cup 10

BARCELONA (Spain)
Barcelona's motto is 'mes que un club,' meaning 'more than a club,' and they have long been a symbol for Catalonia's regional pride. Their bitter rivalry with Real Madrid is a key feature of Spanish football. Coach Johann Cruyff, a playing great, created the winning 'dream team,' featuring Koeman, Pep Guardiola, Hristo Stoichkov, and Michael Laudrup – which many regard as

Barcelona's best-ever team. Frank Rijkaard, Cruyff's protege, later crafted the 2005–06 side that beat Arsenal 2-1 in the Champions League final and won La Liga. Guardiola replaced Rijkaard in 2008, and raised the bar still further thanks to the star quality of Lionel Messi, Andres Iniesta and Xavi. After Guardiola's departure in 2012, Tito Vilanova and Gerardo Martino have kept the ship steady, although Champions League defeats by Bayern Munich in both 2013 and 2014 have signalled the end of the club's European dominance.
Titles: European Cup/Champions League 1992, 2006, 2009, 2011; UEFA/Fairs Cup 1958, 1960, 1966; Cup Winner's Cup 1979, 1982, 1989, 1997; Spanish Champions 22 times; Spanish Cup 26

BAYERN MUNICH (Germany)

Bayern Munich succeeded Ajax as the dominant team in Europe in the mid-1970s, winning the European cup three times in a row. The great Franz Beckenbauer was their captain, supported by prolific striker Gerd Müller and goalkeeper Sepp Maier. Bayern came within a minute of losing the 1974 final to Atletico Madrid, winning the replay 4-0. A year later they beat Leeds United 2-0 in the final and they completed their trio with a 1-0 win over Saint-Etienne. Bayern added a fourth triumph in 2001, when goalkeeper Oliver Kahn defied Valencia in a penalty shoot-out and despite losing the 2012 final to Chelsea on their own ground, Bayern triumphed in London in 2013, beating German rivals Borussia Dortmund thanks to a late winner from Arjen Robben to add to their domestic 'double'. Bayern have been the dominant team in their domestic Bundesliga for more than 40 years.
Titles: European Cup/Champions League 1974, 1975, 1976, 2001, 2013; UEFA Cup Winners' Cup 1967; UEFA Cup 1996; German champions 24 times; German Cup 16

BENFICA (Portugal)

Benfica fans look back on the 1960s as their club's golden years. They succeeded Real Madrid as European champions by beating Barcelona 3-2 in the 1961 final, then retained the trophy with a 5-3 win over Real Madrid. Benfica also reached the final in 1963, 1965, and 1968 and supplied the bulk of the Portugal side that finished third in the 1966 World Cup finals. Benfica's hero was the great striker Eusébio. The team was packed with internationals, with Mario Coluna pulling the strings in midfield. Benfica lost in recent finals to PSV Eindhoven and AC Milan in 1990. In 2013 Benfica made it to the Europa League final but were beaten by Chelsea. Fate dealt its hand once again in the 2014 Europa League final, which Benfica lost to Sevilla on penalties.
Titles: European Cup 1961, 1962; Portuguese champions 32 times; Portuguese Cup 27

BORUSSIA DORTMUND (Germany)

Borussia Dortmund became the first West German team to lift a European trophy after they beat Liverpool in the 1966 Cup Winners' Cup

ABOVE Henrik Larsson, Carles Puyol and Ronaldinho take the Champions League Cup by tickertape storm in 2006

BELOW Arsenal celebrate their 1971 FA Cup final victory

GREAT CLUBS

EUROPE

final. But their greatest day came in 1997, when Ottmar Hitzfeld's side stunned Juventus 3-1 in the Champions League final. Hitzfeld had brought back Matthias Sammer, Andy Möller, Jürgen Koller and Stefan Reuter from Italy to form the core of the team. Five years later, Borussia Dortmund won the Bundesliga and reached the UEFA cup final, losing to Feyenoord. They came perilously close to bankruptcy in 2005, but recovered to win the Bundesliga again in 2011 and 2012, reaching the final of the Champions League under charismatic coach Jurgen Klopp in 2013.

Titles: European Cup 1997; UEFA Cup Winners' Cup 1966; German champions 8 times; German Cup 3

CELTIC (Scotland)

Celtic were the first British club to win the European Cup when they beat Internazionale

2-1 in the 1967 final at Lisbon. The team became known as the 'Lisbon Lions', and were all born within a 30-mile radius of Glasgow. Celtic also reached the final in 1970. They were managed by Jock Stein, and included outstanding figures such as Tommy Gemmell, Billy McNeill, Bobby Murdoch, and Jimmy Johnstone. That team began to break up after losing the 1974 European Cup semi-final to Atletico Madrid. But they still set a domestic record of nine consecutive championships. Celtic revived memories of those glory days with a run to the 2003 UEFA cup final, and they surprised Barcelona with a 2-1 win during the 2012-13 Champions League group stages.

Titles: European Cup 1967; Scottish champions 45 times; Scottish Cup 36; League Cup 14

CHELSEA (England)

Chelsea's recent transformation into a European power has been bankrolled by Russian oil billionaire Roman Abramovich, the club's owner since 2003. His appointment of Portugal's Jose Mourinho as manager a year later galvanised the club. Mourinho spent heavily to win the Premier League in his first season, and delivered another league title in 2006. He left Chelsea in September 2007, despite guiding them to FA Cup and League Cup victories, after falling out with Abramovich. After Mourinho, Israeli Avram Grant took Chelsea to their first Champions League final, but was sacked after their shoot-out defeat by Manchester United. In 2012 they took their first Champions League, beating Bayern Munich on penalties under caretaker coach Roberto di Matteo. Disappointment a year later was eased when they lifted the Europa League under another temporary coach, Rafael Benitez. In 2013 Mourinho returned to Chelsea.

Titles: Champions League 2012, Europa League 2013, Cup Winners' Cup 1971, 1998; English Champions 4 times; FA Cup 7; League Cup 4

BELOW Barcelona's Thierry Henry fails to breach Celtic's defence

DYNAMO KIEV (Ukraine)

Dynamo Kiev were the first club from the former Soviet Union to win a European trophy when they beat Hungary's Ferencváros in the 1975 European Cup winners' Cup final. They saw off Atletico Madrid 3-0 to win the same competition 11 years later. The Ukrainians led non-Russian opposition to the Moscow clubs during the Soviet era, winning 13 championships and nine cup finals. They are seasoned Champions League competitors, despite normally needing to start in the qualifying stages, and reached the semi-final stage in 1999. Andriy Shevchenko was their inspiration with eight goals, earning him a lucrative move to AC Milan.
Titles: Cup Winners' Cup 1975, 1986; Soviet/Ukrainian champions 26 times; Soviet/Ukrainian Cup 18

EVERTON (England)

Everton, formed in 1878, were founder members of the Football League, and one of its most successful clubs for many years. They reached their peak under Howard Kendall in the mid-1980s. They won the FA Cup in 1984, the league title (ahead of their great rivals, Liverpool) and the Cup Winners' Cup a year later, and added another title in 1987. In between, they finished as runner-up to Liverpool in the league and FA Cup. However, the ban on English clubs after the Heysel Stadium disaster denied Everton the chance to build on their European success, and eventually the team broke up. Manager David Moyes steered Everton to a Champions League qualifying place in 2005, but his replacement Roberto Martinez was unable to replicate his success. The 2-0 win over Manchester United in the 1995 FA cup remains their last major honour.
Titles: Cup Winners' Cup 1985; English champions 9 times; FA Cup 5

FEYENOORD (Holland)

Feyenoord became the first Dutch team to win the European Cup when they beat Celtic 2-1 after extra-time in 1970 in Milan. Four years later, they lifted the UEFA Cup after drawing with Tottenham in the first leg in London and winning the return game 2-0. Three of that victorious side, Wim Rijsbergen, Wim Jansen, and Wim van Hanegem, played for Holland in the 1974 World Cup final. Following almost 20 years without further European success, Feyenoord were surprise UEFA Cup winners in 2002, beating Borussia Dortmund 3-2. They have failed to make any impact in Europe since, and have not won the Dutch title since 1999. Instead, they have become a supplier of stars, including talents such as Robin van Persie, Dirk Kuyt and Salomon Kalou to clubs in richer leagues.
Titles: Intercontinental Cup 1970; European Champion Clubs' Cup 1970; UEFA Cup 1974, 2002; Dutch Champions 14 times; Dutch Cup 11

INTERNAZIONALE (Italy)

Internazionale were a dominant world power in the mid-1960s. European champions in 1964 and '65, they were beaten finalists in 1967. However, coach Helenio Herrera's catenaccio tactics were criticised for being too defensive, and they were an unpopular side with neutral spectators, despite fielding greats such as full-back Giacinto Facchetti, midfielder Luis Suarez, and attacker Sandro Mazzola. Internazionale reached another European Cup final in 1972, when they were swept aside by Ajax. They won only two domestic championships between 1972 and 2005, but collected three straight under Roberto Mancini and Jose Mourinho, with the latter lifting the Champions League in 2010, ending a 45-year wait and in the process becoming the first coach to lead an Italian side to a 'treble'.
Titles: Intercontinental Cup 1964, 1965; European Cup 1964, 1965, 2010; UEFA Cup 1991, 1994, 1998; Italian champions 18 times; Italian Cup 7

JUVENTUS (Italy)

Juventus boast an enviable record of appearing in seven European Cup finals. The tragedy of the Heysel Stadium disaster dwarfed their first success, when Michel Platini's goal edged out Liverpool in the 1985 final. They won again in 1996, when Marcello Lippi's team beat Ajax on penalties. Juventus have also lost finals to Ajax, Hamburg, Borussia Dortmund, Real Madrid, and AC Milan, most recently in 2003. They have amassed a record number of Italian titles, but recent successes have been dogged by controversy. Their three title wins between 1995 and 1998 were the subject of a doping enquiry. In 2006, Juventus were stripped of their 2005 and 2006 Serie A titles following a match-fixing scandal. The punishment included

ABOVE Alessandro Del Piero of Juventus celebrates a goal against Celtic in 2001

GREAT CLUBS

EUROPE

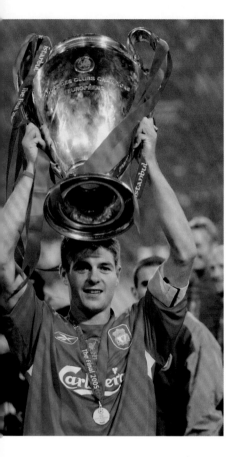

ABOVE Liverpool captain Steven Gerrard
lifts the 2005 European Cup in Istanbul

relegation, sending them to Serie B for the first time. Despite a 30-point deduction, they won promotion and returned to the top of Serie A, going unbeaten through the 2012-13 campaign.
Titles: Intercontinental Cup 1985, 1996; European Cup/Champions League 1985, 1996; Cup Winners' Cup 1984; UEFA/Fairs Cup 1977, 1990, 1993; Italian champions 30 times; Italian Cup 9

LIVERPOOL (England)
Liverpool remain the most successful English club in European competition. They have lifted the European Cup five times, the UEFA Cup three times, and have a hat-trick of European Super Cup prizes. Manager Bob Paisley, who succeeded the great Bill Shankly, was the architect of their success, steering Liverpool to a hat-trick of triumphs in 1977, 1978, and 1981 before handing over to Joe Fagan for their 1984 triumph. The Steven Gerrard-inspired comeback known as "the Miracle of Istanbul" brought Liverpool their fifth European Cup, and their first of the Champions League era in 2005. Such stars as Kenny Dalglish, Alan Hansen, Ian Rush, Graeme Souness and Phil Thompson then helped Liverpool to win a total of 18 championships. They have not won the league since 1990 and ending that run has become the club's priority. They reached second spot in the Premier League table for the 2013-14 season.
Titles: European Cup/Champions League 1977, 1978, 1981, 1984, 2005; UEFA Cup 1973, 1976, 2001; English champions 18 times; FA Cup 7; League Cup 7

LYON (France)
Lyon monopolised French football from 2002 for seven straight seasons, a domestic record. In 2008, they completed a league and cup 'double'. The 2002 title was Lyon's first, and a realisation of the dreams of Jean-Michel Aulas, club president since 1987. Despite that dominance, Lyon failed to

dominate in Europe, regularly losing key players to Champions League rivals, such as Michael Essien to Chelsea and Karim Benzema to Real Madrid.
Titles: French champions 7 times; French cup 5

MANCHESTER CITY (England)
Life has rarely been dull for fans of Man City. Recent history has seen them suffer the indignity of dropping into the third tier of English football before climbing back to the Premier League. They were relegated again, only for Kevin Keegan to lead them up again in 2002. A huge injection of cash by new Arab owners in 2008 elevated City into the big time, and they immediately sought to challenge for England's top honours. They won their first league title in 44 years in 2012 under Roberto Mancini, bringing back the glory years of the late 1960s when manager Joe Mercer guided them to the championship in 1968, the FA Cup in 1969 and the European Cup Winners' Cup and League Cup the next season. Mancini was replaced by Manuel Pellegrini in 2013, who won the 2013-14 Premier League season.
Titles: Cup Winner's Cup 1970; English champions 5; FA Cup 5; League Cup 4

MANCHESTER UNITED (England)
Scottish managers have crafted Manchester United's record-breaking post-war achievements. Sir Matt Busby built the team known as 'the Busby Babes' who won two championships and reached the European cup semi-finals twice, before being torn apart by the Munich air disaster in 1958. Busby went on to create another great side – featuring Bobby Charlton, Denis Law and George Best – which won two more championships and became the first English team to lift the European Cup, ten years after Munich. Sir Alex Ferguson then achieved greatness in his own style after delivering Manchester United's first league title for 26 years in 1993. His sides dominated the lucrative Premier League era. Ferguson added

two Champions League triumphs – in 1999 and 2008, the first bringing the club a unique 'treble', adding to the prizes of the Premier League and FA Cup. Ferguson retired in 2013, to be succeeded by David Moyes. But Moyes did not replicate Ferguson's success and the side was unable to achieve a top-four finish after being Premier League winners the season before. Moyes was said to have lost the support of his dressing room, which was followed by large sections of the club's fans. Moyes was sacked in 2014 after only 10 months in charge and replaced by Dutchman Van gaal.

Titles: European Cup/Champions League 1968, 1999, 2008; Cup Winners' Cup 1991; English champions 20 times; FA Cup 11; League Cup 4

AC MILAN (Italy)

AC Milan come second only to Real Madrid in terms of Champions League successes, having captured the prize seven times and appeared in four other finals. They first lifted it in 1963 by deposing holders Benfica 2-1, and six years later crushed Ajax Amsterdam 4-1. They had to wait 20 years for their next victory, when the Dutch trio of Ruud Gullit, Frank Rijkaard, and Marco van Basten inspired Arrigo Sacchi's cultured side to a 4-0 win over Steaua Bucharest, beating Benfica to retain the trophy a year later. AC Milan triumphed again in 1994, tearing Barcelona apart 4-0 under Fabio Capello. Defeat by Ajax Amsterdam the following year signalled the end of an era. The Dutchmen had already gone, but two defenders remained who would star in the next decade – Alessandro Costacurta and Paolo Maldini. Milan edged past Juventus on penalty kicks in 2003, then lost one of the most dramatic finals in 2005; having led Liverpool 3-0, they were defeated on penalties. They gained revenge two years later, winning 2-1 as Maldini collected his fifth winner's medal in the competition.

Titles: European Cup/Champions League 1963, 1969, 1989, 1990, 1994, 2003, 2007; European Cup Winners' Cup 1968, 1973; Italian champions 18 times; Italian Cup 5

OLYMPIQUE MARSEILLE (France)

Marseille's greatest achievement also led to their greatest crisis. They became the only French team

ABOVE Andrea Pirlo of AC Milan takes a free kick against Atalanta in 2008

to have won the Champions League when they saw off AC Milan in the 1993 final. Club president Bernard Tapie was jailed for his involvement in a match-fixing scandal which saw the club relegated. The club, who had won the previous five championships, were also stripped of their domestic crown. UEFA disqualified them from competing for a short period, but they returned to reach the UEFA Cup final in 1999 and 2004.

Titles: Champions League 1993; French champions 9 times; French Cup 10

PORTO (Portugal)

Porto tasted glory under Jose Mourinho as the new century unfolded. He steered them to the championship and a 2003 UEFA Cup final victory over Celtic. A year later, they were crowned champions of both Portugal and Europe, destroying AS Monaco 3-0 in the Champions League final, to deliver Porto's second such triumph. Mourinho then left for big-spending Chelsea, taking defensive duo Paulo Ferreira and Ricardo Carvalho with him, while playmaker Deco left for Barcelona. Still a Champions League regular, Porto have supplied many more of Europe's top players in recent seasons, notably Radamel Falcao, who helped them to the 2011 Europa League.

Titles: European Cup/Champions League 1987,

EUROPE

2004; UEFA Cup/Europa League 2003, 2011; Portuguese Champions 27 times; Portuguese Cup 16

PSV EINDHOVEN (Holland)

PSV broke the dominance of Ajax and Feyenoord, Holland's 'Big two' in the 1970s, when they won three championships in four seasons, and snatched the UEFA cup in 1978 with a 3-0 aggregate win over Bastia. PSV's greatest moment came ten years later, when they beat Benfica on penalties in the European Cup final, coached by Guus Hiddink.
The side have continued to challenge in the UEFA Champions League despite losing stars to England (Arjen Robben and Park Ji-Sung), Germany (Mark Van Bommel), and Spain (Arouna Kone). They lost on away goals to AC Milan in the 2005 semi-finals and reached the quarter-finals two years later.
Titles: European Champion Clubs' Cup 1988; UEFA Cup 1978; Dutch champions 21 times; Dutch cup 9

RANGERS (Scotland)

Rangers' run to the 2008 UEFA Cup final, which they lost 2-0 to Zenit St. Petersburg, marked the end of a 36-year gap since their last appearance in a European showpiece. In the previous final, they beat Dynamo Moscow 3-2 to lift the European Cup Winners' Cup – their only European prize.
In 1961, Rangers had lost the first European Cup Winners' Cup final to Fiorentina. A year earlier, Rangers reached the European Cup semi-finals, but crashed 12-4 on aggregate to Eintracht Frankfurt. They made their biggest impact on the Champions League in 1993, when they finished a point behind winners Marseille in the last-eight group stage.
Rangers have won a record 51 Scottish League titles, but were relegated to Scotland's lowest tier amid financial scandal in 2012.
Titles: Cup Winners' Cup 1972; Scottish champions 54 times; Scottish Cup 33; League Cup 27

RIGHT Jorge Costa and Vitor Baia lead Porto's European victory parade in 2004

REAL MADRID (Spain)

Real Madrid are the best-known club in the world. They won each of the first five finals of the European Cup – defeating Reims twice, Fiorentina, AC Milan, and Eintracht Frankfurt. Real were guided by visionary president Santiago Bernabeu, with the team ably led by the legendary Argentinian forward Alfredo di Stefano – who played in all five finals. The most renowned final was the 7-3 victory over Frankfurt in 1960, when di Stefano hit a hat-trick and Hungary great Ferenc Puskás netted four goals. Winger Paco Gento was the only attacking link with that golden past when Real Madrid's new-look team edged Partizan Belgrade 2-1 to win the trophy again six years later. They had to wait until 1998 for their next success, when Predrag Mijatovic scored the clincher against Juventus. Vicente del Bosque revived past glories, steering Real Madrid to victories in 2000 and 2002, but was sacked after their 2003 semi-final loss, and club president Florentino Perez put together a star-studded side with the top players known as 'Galacticos.' The great Jose Mourinho failed to win the Champions League, instead falling under the shadow of Barcelona and Bayern Munich. Carlo Ancelotti began his tenure as manager in 2013 and clinched Real's tenth European victory in 2014, beating Madrid rivals, Atletico, in the final.
Titles: European Cup/Champions League 1956, 1957, 1958, 1959, 1960, 1966, 1998, 2000, 2002, 2014; UEFA Cup 1985, 1986; Spanish champions 32 times; Spanish Cup 19

AS ROMA (Italy)

AS Roma have enjoyed their most successful decade recently, winning Serie A in 2001 and finishing runners-up five times since. The fulcrum of the club's success has been the excellence of forward Francesco Totti, who holds club records for games and goals. After a dip in form, Roma looked back to their best under French coach Rudi Garcia during 2013-14.
Titles: Fairs Cup 1961; Italian champions 3 times; Italian Cup 9

TOTTENHAM HOTSPUR (England)

Tottenham Hotspur became the first English club to win a European trophy when they beat Atletico Madrid 5-1 in the 1963 European Cup Winners'

Cup final. The team, built by Bill Nicholson and skippered by Danny Blanchflower, are considered Tottenham's best ever. They won the first league and cup 'double' of the 20th century in 1961, collecting the FA Cup again the following season, and reached the European Cup semi-final. Tottenham have since added two UEFA Cup victories to their European honours, and qualified for their first Champions League campaign in 2010, reaching the quarter-finals thanks largely to the form of Gareth Bale and Luka Modric who have both since been sold to Real Madrid.
Titles: European Cup Winner's Cup 1963; UEFA Cup 1972, 1984; English champions 2 times; FA Cup 8; League Cup 4

ABOVE Tottenham Hotspurs' double-winning players enjoy their open-top bus parade in 1961

GREAT CLUB MOMENTS

ABOVE Tottenham's Jimmy Greaves shoots for goal against Burnley

BELOW Celtic keeper Ronnie Simpson defies Internazionale in Lisbon

ABOVE Zico (left) is a legendary figure for Flamengo and Brazil

LEFT Benfica's Portugal hero Eusébio bears down on goal

BELOW Manchester United parade the Champions Cup in 1968

ABOVE Hugo Sanchez top-scored for Mexico, Real and Atletico Madrid

RIGHT Carles Puyol and Ronaldinho raise the Champions Cup

BELOW Alex (Santos) tackles Boca's Carlos Tevez

RIGHT David Beckham takes to the wing for LA Galaxy

ABOVE Milan forward Kaka eludes Inter's Nelson Rivas

ABOVE RIGHT Etoile Sahel carry off the African Super Cup

AMERICAS

BOCA JUNIORS (Argentina)

No South American club has won more international titles than the Argentinian club from la Bombonera, the Buenos Aires stadium whose affectionate nickname translates as 'the Chocolate Box'. Their 'Superclásico' rivalry with River Plate is one of the fiercest in the world, with Boca Juniors' supporters considering themselves as the city's working-class underdogs. Diego Maradona spent a title-winning season with the club before leaving for Spain in 1982, returning 13 years later. Juan Román Riquelme was a modern-day heir whose return for a second spell led to Copa Libertadores glory in 2007, and has a statue outside the stadium.
Titles: Copa Libertadores 1977, 1978, 2000, 2001, 2003, 2007; Copa Sudamericana 2004, 2005; Argentine league 30 times

COLO COLO (Chile)

The "Snow Whites" of Santiago became the first, and so far only, Chilean club to win the Copa Libertadores – the South American equivalent of the UEFA Champions League – in 1991 when they beat Paraguay's Olimpia Asuncion 3-0 on aggregate. They are Chile's most successful club, with 41 domestic trophies and the only club to have contested every season without relegation since the league was founded in 1933.
Titles: Copa Libertadores 1991; Chilean league 30 times; Chilean Cup 10

FLAMENGO (Brazil)

Flamengo began life in 1895 as a rowing club but embraced football 16 years later, after a breakaway by aggrieved members of neighbouring Fluminense. They have since become Brazil's best-loved club, with an estimated fanbase of 40 million. It was not until the late 1970s and early 1980s that they extended their domestic brilliance to the international arena, inspired by the brilliance of Zico.
Titles: Copa Libertadores 1981; Brazilian league 6 times, Brazilian Cup 3

INDEPENDIENTE (Argentina)

Years of decline and debts forced Independiente to sell wonder-kid Sergio Aguero to Atletico Madrid in 2006, yet the club's history remains as glorious as any in Argentina – including a record seven Copa Libertadores titles. These include four in a row between 1972 and 1975 that were inspired by midfielder Ricardo Bochini, who played for 20 years with the club. They have also been home to the World Cup-winning trio of Daniel Bertoni, Jorge Burruchaga and Oscar Ortiz.
Titles: Copa Libertadores 1964, 1965, 1972, 1973, 1974, 1975, 1984; Argentine league 16 times

PEÑAROL (Uruguay)

Uruguay's most prestigious club provided the two scorers when Brazil were amazingly beaten in the 1950 World Cup finals, namely Alcides Ghigghia and Juan Schiaffino. At times in the 1960s, Peñarol could even outshine Pelé and Santos, including a 5-0 win in 1963, featuring a hat-trick by Alberto Spencer. He remains the all-time top scorer in the Copa Libertadores, leading the Montevideo club to three of their five triumphs. Peñarol have also been crowned World Club champions three times.
Titles: Copa Libertadores 1960, 1961, 1966, 1982, 1987; Uruguayan league 49 times

RIVER PLATE (Argentina)

Along with Buenos Aires arch-rivals Boca Juniors, River Plate remain one of Argentina's biggest, best-supported teams. Their formidable five-man forward line of the early 1940s was dubbed 'La Máquina' (the Machine) but a sixth striker that decade was perhaps their greatest of all, Alfredo di Stefano. Argentina's 1978 World Cup-winning captain Daniel Passarella spearheaded a club revival in the 1970s, before boyhood-fan Hernan Crespo shot to fame at the Estadio Monumental in the 1990s. 1986 was a perfect year for River Plate, not only were Argentina crowned world champions, but River captured the league, the Copa Libertadores and the World Club Cup, beating

LEFT Pelé takes aim for Santos in 1973

Steaua Bucharest. Recent years have brought struggles, however, and they were relegated from the top flight for the first time ever in 2011, though they returned a year later.
Titles: Copa Libertadores 1986, 1996; Supercopa Sudamericana 1997; Argentine league 35 times

SANTOS (Brazil)

For much of the 1960s, Santos were the side the whole world wanted to see – largely thanks to their iconic number 10, Pelé. As well as clinching two world club titles, beating Benfica and AC Milan, and several state championships, the Brazilian entertainers toured the world almost non-stop to play money-making exhibition matches for huge crowds. Pelé's departure in 1972 inevitably signalled an end to the glory days, and they had to wait until 2002 for their next Brazilian league title. In recent years the club has produced such young stars as Robinho, Elano, Diego and Neymar, a star of the 2014 World Cup who helped the side to its third Copa Libertadores in 2011.
Titles: Copa Libertadores 1962, 1963, 2011; Copa CONMEBOL 1998; Brazilian champions 8 times, Brazilian Cup 1

SÃO PAULO (Brazil)

Brasilia is the country's capital, Rio's clubs have the most fervent support, and neighbours Santos boasted Pelé, but São Paulo can claim to be Brazil's most successful club. Leonidas da Silva in the 1940s, Gerson in the 1970s, Careca in the 1980s and more recently Kaka in the 2000s have contributed to their collection of domestic and world titles. Their Copa Libertadores win in 2005 made them the first Brazilian club to claim a hat-trick of titles, and the first team to beat a side from the same country in the final, Atletico Paranaense.
Titles: Copa Libertadores 1992, 1993, 2005; Copa Sudamericana 2012; Brazilian champions 6 times

VASCO DA GAMA (Brazil)

Vasco da Gama was founded in 1898 by Portuguese immigrants, taking their name from the revered Portuguese explorer of the 14th and 15th centuries, and call for much of their support on Rio's Portuguese communities. World cup-winning striker Romario started his career at Vasco in 1985 and retired in 2008 after his fourth term at the club, which included the goal he claimed was the 1,000th of his career. But his 316 goals for Vasco da Gama were less than half the tally of their leading goalscorer, Roberto Dinamite. he scored 698 in 1,110 games between 1971 and 1993. Vasco have not won the league since 2000, but did lift the domestic cup in 2011.
Titles: Copa Libertadores 1998; Brazilian champions 4 times, Brazilian cup 1

GREAT CLUBS

REST OF THE WORLD

ABOVE Jaime Moreno of DC United looks for an opening against the New York Red Bulls

AL-AHLY (Egypt)

Llittle wonder the Cairo side were named in 2000 as the Confederation of African Football's club of the century. Egypt's so-called 'people's club' has won a record five African Club Championships, and a major haul of domestic titles. They even managed to remain unbeaten from 1974 to 1977. The 'red devils,' whose former players include Egypt's record scorer Hossam Hassan, have a ferocious rivalry with city rivals Zamalek, and have recently had the upper hand, lifting the past two Champions League titles.
Titles: African Champions League 1982, 1987, 2001, 2005, 2006, 2008, 2012, 2013; African Cup Winners' Cup 1984, 1985, 1986, 1993; Egyptian league 36 times, Egyptian Cup 35

CLUB AMERICA (Mexico)

Club America have been Mexico's big spenders since a 1959 takeover by television giant Televisa. Until recent years at least, such power guaranteed success, including a record five crowns as CONCACAF champions (the same number won by rivals Cruz Azul) and 11 league titles (a joint record with Chivas Guadalajara). Big-name foreign imports have included Argentina's Oscar Ruggeri, Chilean Ivan Zamorano, and Romania's Ilie Dumitrescu. But they have also developed home-grown talent such as Mexican playmaker Cuauhtemoc Blanco. Club America play at the huge Azteca Stadium in Mexico City, the only stadium to have hosted two World Cup finals.
Titles: CONCACAF Champions Cup/ Champions League 1978, 1987, 1991, 1993, 2006; CONCACAF Cup Winners' Cup 2001; Mexican league 11 times, Mexican Cup 5

DC UNITED (United States)

Captain John Harkes, returning home from the English Premier League, and coach Bruce Arena led the Washington DC-based club to the first two MLS titles in 1996 and 1997. They also became the first US club to win the CONCACAF Champions'

Cup in 1998. But trophies have proved harder to come by since Arena left to become national coach in 1998, despite high-profile signings such as iconic Hristo Stoichkov and Freddy Adu – who made his debut aged 14. Other notable former players include Bolivian pair Jaime Moreno and Marco Etcheverry.
Titles: CONCACAF Champions Cup 1998; US MLS Cup four times; US Open Cup 3

ETOILE DU SAHEL (Tunisia)

Tunisia may have underachieved internationally, with only one African Cup of Nations triumph, but their oldest club has proved the pride of a nation, with impressive performances in all continental competitions. They achieved surprise Champions League glory in 2007, beating Egyptian holders Al-Ahly, making them the first club to have won each of the African Federation's club trophies.
Titles: African Champions League 2007; African Cup Winners' Cup 1997, 2003; Tunisian league 9; President's Cup 8

LOS ANGELES GALAXY (United States)

LA Galaxy pulled off the most high-profile signing in MLS history when world superstar, England's iconic David Beckham, joined from Real Madrid in 2007. Another great, Holland's Ruud Gullit, was then appointed LA Galaxy coach after a disappointing first season for Beckham. The midfielder's arrival helped the club sell 700 times as many replica shirts as before, bringing global attention to the MLS for the first time. Beckham left after lifting the MLS Cup in 2012, by which time he had been joined by Robbie Keane from Tottenham Hotspur.
Titles: CONCACAF Champions Cup 2000; MLS Cup 2002, 2005, 2011, 2012; US Open Cup 2

KAIZER CHIEFS (South Africa)

Kaizer Chiefs, one of South Africa's first professional clubs, take their name from the

former international midfielder, Kaizer Motaung. He co-founded the club in 1970 after returning from a spell in the US. he has since served them as a player, in three separate stints as coach, and now as club president. The Chiefs passionately contest the Soweto derby with Orlando Pirates, another of Motaung's old teams. Their home at Johannesburg's FNB Stadium was rebuilt as Soccer City to host the 2010 World Cup final between Spain and Holland.
Titles: African Cup Winners' Cup 2001; South African league 3; Nedbank Cup 13

POHANG STEELERS (South Korea)
Pohang Steelers dominated in Korea during the 1970s and '80s, then suffered a 15-year barren spell in the K league until their 2007 title triumph. In 1997, they became the third South Korean team to win the Asian Champions League by beating compatriots and defending champions Seongham Ilhwa Chunma. They retained the trophy the following year against China's Dalian Wanda. Crucial to their success in the 1990s was reliable defender Hong-Myung Bo, who went on to become his country's most-capped player, and now coaches his country.
Titles: Asian Champions League 1997, 1998, 2009; South Korean league 5; Korean FA Cup 4

UNAM PUMAS (Mexico)
UNAM Pumas, the club affiliated to Latin America's largest university, has long put a useful emphasis on youth and proudly produced Mexican legends such as Luis Garcia, Jorge Campos and Hugo Sanchez. The inspirational striker scored 96 goals for UNAM Pumas from 1976 to 1981, then returned as coach 19 years later, guiding the club to four trophies in 2004. Colourful goalkeeper Campos loved to roam upfield but also occasionally played in attack with 35 goals to his credit in 199 games. UNAM Pumas' home in Mexico City was the main venue for the 1968 Olympic Games.
Titles: CONCACAF Champions Cup 1980, 1982, 1989; Copa Interamericana 1981; Mexican league 7, Mexican Cup 1

URAWA RED DIAMONDS (Japan)
Urawa Red Diamonds won four league titles and four Emperor's Cups before the Japanese game turned professional in 1993. They made a bad start

in the J league, finishing bottom in the first two seasons. The team, nicknamed 'the Nearly Men' lived up to their image by just missing out on the 2004 and 2005 titles, but they finally sparkled to become J league champions in 2006 and win the Asian Champions League in 2007. Star players have included Japanese midfielder Shinji Ono and Brazilian striker Edmundo.
Titles: Asian Champions League 2007; Japanese League 5; Emperor's Cup 6; J league Cup 1

AL-HILAL (Saudi Arabia)
One of the most accomplished Asian sides and the club most widely followed in Saudi Arabia, Al-Hilal has over 55 major trophies to its name. Known locally as Al-Zaeem, or 'The Boss', the side boasts players such as 2000 AFC player of the year Nawaf Al Temyat, four-time World Cup player Sami Al Jabber and goalkeeper Mohamed Al Deayea, who holds the record for most appearances with the club.
Titles: 13 Saudi Premier Leagues: 1977- 2011; Asian Club Championships 1992, 2000; 2 Asian Cup Winners' Cups 1997, 2002; 2 Asian Super Cups 1997, 2000; 6 Saudi King's Cups 196-1989; 7 Saudi Federation Cups: 1987-2006; 11 Saudi Crown Prince Cups 1994-2013
2 Arab Champions' Cups 1994, 1995.

ABOVE Urawa Reds Diamonds take the glory after their Asian Champions League triumph in 2007

GREAT CLUBS

REST OF THE WORLD

ESPERANCE SPORTIVE DE TUNIS
(Tunisia)

Esperance ST was formed in 1919 as the first club to be run by Tunisians without assistance from the French colonists. As such, the club is one of the most celebrated in Tunisia. The club today retains its place as the country's best, with eight league titles, three President's Cups and a Tunisian Super Cup won in the last decade alone. The club plays its football in the multi-purpose Stade Olympique d'El Menzah, which has a 45,000-person capacity.
Titles: 26 Tunisian championships 1942-2014; 14 Tunisian Cups 1939-2011; 2 Tunisian Super Cups 1993, 2001; 2 CAF Champions Leagues 1994, 2011; 1 African Cup Winners Cup 1998; 1 CAF Super Cup 1995; 1 CAF Cup 1997.

ESTEGHLAL TEHRAN (Iran)

Tehran-based Esteghlal is the biggest club in Iran, alongside its city rival Persepolis. The pair usually sit at the top of the country's premier league known as the Iran Pro League. Esteghlal has been a consistent winner not only of domestic club competitions, but also of the Asian Club Championship, winning it twice. These Asian Club wins are proudly displayed as two golden stars on the club's badge. Esteghlal plays its football in the Azadi Stadium, which was constructed in 1971 and has a capacity of 90,000. Persepolis and the Iranian national team also share the stadium.
Titles: 7 League championships 1975, 1990, 1999, 2001, 2006, 2009, 2013; 6 Hazfi Cups 1977, 1996, 2000, 2002, 2008, 2012; 2 Asian Club Championships: 1971, 1991.

KASHIMA ANTLERS (Japan)

Seven-time winners of the Japanese J. League, the Kashima Antlers has been the country's highest-profile team since the club's inception in 1993. With close links to South American football through their various Brazilian players – Zico, Leonardo, Jorginho, and Mazinho – the Kashima

Antlers are the only Japanese side to have finished in the top five of the teams playing in Japan's top flight since the professional league was founded in 1993. The Kashima Antlers' 40,700-capacity Kashima stadium, constructed in 1993, is Japan's only stadium built solely for football.
Titles: 7 J. League championships 1996, 1998, 2000, 2001, 2007, 2008, 2009; 4 Emperor's Cups 1997, 2000, 2007, 2010; 4 J. League Cups 1997, 2000, 2002, 2011; 3 J. League Super Cups: 1997, 1998, 1999; 1 A3 Champions Cup 2003.

NEW YORK RED BULLS (United States)

Formed as a founding member of Major League Soccer in 1996 (MLS), the New York Red Bulls are one of two New York league sides, which includes rivals New York City FC. The side's most recent significant trophy was the Supporters' Shield in 2013. The team has undergone several name changes which include the MetroStars and achieved their best season result when they reached the MLS Cup final in 2008. The team is known for its big name players which have often been signed for major league teams in Europe and South America. These include Thierry Henry, Giovanni Savarese, Adolfo Valencia and Youri Djorkaeff.
Titles: Supporters' Shield 2013; MLS Eastern Conference 2000, 2010, 2013; MLS Western Conference 2008.

SEONGNAM FC (Korea)

Formed in 1989 as Seongnam Ilhwa Chunma, cynics considered the club had been created by the Ilhwa Company simply as a way of selling its Chunma drinks. Over 20 years later, Seongnam Ilhwa Chunma are easily Korea's most successful K League club, with over 16 trophies to their name, including seven national titles. Recently, Shin Tae-Yong, the legendary captain, has taken over the club's coaching reins and reinvigorated the sides by signing several young players. In 2014, the club

BELOW Kashima Antlers players celebrate scoring a third goal in a Championship match against Sao Paulo FC.

ABOVE Toronto FC players celebrate scoring a goal against Vancouver Whitecaps in the MLS.

was bought by the Seongnam Government and officially renamed Seongnam FC.
Titles 7 Korean league championships 1993-2006; 2 Korean FA Cups 1999, 2011; 1 Korean Super Cup 2002; 3 Korean League Cups 1992, 2002, 2004; 2 AFC Asian Club Championships: 1995, 2010; 1 AFC Asian Super Cup 1996.

TOUT PUISSANT MAZEMBE (Congo)

Founded in 1939 by Benedictine monks, TP Mazembe hails from the mining region of the country's Katanga province. Four-time winner of the CAF Champions League, TP Mazembe is the most successful club in sub-Saharan Africa and a close rival of north African teams Al-Ahly and Zamalek, who have won a similar number of titles. TP Mazembe plays its football in the 18,500-capacity Stade TP Mazembe and often signs its players from Congolese feeder club CS Don Bosco.
Titles: 11 DR Congo League 1966- 2011; 5 DR Congo Cups 1966, 1967, 1976, 1979, 2000; 4 CAF Champions Leagues 1967, 1968, 2009, 2010; 1 CAF Cup Winners' Cup 1980; 2 CAF Super Cups 2010, 2011 FIFA Club World Cup runners-up 2010.

TORONTO FC (Canada)

The club Toronto FC was officially announced in 2006 after a public vote on its name. More commonly known as 'The Reds' and 'TFC', Toronto FC was the first Canadian side to play in the North American Major Soccer League after the league's expansion in 2007. The team has won four consecutive Canadian Championships and reached the semi-finals of the 2011-12 CONCACAF Champions League. Toronto FC plays its home matches at the football stadium BMO Field which is located on the shores of Lake Toronto. Recent big-name signings from overseas to play with the club have included Brazilian goalkeeper Julio Cesar and ex-England and Tottenham Hotspur striker Jermain Defoe. Titles: Canadian Championship 2009, 2010, 2011, 2012; Trillium Cup 2011.

RIGHT Tout-Puissant celebrate their CAF Champions League final victory in 2010.

GREAT
PLAYERS

Every generation has its share of great players whose
footballing prowess puts them head and shoulders above
the rest. These are the sport's superstars, who use their
individual skills to enthrall the crowds and lead their teams
to victory. The most gifted players can have it all – fame,
fortune and the adulation of millions. But football fans are
fickle and can turn on a player who doesn't consistently
perform well. The greatest football players are therefore
often those who have overcome slumps in form, off-
pitch controversy, and the odd red card, to forever win a
place in the history books and the hearts of their fans.

ABOVE Gabriel Batistuta

BELOW RIGHT Franz Beckenbauer

DAVID ALABA (born 25 June 1992)

Austria: 31 games, 6 goals

One of the rising stars of Austrian football, David Alaba made his debut for the senior national team in 2009, making him the youngest ever player in Austrian history to do so. At the age of 19, Alaba was voted 2011 Austrian Footballer of the Year. He scored his first goal for his country in 2012 against Kazakhstan and scored five more in the following two years. Alaba has played in the positions of central midfield as well as right and left wing for his country. More recently, Alaba has played at left-back for his club side, Bayern Munich. He is under contract with the club until 2018.

GARETH BALE (born 16 June 1989)

Wales: 44 games, 12 goals

When he signed to Real Madrid in 2013, Welsh footballer Gareth Bale was proclaimed the 'Most Expensive Footballer In The World'. The transfer figure paid to his former club side Tottenham Hotspur was reported to be a record-breaking £85.3 million, although the exact figure has never been released by Real Madrid. Bale started his professional career at Southampton as left-back, although he later became more of an attacking player, playing in both midfield and on the wings. He was awarded the PFA Players' Player of the Year in 2011 and 2013.

MARCO VAN BASTEN

(born 31 October 1964)

Holland: 58 games, 24 goals

Marco Van Basten scored one of the finest goals in international history when he volleyed home Holland's second in their victory over the Soviet Union in the final of the 1988 European Championship. The goal sealed Van Basten's reputation as one of the finest centre forwards to grace European football, not only with Holland but also with top club sides Ajax Amsterdam and Milan. Injury forced his premature retirement.

GABRIEL BATISTUTA

(born 1 February, 1969)

Argentina 78 games, 56 goals

Nicknamed "Batigol", Gabriel Batistuta led the Argentine line at three consecutive World Cups and hit a hat-trick on his tournament debut in a 4-0 win over Greece. Four years later, he became the first player to score hat-tricks in two different tournaments, when he repeated the feat in a 5-0 thrashing of Jamaica. In total, Batistuta netted 10 goals at the World Cup, but his international career ended in disappointment when Argentina were eliminated at the group stage in 2002.

FRANZ BECKENBAUER

(born 11 September 1945)

West Germany: 103 games, 14 goals

Franz Beckenbauer is one of the few defenders guaranteed a place in any football hall of fame. Initially a playmaker, 'Der Kaiser' was converted into a creative sweeper by Yugoslavian coach Tschik Čajkovski at Bayern Munich in the 1960s. With more than 100 international appearances, he appeared in two World Cup finals and lifted the trophy as the West German captain in 1974 and

again as national coach in 1990. In recent years, he has served as president of Bayern, as a member of the FIFA executive and has chaired the organising committee for the 2006 World Cup.

DAVID BECKHAM (born 2 May 1975)
England: 115 games, 17 goals
A boyhood Manchester United fan, David Beckham went on to win a historic treble with the club in 1999. He was subsequently sold to Real Madrid in 2003, winning the Spanish league in the last of his four seasons with the club, then joined LA Galaxy. Beckham played in three World Cup finals for England, which included a controversial sending off against Argentina in 1998.

GEORGE BEST
(born 22 May 1946, died 25 November 2005)
Northern Ireland: 37 games, 9 goals
Best was arguably the greatest player never to have made an appearance in the World Cup finals. A magical talent, one of the most exciting to grace English football, he made his Manchester United debut as a winger aged 17 in 1963 and went on to win the European Champion Clubs' Cup in 1968 and two league titles, before being driven out of the British game by the pressures of his own fame. His greatest exploit was in United's 5-1 thrashing of Benfica in Lisbon in a European Champion Clubs Cup quarter-final in 1966. He was voted European Footballer of the Year in 1968.

ANTONIO CARBAJAL (born 7 June 1929)
Mexico: 48 games, no goals
Antonio Carbajal became the first player to appear in the finals of five World Cup competitions, but ended up on the winning side only once. The goalkeeper's debut in the finals was against Brazil in 1950, when he conceded four goals. He played in the 1954, 1958, and 1962 World Cup finals before bowing out after a goalless draw against Uruguay in the 1966 finals.

ROBERTO CARLOS (born 10 April 1973)
Brazil: 125 games, 11 goals
Roberto Carlos da Silva Rocha proved to be one of Brazil's most loved players due to the power of his shooting and the exuberance of his attacking play from left-back. He played in three World

ABOVE George Best

Cups, where, with Cafu on the right, he became a Brazilian icon and lifted the 2002 trophy in Japan, having scored against China in the group stages with a trademark free-kick. He retired from international football after Brazil were eliminated by France in the 2006 World Cup quarter-final.

PETR CECH (born 20 May 1982)
Czech Republic: 107 games, 0 goals
Petr Cech is the second most-capped player in the history of Czech football, and represented his country at the 2006 World Cup, as well as Euro 2004, 2008 and 2012. Cech played for club sides Blsany, Sparta Prague and Rennes before joining Chelsea in 2004, a team he has made over 450 appearances for. He was voted best goalkeeper for the 2004-05, 2006-07 and 2007-08 seasons of the UEFA Champions League. Cech's goalkeeping records include, over 100 clean sheets in 180 English Premier League games and over 220 clean sheets for Chelsea across all competitions.

SIR BOBBY CHARLTON
(born 11 October 1937)
England: 106 games, 49 goals

Having overcome the tragedy of the Munich air disaster in 1958, Charlton helped lead the reconstruction of the devastated Manchester United side. At international level, his powerful shooting had helped England to their sole World Cup success, alongside his brother Jack, a defender. With 49 international goals, he remains England's top goalscorer of all time and went on to play in the 1970 tournament in Mexico. He was substituted by manager Alf Ramsey with England leading West Germany, only for the Germans to come from behind to win 3-2.

BELOW Sir Bobby Charlton

JOSÉ LUIS CHILAVERT (born 27 July 1965)
Paraguay: 74 games, 8 goals

José Luis Chilavert was renowned for his scoring achievements despite being a goalkeeper. His ultimate ambition was to score a goal in the World Cup finals, but he failed, even though he had scored four in qualifying matches for the 2002 tournament. He was voted the world's top goalkeeper three times and was included in the 1998 team of the tournament.

JOHAN CRUYFF (born 25 April 1947)
Holland: 48 games, 33 goals

Johan Cruyff, son of a cleaner at the Ajax Amsterdam offices, grew up to be the epitome of Holland's 'Total Football' revolution, as well as being voted European Footballer of the Year three times in the 1970s. He led his nation to the final of the 1974 World Cup, but they were beaten by hosts West Germany. Cruyff controversially refused to play in the 1978 World Cup finals in Argentina because of the kidnap threats made to him and his family. Holland reached the final, but were once again beaten by the hosts. Critics believe that with his presence they could have returned from South America with the coveted trophy.

TEÓFILO CUBILLAS (born 8 March 1949)
Peru: 81 games, 26 goals

Teófilo Cubillas shot to stardom as an inside forward in the outstanding Peru team that reached the 1970 World Cup quarter-finals, scoring in all four of his country's games and five goals in total, including against eventual champions Brazil. Just 21, he was named the best young player in the tournament and returned in 1978 when he scored twice against Scotland and scored a hat-trick against Iran.

KENNY DALGLISH (born 4 March 1951)
Scotland: 102 games, 30 goals

Kenny Dalglish achieved a remarkable feat by

winning league titles as both a player and a manager in England with Liverpool and in Scotland with Celtic. A nimble, quick-thinking forward, Dalglish moved from Glasgow to Anfield in 1978 as replacement at Liverpool for the legendary Kevin Keegan. He duly proved that he could fill the boots of the Kop hero – he was the club's leading scorer in his first season. After a glittering playing career for Liverpool, he successfully made the transition to managing the club in 1985, and became the only player-manager in modern times to steer his club to a domestic double in both league and FA Cup. His glittering career saw him equal the scoring record with Denis Law for Scotland, but he stands alone with the record for most appearances.

DIDI (born 8 October 1929, died 12 May 2001)
Brazil: 68 games, 20 goals
Didi, full name Waldyr Pereira, won the World Cup twice with Brazil in 1958 and 1962, having also played in 1954. Brazil might not have even been at the finals in 1958 at all but for a remarkable free-kick from the midfielder that bent in the air and flew into the net against Peru in a qualifying tie. The 'Falling Leaf' became Didi's trademark and has been copied by players all over the world ever since. He is regarded as among his country's best ever midfield players and was voted the best player of the tournament in Sweden in '58, his performances, however, were overshadowed by the 17-year-old Pele.

DIDIER DROGBA (born 11 March 1978)
Ivory Coast: 52 games, 33 goals
Didier Drogba was a late starter, not making his professional breakthrough until he was 20 with French club Le Mans. He moved on to Guingamp in the French first division at the age of 24 before being bought by Marseille, who he led to the 2004 UEFA Cup final. His next step was a transfer to newly-enriched Chelsea for a then club record $48 million (£24 million). He scored over 70 goals in four seasons for the club and has won the Premier League, FA Cup, and League Cup. He was named African Player of the Year in 2007.

LANDON DONOVAN (born 4 March 1982)
United States: 100 games, 35 goals
Landon Donovan is the long-serving, outstanding international that US football has been waiting for. He debuted at the World Cup in 2002, helping his country beat the highly-rated Portugal before scoring in the 2-0 win over Mexico. He was named the tournament's best young player and returned in 2006 for a disappointing campaign, before scoring three further times in South Africa in 2010 as the US again reached the knockout rounds. No player from the American qualifying region has scored as many World Cup goals as Donovan.

CHRISTIAN ERIKSEN
(born 14 February 1992)
Denmark: 44 games, 4 goals
Midfielder Christian Eriksen made a name for himself at club side Ajax before signing for Tottenham Hotspur in 2013. He made his debut for Denmark in 2010, making him the youngest player of the World Cup in South Africa. In 2010, Eriksen won AFC Ajax Talent of the Future, and in 2011, Ajax Talent of the Year and Dutch Football Talent of the Year. He was awarded the Dutch Bronze Boot in 2012 and in 2013, Danish Footballer of the Year. With Ajax, Eriksen won the Dutch Eredivisie in 2010-11, 2011-12 and 2012-13.

ABOVE Teófilo Cubillas

BELOW Didi

GREAT PLAYERS

ABOVE Eusébio

RIGHT Garrincha

SAMUEL ETO'O (born 10 March 1981)
Cameroon: 76 games, 31 goals
Samuel Eto'o is an explosive Cameroonian
striker who was brought to Europe by Real
Madrid. However, he failed to impress the club and
was sold. He has made them regret it with four
wonderful seasons each at Mallorca and then
Barcelona. In 2006, Eto'o won the Golden Boot
as Europe's leading league scorer with 26 goals,
helping to fire Barcelona to their Champions
League success over Arsenal as well as winning the
Spanish Super Cup.

EUSÉBIO
(born 25 January 1942, died 5 January 1914)
Portugal: 64 games, 41 goals
Eusébio da Silva Ferreira, a Mozambican-born
Portuguese striker, was nicknamed the 'Black
Panther' for his valuable goals. A star for club side
Benfica, he guided Portugal to third place at the
1966 World Cup and won the Golden Boot as top
scorer in the competition with nine goals. His finest
performance was in the memorable quarter-final
against North Korea. The Koreans raced to a 3-0
lead before Eusébio came on and scored four goals
to give his country a 5-3 victory.

JUST FONTAINE (born 18 August 1933)
France: 21 games, 30 goals
Just Fontaine was a fast, brave forward who wrote
his name into World Cup history by scoring 13
goals for third-placed France in the 1958 finals –
Fontaine scored in all six games. His goalscoring
record remains unbeaten. Fontaine, born in
Morocco, only got his chance in the 1958 World
Cup finals because Reims team-mate Rene Bliard
was ruled out with an ankle injury. Fontaine's
career was ended prematurely in 1961 due to two
serious leg fractures.

ENZO FRANCESCOLI
(born 12 November 1961)
Uruguay: 72 games, 15 goals

Enzo Francescoli, nicknamed "The Prince", is
arguably the last great Uruguayan player. However,
he played the majority of his club career in
Argentina, France, and Italy. He played the 1989-90
season with Olympique Marseille, where he was
the footballing hero and inspiration for the teenage
Zinedine Zidane. A tall, graceful inside forward,
Francescoli was a three-times winner of the Copa
America with Uruguay and played twice at the
World Cup finals. He was voted South American
Player of the Year in both 1984 and 1995.

GARRINCHA
(born 28 October 1933, died 20 January 1983)
Brazil: 50 games, 12 goals
Garrincha, full name Manoel dos Santos Francisco,
lived a life that was a tale of triumph and tragedy.
Nicknamed "the Little Bird", he won the World
Cup in 1958 and 1962, with his goals and creativity
proving to be decisive. His dribbling ability was
unmatched, despite birth defects that left him bow-

legged and with one limb six centimetres shorter than the other. Yet his love of the good life meant he was also his own worst enemy and a nightmare for coaches. He tragically died of alcohol poisoning.

FRANCISCO GENTO

(born 21 October 1933)

Spain: 43 games, 5 goals

"Paco" Gento set a record in 1966 when, as captain of Real Madrid, he collected a sixth European Champion Clubs' Cup Winner's medal. Gento, from Santander in northern Spain, was nicknamed "El Supersonico" for his electric pace on the left wing. His distracting effect created valuable extra space to assist the goalscoring exploits of team-mates such as Alfredo Di Stefano and Ferenc Puskás. Gento was a key figure in Real Madrid's triumphs of the 1950s and 1960s, scoring 126 goals in 428 games over 18 years. He won the domestic league title 12 times, represented Spain in the 1962 and 1966 World Cup finals, and played a key role in the side that dominated the first five European Champion Clubs' Cup finals with successive victories in the late 1950s.

RUUD GULLIT (born 1 September 1962)

Holland: 66 games, 17 goals

Ruud Gullit was hailed as Europe's finest player in the late 1980s, when he moved from Dutch football to help inspire a revival at AC Milan. Gullit, World Player of the Year in 1987 and 1989, was a favourite of AC Milan owner Silvio Berlusconi, winning two European Champion Clubs' Cups and three Italian league titles. He captained Holland in the 1988 European Championship, heading home the opening goal in the 2-0 victory over Russia in the final. He moved to Chelsea as a player and later became their coach – he was the first non-British manager to win the FA Cup. He subsequently had brief spells as manager of Newcastle United and Dutch giants Feyenoord.

GHEORGHE HAGI (born 5 February 1965)

Romania: 125 games, 35 goals

Gheorghe Hagi was nicknamed the 'Maradona of the Carpathians' during the late 1980s because of his cultured left foot and silky skills. His huge self-confidence helped him to push forward from midfield to score goals, but his main strength lay in his skill and vision as a playmaker. Such outstanding

ABOVE Gheorghe Hagi

talent earned special permission, in a restrictive political era, to move abroad to ply his trade. He played for Real Madrid, moved to Brescia in Italy, and then on to Barcelona before ending his career at Turkish side Galatasaray. Hagi was the fulcrum of the Romanian side that reached the quarter-final stage of the 1994 World Cup.

HOSSAM HASSAN (born 10 August 1966)

Egypt: 170 games, 69 goals

Hossam Hassan is the world's second most-capped player with 170 appearances for the Pharaohs, just behind Mohammed Al Deayea's 181 games for Saudi Arabia. He has yet to announce retirement and continues to break Egyptian records: winning 41 titles as a player, playing 21 matches over seven African Nations' Cup competitions, and being the oldest scorer in an Egyptian national shirt. Hossam has also played for Paok Saloniki in Greece, Neuchatel Xamax in Switzerland, and El-Ain in the UAE.

ABOVE Ferenc Puskás

RIGHT Thierry Henry

THIERRY HENRY (born 17 August 1977)
France: 100 games, 44 goals
A raw and pacy winger, Thierry Henry had impressed at club level and earned a first international call-up as a 20-year-old just eight months before the 1998 World Cup. He earned a place in the squad and scored three times in the group stages, appearing both out wide and as a centre-forward, but was an unused substitute in the final as France beat Brazil 3-0. A goalless 2002 campaign meant an early exit for the defending champions, but he returned in 2006 as the lone striker, his three goals helping France to the final where they were beaten on penalties by Italy. France's 2010 campaign was another poor one and, no longer an automatic starter, Henry made just one substitute appearance as they were eliminated in the group stages.

SIR GEOFF HURST (born 8 December 1941)
England: 49 games, 24 goals
Sir Geoff Hurst remains the only player to have scored a hat-trick in a World Cup final, an achievement which ultimately earned him a belated knighthood. Hurst only came into the 1966 England side because first-choice forward Jimmy Greaves was injured. His header had drawn England level against West Germany before he controversially put England ahead in extra-time, his shot bouncing down off the crossbar and on to the line, before he raced away to hit a late third, and England's fourth. As well as his match-winning performance in the final, Hurst scored what proved to be the decisive goal in the quarter-final against Argentina.

ZLATAN IBRAHIMOVIC (born 3 October 1981)
Sweden: 97 games, 44 goals
One of the world's best strikers, Zlatan Ibrahimovic became a high-profile club player at Internazionale

and AC Milan, after first playing first at Malmo FF, Ajax and Juventus. In 2009, Ibrahimovic joined Barcelona in a swap deal with Samuel Eto'o. Although the contract was for five years, Ibrahimovic fell out with manager Pep Guardiola and was sold to French club PSG in 2012. He is captain of the Swedish national team and has won multiple awards, including the 2012 Golden Boot and the FIFA Puskás Award; won for an outstanding bicycle-kick goal against England.

BRANISLAV IVANOVIC (born 22 February 1984)
Serbia: 68 games, 7 goals
A multi-position defender, Branislav Ivanovic has carved out a name for himself as one of the English Premier League's most dependable players, despite being a virtual unknown when he signed for Chelsea in 2008. Prior to the move to Chelsea, Ivanovic played for Serbian sides Remont, FK Srem and OFK Beograd as well as short spell at Lokomotiv Moscow. He was a key player for Serbia

during the 2010 World Cup in South Africa – his country's first international tournament since becoming an independent nation.

JAIRZINHO (born 25 December 1944)
Brazil: 81 games, 33 goals
Jairzinho, full name Jair Ventura Filho, was the free-scoring successor to the Brazilian tradition of great outside rights, from Julinho in the mid-1950s to Garrincha in the late 1950s and 1960s. In 1970, he recovered twice from a broken right leg and became the only player to score in every round of the World Cup finals in Mexico, scoring seven goals overall. Jairzinho, nicknamed 'God', also played in the World Cup finals of 1966 and 1974, and famously discovered an outstanding 12-year-old in Rio de Janeiro, a talent called Ronaldo.

STEVAN JOVETIC (born 21 August 1988)
Montenegro: 30 games, 12 goals
Striker Stevan Jovetic won the honour of scoring his first goal during Montenegro's first match as an independent country – a 2008 3-3 draw with Hungary. Jovetic emerged as one of Europe's most promising young players after playing for clubs sides Mladost Podgorica, Partizan Belgrade and Fiorentina. Jovetic won public acclaim during the 2009-10 Champions League season, but then suffered a cruciate ligament injury that kept him out for the whole of the following season. Jovetic won back his place in the Fiorentina side in 2011, but was then snapped up by Manchester City in 2013.

KAKÁ (born 22 April 1982)
Brazil: 59 games, 22 goals
Kaká, full name Ricardo Izecson dos Santos Leite, was generally hailed as having established himself as the world's top player in 2007. During 2007, he set up AC Milan's victory in the European Champions League and was voted both FIFA Player of the Year and European Player of the Year. The supremely gifted Brazilian forward originally made his name with São Paulo, following a remarkable recovery from a swimming pool accident that left him temporarily paralysed. AC Milan paid a relatively low $10 million (£5 million) for him in 2003.

ABOVE Mario Kempes

MARIO KEMPES (born 15 July 1954)
Argentina: 43 games, 20 goals
Forward Mario Kempes emerged at the 1974 World Cup finals, but it is his performances four years later for which he is remembered. As Cesar Luis Menotti's only foreign-based player called up to the squad, he was under pressure to perform, but did so magnificently to take the Golden Boot with six goals, including a brace in the final against Holland. Powerful, direct and clinical, Kempes returned to the squad in 1982, and played 18 World Cup games in total.

GREAT PLAYERS

ABOVE Miroslav Klose

RIGHT Robert Lewandowski

MIROSLAV KLOSE (born 9 June 1978)
Germany: 137 games, 71 goals
Born in Poland, Klose opted to play for Germany in 2001 and sprang to prominence at the World Cup in 2002, where he became the first player to score five headed goals at one finals, including a hat-trick against Saudi Arabia in an 8-0 win. Germany were eventually beaten in the final by Brazil. On home soil in 2006, he added another five as he took the Golden Boot and a second successive appearance in the All-Star XI. In 2010, Germany reached the semi-finals and Klose was among the goals again, scoring against Australia, England and Argentina to help his country to a second successive third-place finish. In Brazil 2014, Klose scored two vital goals for the Germans on their way to World Cup victory, reaching a record-breaking 16 World Cup goals.

RAYMOND KOPA (born 13 October 1931)
France: 45 games, 18 goals
Raymond Kopa was the son of a Polish mining family from northern France. His talent was first spotted by Angers, who then sold him on to Reims in 1950. He was sold to Real Madrid after the Spanish club defeated Reims in the European Champion Clubs' Cup final in 1956. At Real Madrid he won the European Champion Clubs Cup three times and was crowned 1958 European Footballer of the Year. Kopa won four French and two Spanish league titles.

HANS KRANKL (born 14 February 1953)
Austria: 69 games, 34 goals
Hans Krankl was one of the great Austrian centre forwards. In 1978 he scored 41 goals for Rapid Vienna, winning the Golden Boot as Europe's leading league scorer. He starred for Austria at the World Cup finals in Argentina, where he netted the winning goal against West Germany – Austria's first victory over their neighbours for 37 years. He went on to play for Barcelona, where he won the

1979 European Cup Winners' Cup.

MICHAEL LAUDRUP (born 15 June 1964)
Denmark: 104 games, 37 goals
Michael Laudrup stood out in Denmark's outstanding team that reached the semi-finals of the 1984 European Championship and the second round at the 1986 World Cup finals. He achieved club success with Juventus before moving to Lazio, and he was part of Johan Cruyff's 'Dream Team' at Barcelona where he won four league titles. He also played for Real Madrid and Ajax.

DENIS LAW (born 24 February 1940)
Scotland: 55 games, 30 goals
Denis Law, despite the competing talents of Bobby Charlton and George Best, was the king of Old Trafford in the 1960s. His ebullient personality, and his ability to create chances and goals out of nothing, earned him the adulation of Manchester United fans. Law started at Huddersfield Town, and had brief spells at Manchester City and Torino before being brought to Manchester United in 1962. He repaid the club's financial investment with 171 goals in 309 league games. He won the European Footballer of the Year prize in 1964.

ROBERT LEWANDOWSKI

(born 21 August 1988)

Poland: 60 games, 44 goals

Striker Robert Lewandowski grabbed the attention of the world's football community when he scored four goals against Real Madrid in a Champions League match in April 2013. Despite helping his club Borussia Dortmund go on to reach the Champions League final in 2013, they were beaten by rivals Bayern Munich – the team Lewandowski went on to sign for in the 2014-15 season. Lewandowski has also played for Polish clubs sides Znicz Pruszkow and Lech Poznan and been one of the main scorers for his national team, netting no less than one goal in every three matches.

GARY LINEKER (born 30 November 1960)

England: 80 games, 48 goals

The only Englishman to win a World Cup Golden Boot, Lineker struck six times in Mexico in 1986, including a hat-trick against Poland, all three goals scored from within the six-yard box, when their campaign was struggling. He added two more against Paraguay in the knockout round, before England were cheated by Diego Maradona's infamous 'Hand of God' goal. Lineker did score a consolation to take his tally to six and he added four more in Italy in 1990 as England went one better to the semi-finals. He ended his international career with 48 goals, one less than Sir Bobby Charlton.

LEFT Gary Lineker

DIEGO MARADONA

(born 30 October 1960)

Argentina: 91 games, 34 goals

Diego Maradona ranks among the greatest ever players, despite a career shrouded in controversy. Small but strong, Maradona was entirely left-footed and his dribbling ability made him almost impossible to shake off the ball. Captain and inspiration of the Argentine side that lifted the 1986 World Cup, his second strike against England is considered to be one of the all-time great finals goals, though the infamous 'Hand of God' is what most people remember from that quarter-final tie. Such was Maradona's importance to his side, he scored twice more in the semi, and was involved in 10 of their 14 goals in total. A runner-up in the 1990 World Cup, he was suspended from the sport in 1991 after failing a drugs test, and three years later failed a World Cup finals' doping test, having scored in a 4-0 win over Greece. He played 21 World Cup games in total.

JOSEF MASOPUST (born 9 February 1931)

Czechoslovakia: 63 games, 10 goals

Josef Masopust was a midfield heir in the 1950s and early 1960s to the great pre-war traditions of Czech football. An attacking midfielder, he reached his peak at the 1962 World Cup in Chile, where he helped to inspire his side all the way to the final.

BELOW Josef Masopust

ABOVE Roger Milla

BELOW Giuseppe Meazza

Although he opened the scoring against Brazil for an unexpected lead, the holders fought back to triumph 3-1. Masopust won the 1962 Footballer of the Year award following his outstanding displays in Chile, where he was nicknamed 'the Czech Knight'.

LOTHAR MATTHAUS

(born 21 March, 1961)

Germany: 150 games, 23 goals

Having led West Germany to the World Cup in Italy in 1990, Matthaus became the first and only outfield player to play in five different tournaments in 1998. Nobody has played as many as his 25 World Cup matches. An energetic and disciplined midfielder, Matthaus collected a runners-up medal in both 1982 and 1986, playing in the latter, before captaining his country to success four years later. Quarter-final exits in 1994 and 1998 followed for one of his country's most-capped players ever.

SIR STANLEY MATTHEWS

(born 1 February 1915, died 23 February 2000)

England: 54 games, 11 goals

Sir Stanley Matthews was the first active player to be knighted as reward for extraordinary service to the game both before and after World War II. He was an outside right whose mesmerising talent earned him the nickname the "Wizard of Dribble." Matthews achieved his ambition to win the FA Cup with Blackpool in 1953, when, aged 38, he famously rescued his side from a 3-1 deficit by setting up three goals. In 1956, he received the inaugural European Player of the Year. His fitness and enthusiasm saw him play at the 1954 World Cup finals and then lead his original club, Stoke City, to promotion back into the old First Division in 1962.

GIUSEPPE MEAZZA

(born 23 August 1910, died 21 August 1979)

Italy: 53 game, 33 goals

Giuseppe Meazza is one of only two Italian players

– Giovanni Ferrari is the other – to have won the World Cup for the Azzurri both at home and also away from Italy. Meazza was a powerful, goalscoring inside forward with Internazionale in the 1930s, scoring 287 goals in 408 games for the club. He was a World Cup winner at home in 1934 and was the captain in France when Italy triumphed in 1938, scoring three goals at the finals overall.

ROGER MILLA (born 20 May 1952)

Cameroon: 102 games, 28 goals

Roger Milla had long been an African hero before his goal-celebrating dance around the corner flags brought him global fame at the 1990 World Cup. Milla scored four times at those finals, making him the oldest ever World Cup goalscorer at the age of 38. He returned to the World Cup finals four years later, before retiring with an impressive career record: he twice picked up the African Player of the Year award (1976 and 1990) and in 2007 was voted the best African Player of the last 50 years.

BOBBY MOORE (born 12 April 1941, died 24 February 1993)

England: 108 games, 2 goals

Bobby Moore proved to be an ideal captain for England, leading them to glory at the 1966 World Cup and also during their unsuccessful defence of the trophy in 1970. Respected by his teammates and opponents alike for his tough tackling and silky skills, Moore was regarded as among the best defenders in the world. A bronze statue of Moore stands outside the new Wembley Stadium. Nobody has led England more times than Moore's 90.

GERD MÜLLER (born 3 November 1945)

West Germany: 62 games, 68 goals

Gerd Müller was the most prolific goalscorer in modern German football. Müller scored 10 times at the 1970 World Cup finals in Mexico – hitting successive hat-tricks against Bulgaria and Peru – to finish as the highest scorer and win the Golden Boot. He also scored the winning goal for West Germany in the 1974 World Cup final victory over Holland, taking his total tally to 14. Short and stocky, he was nicknamed 'Der Bomber' by the adoring German public.

HONG MYUNG-BO

(born 12 February 1969)

South Korea: 135 games, 9 goals

Hong Myung-Bo was the first Asian player to appear in four World Cups. Originally a powerful defensive midfielder, he was soon switched to central defence. He made his international debut in 1990 and was chosen to be part of the Korea Republic World Cup squad in Italy later that year. He earned international admiration for his displays in the 1994 and 1998 World Cup finals, despite the first round exits, and was a national hero long before he captained Korea Republic to the final four on home territory at the 2002 World Cup finals. He coached his country in Brazil in 2014.

HIDETOSHI NAKATA

(born 22 January 1977)

Japan: 77 games, 11 goals

Hidetoshi Nakata was the first Japanese player to make a major impact in Europe. Nakata had been hailed Asian Player of the Year before his 1998 World Cup finals debut. He played in the next two World Cup finals, announcing his shock retirement immediately after the 2006 World Cup match against Brazil in Germany. Nakata played seven seasons for various sides in Italy's Serie A and had a short spell in England's Premier League with Bolton Wanderers.

JAY-JAY OKOCHA (born 14 August 1973)

Nigeria: 74 games, 14 goals

Augustine 'Jay-Jay' Okocha provided the midfield command that lifted Nigeria's "Super Eagles" out of the also-rans of Africa to regular appearances at the World Cup finals. He played in the 1994, 1998 and 2002 finals, regularly lighting up games with his flair, dribbling and passing. Okocha was the mercurial playmaker around which the side was built and after reaching the knockout rounds at their first finals tournament, he helped Nigeria win the 1996 Olympic gold medal, before reaching the last 16 of the World Cup finals once more in 1998.

SAEED AL-OWAIRAN (born 19 August 1967)

Saudi Arabia: 50 games, 24 goals

Saeed Al-Owairan won the accolade of Asian Player of the Year in 1994, largely thanks to his memorable solo strike against Belgium in that year's World Cup finals. His goal for Saudi Arabia was comparable to Diego Maradona's sensational strike against England in 1986 and has been voted the sixth best World Cup goal of all time.

PELÉ (born 23 October 1940)

Brazil: 92 games, 77 goals

Pelé, full name Edson Arantes do Nascimento, is synonymous with the World Cup. One of few who could realistically claim to be the best footballer who ever played, he was a World Cup winner at 17 – scoring twice in the 5-2 victory over Sweden in the 1958 final, including a brilliant flick over a defender's head and volley into the bottom corner. Injury prevented Pelé playing in the 1962 World Cup final and he endured an unhappy tournament in 1966, when he was the subject of rough marking by Portuguese defenders, but he was back at his best in 1970 and scored in the 4-1 win over Italy. He is the only player to have three World Cup winner's medals.

FERENC PUSKÁS

(born 2 April 1927, died 17 November 2006)

Hungary: 85 games, 84 goals

Spain: 4 games, no goals

Ferenc Puskás is one of the game's all-time greats, famed for his goals, his leadership and the way that he reconstructed his career after the 1956 Hungarian Revolution. Puskás and Hungary were unbeaten for four years going into the 1954 World Cup finals as Olympic champions, but fell 3-2 to West Germany in the final, despite leading 2-0 inside the first 10 minutes. Puskas had opened the scoring in the final, despite not being fully fit.

ABOVE Hong Myung-Bo

BELOW Jay-Jay Okocha

GREAT PLAYERS

ABOVE Ronaldo

once more in 2006, when Brazil were beaten by France in the quarter-finals.

RONALDO (born 22 September 1976)
Brazil: 97 games, 62 goals
Ronaldo Luis Nazário de Lima was discovered as a 12-year-old by World Cup-winning hero Jairzinho. Five years later, he was at the 1994 World Cup, albeit as a non-playing member of the winning Brazilian squad. In 1998, he was the best player in the world, his pace, power and clinical finishing making Brazil the favourites, but before the final against France he was taken ill, played anyway and was anonymous as his side lost 3-0. Ronaldo made amends by scoring twice in the 2002 World Cup final win over Germany and nine times in total, adding a 15th goal at the 2006 World Cup finals.

CRISTIANO RONALDO
(born 5 February 1985)
Portugal: 55 games, 20 goals
Cristiano Ronaldo became Britain's most expensive teenager when, aged 18, he cost Manchester United the remarkable sum of $25 million (£12.4 million) in 2003. At first, the self-indulgence of his trickery on the right wing frustrated fans and teammates alike, but once he adapted to the difficult demands of the English game, he proved to be equally dangerous on the left wing and a real handful to deal with in the air. In the 2007–08 season, he scored 42 goals in all competitions, which helped guide Manchester United to a double of the English league title and the Champions League.

PAOLO ROSSI (born 23 September 1956)
Italy: 48 games, 20 goals
Paolo Rossi looked a great prospect after the 1978 World Cup finals, but he was banned for two years over a match-fixing scandal. The striker only returned to top-class action weeks before the 1982 World Cup finals kicked off, and he

RONALDINHO (born 21 March 1980)
Brazil: 80 games, 32 goals
Ronaldinho, full name Ronaldo de Assis Moreira, was the third of 'the three Rs' in the Brazil team of 2002, joining Rivaldo and Ronaldo in attack. Incredibly talented, he scored in the group game win over China and netted the winner against England in the quarter-final with a long-range free-kick before being sent off, returning for the final and a 2-0 win over Germany. Ronaldinho was voted FIFA World Player of the Year in 2004 and 2005 and was in the squad

started slowly, yet finished as the top scorer with six goals to his credit. These strikes included a hat-trick to deliver the knock-out blow to Brazil in the quarter-final, one of the all-time great World Cup encounters, before scoring both Italian goals against Poland in the semi and the opener against Germany in the final. A stunning return from the wilderness had seen Rossi lead his country to their first World Cup in 44 years.

HUGO SÁNCHEZ (born 11 July 1958)
Mexico: 58 games, 29 goals
Hugo Sánchez numbers among the most prolific scorers in the history of Mexican football and as one of its greatest personalities. He led the attack in three World Cup finals, in 1978, 1986 and as a veteran in 1994.

HECTOR SCARONE
(born 1 January 1900, died 4 April 1967)
Uruguay: 51 games, 31 goals
Hector Scarone, nicknamed 'the Magician', was the original star of the World Cup after leading Uruguay to victory over Argentina in the inaugural finals in 1930, scoring in a 4-0 win over Romania. His all-time Uruguayan goalscoring record was only broken in 2011.

MATTHIAS SINDELAR
(born 10 February 1903, died 23 January 1939)

Austria: 43 games, 27 goals
Matthias Sindelar was the inspirational forward of the Austrian 'Wunderteam' that ruled European football in the late 1920s and early 1930s. Sindelar, nicknamed the 'Man of Paper' because of his delicate build, was a World Cup semi-finalist in 1934, but suffered at the bruising hands of his marker, Italian Luis Monti. Five years later he died of carbon monoxide poisoning in his Viennese apartment in unexplained circumstances.

ALFREDO DI STEFANO
(born 4 July 1926, died 7 July 2014)
Argentina: 6 games, 6 goals
Spain: 31 games, 23 goals
Alfredo Di Stefano remains, for many experts, the greatest ever player because of his all-action performances as a pitch-roaming, high-scoring centre forward. He starred for Argentina's River Plate and Colombia's Millonarios, before inspiring Real Madrid to victory in the first five European Champion Clubs' Cup competitions. Di Stefano scored in all five finals, and totalled 216 league goals for Real Madrid over 11 years.

HRISTO STOICHKOV
(born 8 February 1966)
Bulgaria: 83 games, 37 goals

LEFT Hristo Stoichkov

ABOVE Paolo Rossi

BELOW Alfredo di Stefano

ABOVE Obdulio Varela

RIGHT Lev Yashin

America in 1994. A 3-0 defeat to Nigeria in their opening group game suggested they would struggle, but wins over Greece and Argentina, with three goals from the forward, sent them into the knockout stages for the first time. Stoichkov's penalty expertise helped eliminate Mexico in a shoot-out before they came from behind, with him scoring again, to beat world champions Germany. Eliminated by Italy in the semis and beaten in the play-off by Sweden, Bulgaria finished fourth, and Stoichkov shared the Golden Boot.

CARLOS VALDERRAMA

(born 2 September 1961)
Colombia: 111 games, 11 goals
Carlos Valderrama, nicknamed 'The Kid', was a colourful character who led Colombia from midfield at the World Cup finals of 1990, 1994, and 1998, all of which ended in disappointment. Valderrama was renowned almost as much for his outrageous, frizzy blonde hair as for his supreme talent, which ensured a 13-year international career.

OBDULIO VARELA

(born 20 September 1917, died 2 August 1996)
Uruguay: 49 games, 10 goals
Obdulio Varela was the attacking centre-half who captained Uruguay to World Cup victory in 1950. Varela apparently told the team to ignore their manager's talk and follow his orders – they bounced back with two goals to spring one of the World Cup's greatest shocks: a 2-1 win over hosts Brazil, despite trailing. He returned to the World Cup in 1954 as a 37-year-old, but injury before the semi-final meant he could not help Uruguay avoid defeat against the great Hungarians.

FRITZ WALTER

(born 31 October 1920, died 17 June 2002)
West Germany: 61 games, 33 goals
Fritz Walter owed his life to national manager Sepp Herberger and repaid him in glory. Walter,

an inside forward from Kaiserslautern who made his international debut just before World War II, was kept away from the front by Herberger's string-pulling before finally being drafted in 1942. He was captured and eventually repatriated by the Soviet army. He relaunched his football career and captained Herberger's West Germany to their unexpected World Cup final victory over the mighty Hungary in 1954.

LEV YASHIN

(born 22 October 1929, died 20 March 1990)
Soviet Union: 78 games, no goals.
Lev Yashin, nicknamed the 'Black Spider' due to his all-black kit and ability to make the most unlikely of saves, ranks as arguably the game's greatest ever goalkeeper, revolutionising the role and constantly barking instructions at his defenders. A veteran of three World Cups, Yashin appeared in 13 finals matches, reaching the quarter-finals twice and the semis once, where they were beaten by West Germany, in 1966. In 1994, FIFA introduced the Lev Yashin Award for the best goalkeeper at a World Cup.

IVAN ZAMORANO (born 18 January 1967)
Chile: 69 games, 34 goals
Ivan Zamorano was Chile's iconic hero in the 1990s, when he led the national team's World Cup attack and starred in European football. Zamorano was brought to Europe by the Swiss club Saint Gallen. After three terms he moved to the Spanish La Liga for six seasons. In 1995 he was the league's top scorer, with 27 goals for Real Madrid. He went on to win the 1998 UEFA Cup with Internazionale before returning to Chile with Colo Colo via a two-year stint in Mexico.

ZICO (born 3 March 1953)
Brazil: 88 games, 66 goals
Zico was arguably the best player in one of the best sides never to win the World Cup, Brazil's 1982 team, which was beaten in the quarter-finals by Italy and Paolo Rossi. A typical number 10, he could create or score prolifically himself and netted four times in the 1982 World Cup, having also been a member of the squad in 1978. In 1986, he was only a substitute for Brazil, who underperformed, and after coming on against France he missed a vital penalty that saw his side eliminated.

ZINEDINE ZIDANE (born June 23, 1972)
France: 108 games, 31 goals
Zidane was the outstanding French playmaker of the late 1990s and early 2000s. He was making headlines until the very last moment of his career – he was sent off in extra-time in the 2006 World Cup Final, his last game, for headbutting Italy's Marco Materazzi, having already opened the scoring with a brilliant chipped penalty. Zidane also scored twice in France's 1998 World Cup final win over Brazil, but was injured for their disastrous 2002 campaign, coming back early to take part in their final group game, although he could not prevent their elimination.

DINO ZOFF (born 28 February 1942)
Italy: 112 games, no goals
Another great goalkeeper, Zoff was Italy's captain when they swept past all opponents at the 1982 World Cup finals. Aged 40, Zoff was the oldest player to win the World Cup after the Azzurri thumped West Germany 3-1 in the final, after which he was voted the best goalkeeper in the tournament. His 112 caps saw him play in three World Cups.

ABOVE LEFT Zinedine Zidane

BELOW Zico

GREAT MANAGERS

Every great football manager has been responsible for putting
together successful teams, improving the skills of his players,
and devising cunning strategies to beat opposing sides. But
once a manager has taken his team to the top level he is
expected to keep it there. Those who do not produce
consistently good results face the wrath of the fans and the
ignominy of a mid-contract sacking. Today, a great manager
is expected to be a media-savvy visionary who can absorb
the high-profile pressures of the job, attract and maintain
the best players, and, of course, win many matches.

TOP Enzo Bearzot

ABOVE Vicente del Bosque

PAGE 164 Guus Hiddink

PAGE 165 Carlos Alberto Parreira

CARLO ANCELOTTI (born 10 June 1959)
Greatest success: winning the league title in three different countries.
A former Roma, Milan and Italian international player, Ancelotti found managerial success with Milan, which he took over in 2001. With Milan, Ancelotti won the Coppa Italia and Champions League in 2003, the Serie A in 2004, and the Champions League again in 2007. After taking over as Chelsea manager in 2009, Ancelotti led the club to a Premier League and FA Cup double. He was sacked by owner Roman Abramovich the following season after Chelsea failed to retain the premier league title. In 2011, Ancelotti became manager of Paris St Germain and won them the Ligue 1 title, before moving to Real Madrid in 2013. Ancelotti's sides typically feature a strong midfield with wide players supporting one lone striker.

ENZO BEARZOT (born 26 September 1927, died 21 December 2010)
Greatest success: 1982 World Cup (Italy)
After a decent playing career and a coaching apprenticeship with the national Under-23 side, Bearzot took charge of the senior Italian team, leading them to a fourth-place finish in Argentina in 1978. Four years later, he famously banned the media from the squad's training camp after a poor start, but performances improved and Italy beat Brazil 3-2 in one of the all-time great World Cup games, before eliminating Argentina and Poland and beating West Germany 3-1 in a scintillating final. It was the first time in 44 years that Italy had been world champions. Bearzot stayed in the job until 1986.

RAFAEL BENITEZ (born 16 April 1960)
Greatest success: winning the league title in three different countries.
Rafael Benitez rose to fame as La Liga winning manager of Valencia in 2002 and 2004. But following an argument over transfer funds Benitez

quit the club to take over Liverpool. Benitez immediately brought the club success with a UEFA Champions League win in 2005, and the FA Cup in 2007. Benitez departed English football to manage Italian side Internazionale in 2010, but was sacked halfway through the season and then became interim Chelsea manager. After winning the Europa League title in 2013, Benitez once again departed for Italian shores when he took over Napoli. Benitez is known as a clever tactician whose sides often expose opposition weaknesses. He favours zonal marking, squad rotation, and is said not to give his players praise easily.

VICENTE DEL BOSQUE
(born 23 December 1950)
Greatest success: 2010 World Cup (Spain)
Del Bosque replaced Luis Aragones as Spanish coach following their success at Euro 2008 and would go on to raise the bar further by bringing the country its first world crown in 2010. Pre-tournament favourites in 2010, Spain were beaten in their opening game against Switzerland, but recovered to top their group, winning each of their knockout matches 1-0 and beating the Dutch after extra-time in the final. After leading the Spanish to Euro 2012 success too, Del Bosque failed in his attempt for a third consecutive major title in 2014.

ANTONIO CONTE (born 31 July 1969)
Greatest success: double Serie A winner 2011–12 and 2012–13 (Juventus)
Antonio Conte ended his successful playing career in 2005 to coach Italian clubs Arezzo, Bari, Atalanta and Sienna. He is best known as the young and upcoming former manager of Juventus, a side he formerly played with and has led to recent glory in Serie A. Under Conte, Juventus have won the Serie A twice, the Supercoppa Italiana twice, and have played a whole season in the league without being beaten. In 2012, Conte was presented with

the Trofeo Maestrelli coaching award. Conte's team management tactics have been compared to Jose Mourinho's, although Conte favours a more attacking style and often employs a 4-3-3 formation.

DIDIER DESCHAMPS

(born 19 November 1965)
Greatest success: Coupe de la Ligue 2010, 2011, 2012 (Marseille)

After a highly successful international career as a club player in France, Italy and England, Deschamps began coaching in 2001 with Monaco. After winning the French League Cup in 2003, Deschamps took over at his old club Juventus – which was facing allegations of match-fixing – and secured the club's Serie A promotion in 2007. Deschamps's best known managerial work was for Marseille, where he was appointed boss in 2009. After ending the side's 18-year wait for the Ligue 1 title, Deschamps went on to secure three Coupe de la Ligue in successive seasons. In 2012, Deschamps succeeded Laurent Blanc as manager of the French national team, and secured his place in the job until 2016 by guiding the side through the initial play-off rounds and into the 2014 World Cup finals.

VICENTE FEOLA

(born 1 November 1909, died 6 November 1975)
Greatest success: 1958 World Cup (Brazil)
The portly Feola guided Brazil to their first World Cup triumph in Sweden, although he took some persuading from senior players to pick both Garrincha and Pelé in the middle of the tournament when they appeared to be floundering. Because of illness, Feola missed their successful defence of the World Cup in 1962. He returned for the luckless 1966 finals in England, when his side went out in the group stage. Feola finished with an outstanding career record of only losing six matches out of the 74 his team played.

LOUIS VAN GAAL (born 8 August 1951)

Greatest success: 1995 Champions League (Ajax)
A long-time advocate of the attacking style inherent in 'total football', van Gaal has managed club sides Ajax, Barcelona, AZ Alkmaar, Bayern Munich and Manchester United. In his six years at Ajax, van Gaal won three Eredivisie crowns, the Dutch Cup, the 1992 UEFA Cup and the 1995 UEFA Champions League. Under van Gaal, Barcelona became champions of La Liga for the two seasons between 1997 and 1999, and Bayern Munich the champions of the Bundesliga in 2010. Despite being unable to lead the national team through the 2002 World Cup qualifying round, van Gaal was once again appointed manager of the Netherlands side in 2012. Van Gaal said he was only interested in keeping the position until the end of the 2014 World Cup.

ABOVE Louis Van Gaal

LEFT BELOW Rafael Benitez

GREAT MANAGERS

ABOVE Sepp Herberger

RIGHT Guus Hiddink

PEP GUARDIOLA (born 18 January 1971)
Greatest success: winning six trophies across six competitions in one year.
A former Spanish and Barcelona midfielder, Pep Guardiola became the high-profile manager of the club in 2008. Guardiola is a proponent of the high-possession, short passing style of football called "tika-taka", which he learned under mentor Johan Cruyff. Guardiola used tiki-taka to deadly effect during his four years with Barcelona, becoming the first manager to win in one year the six trophies: the Spanish League, the Copa de Rey, the Champions League, the Spanish Super Cup, the European Super Cup and the Club World Cup, all in 2009. Citing exhaustion, Guardiola quit Barcelona for a year's sabbatical in 2012, to then rejoin club football as Bayern Munich manager in 2013. In Guardiola's first season, Bayern became champions of the Bundesliga and winners of the Club World Cup.

JOSEF "SEPP" HERBERGER
(born 28 March 1897, died 20 April 1977)
Greatest success: 1954 World Cup (West Germany)
Herberger became manager of Germany in 1938 and used all his sports and political influence to try to keep his players away from the battle fronts during World War II. He returned as national manager after the war and won West Germany's first World Cup in 1954. The final was aptly labelled the 'Miracle of Berne' after his team came from two goals down to defeat the famous Hungarian side 3-2, thanks in no small part to their removable, screw-in studs designed by German manufacturer Adidas.

GUUS HIDDINK (born 8 November 1946)
Greatest success: 2002 semi-finals (South Korea)
Hiddink is a coaching icon around the world, having achieved back-to-back World Cup semi-final appearances in 1998 and 2002. With his

native Dutch team in 1998, he reached the last four, playing an entertaining and attacking brand of football, eliminating Yugoslavia and Argentina after topping the group, before coming unstuck on penalties against Brazil in the semis. Holland were beaten into fourth place by Croatia. Four years later, Hiddink was in charge of hosts South Korea, who were tipped to struggle. However, group stage wins over Poland and Portugal brought unexpected momentum and Italy were controversially beaten after extra-time before Spain were knocked out on penalties. Germany ended the party at the semi-final stage and Turkey took third place in the play-offs, but in Korea, Hiddink remains a hero and became the first person ever to be given an honorary citizenship. He also led Australia to their first World Cup in 32 years in 2006.

OTTMAR HITZFELD (born 12 January 1949)
Greatest success: double Champions League winner, 1997 (Borussia Dortmund) and 2001 (Bayern Munich).
Known as 'The General', Ottmar Hitzfeld is one of the most successful managers in German football. Beginning his coaching career in 1983, Hitzfeld

has won 18 major titles with Grasshopper Club Zurich, Borussia Dortmund and Bayern Munich. He is one of only four managers to win the Champions League with two different clubs and has been voted as 'World Coach of the Year' twice. In 2008, Hitzfeld became manager of the Swiss national team and took the side to the 2010 World Cup where they were eliminated in the group stage. Switzerland failed to qualify for Euro 2012, although Hitzfeld led the side to a place in the 2014 World Cup finals – his last competition as a manager before retirement.

AIMÉ JACQUET (born 27 November 1941)
Greatest success: 1998 World Cup (France)
France had not qualified for the 1994 World Cup and Jacquet was appointed shortly after this disappointment, initially on a temporary basis. Early results and a good showing at Euro 96 were encouraging, though the lead-up to the 1998 World Cup, to be played on home soil, brought complaints from the French public about Jacquet's side's lack of cohesion. They need not have worried, as, inspired by Zinedine Zidane, they won all three group games, beat Paraguay after extra-time and Italy on penalties. Croatia were beaten 2-1 in the semi-finals thanks to two goals from defender Lilian Thuram. Brazil were then swept away in the final with a stunning performance, as Zidane scored twice in the first half before Emmanuel Petit wrapped up the win in injury time. Jacquet retired afterwards, as a world champion.

JURGEN KLOPP (born 16 June 1967)
Greatest success: Bundesliga titles in 2011 and 2012 (Borussia Dortmund)
Despite only featuring as a second league player 'Kloppo', as he is known in Germany, had more success as a club manager. In 2001, Klopp stopped Mainz being relegated to the third tier of German football, and in 2007 promoted them into the Bundesliga. A popular and passionate football pundit, Klopp took over as Borussia Dortmund manager in 2008 and made the club Bundesliga champions in 2011 and 2012. In the 2012–13 season, Klopp built on his successful record by meeting rival Bundesliga team Bayern Munich in a Champions League final – although Dortmund lost the match. Despite losing some of his best

players to rival clubs and being tipped to replace outgoing managers in the English Premier League, Klopp reconfirmed his commitment to Dortmund in 2014.

MARCELLO LIPPI (born 12 April 1948)
Greatest success: 2006 World Cup (Italy)
A distinguished club coaching career led to Lippi's appointment as Italy's national team coach for 2006. Scandal in the domestic game lowered expectations ahead of the finals, but Lippi created an impressive sense of unity and Italy performed well, topping their group before beating Australia and Ukraine. Italy met hosts Germany, who had impressed with their attacking football, in the semi-finals but two goals in extra time put the Italians into the final. Falling behind to a penalty, they equalised through Marco Materazzi before Fabio Grosso struck the winning penalty to win the shoot-out 5-3. It was the Italians' first success in a shoot-out from five attempts. Lippi left his post immediately afterwards but returned in 2008 as he led Italy to the 2010 World Cup in South Africa, although this time they underperformed and were eliminated at the group stage.

JOACHIM LOW (born 3 February 1960)
Greatest success: 2014 World Cup winners (Germany)
Brought into the German national side in 2004 as assistant coach, Joachim Low developed an attacking style of football with manager Jurgen Klinsmann that gave the team a successful campaign at the 2005 Confederations Cup and 2006 World Cup. Low took over as German manager in 2010 and immediately introduced a 'B team' of aspiring first team players into the side, as well as an enhanced fitness coach, a business manager and a mental coach, who prepared the team before stressful matches. Despite being tipped as favourites, Low's Germany were not able to win Euro 2008, Euro 2012 or the 2010 World Cup. Low is thought of as a footballing tactician and strategist, who is responsible for overhauling the defensive playing style formerly employed by the German team. His 2014 German side entertained throughout the tournament, including a 7-1 thrashing of Brazil in the semi-finals, before winning the trophy, beating Argentina 1-0 in extra-time.

ABOVE Joachim Low

GREAT MANAGERS

ABOVE Bora Miluntinović

ROBERTO MANCINI

(born 27 November 1964)

Greatest success: English Premier League 2012 (Manchester City)

Roberto Mancini spent the majority of his playing career in Italy's Serie A before taking up club coaching under Sven-Goran Eriksson at Lazio. As a manager he led Florentina, Lazio and Internazionale to Coppa Italia wins. With Internazionale, Mancini also won two league titles and a record-breaking run of 17 match wins in a row. In 2009, Mancini became manager of Manchester City and led the team to the league title in 2012. After losing the FA Cup to Wigan Athletic in 2013, Mancini was sacked from Manchester City and moved to Turkey, where he signed a three-year deal with club side Galatasaray. Mancini's teams play defensive football and tend to build up attacks from the back line.

CÉSAR LUIS MENOTTI

(born 5 November 1938)

Greatest success: 1978 World Cup (Argentina)

In 1978, the left-leaning César Luis Menotti made himself immune from action by the ruling military junta because he was busy leading Argentina to their first-ever World Cup success. Menotti believed in positive, attacking football, which set him at odds with other top Argentinian coaches of the era such as Juan Carlos Lorenzo and Osvaldo Zubeldía, and they beat the great Dutch side of the 1970s in the final after thrashing Peru 6-0 in their final group game. Menotti quit after Argentina's shock second-round group exit at the 1982 finals in Spain, suffering defeat at the hands of Brazil and Italy.

RINUS MICHELS

(born 9 February 1928, died March 2005)

Greatest success: 1988 UEFA European Football Championship (Netherlands)

Rinus Michels is the manager credited for inventing the influential 'total football' system, whereby any outfield player is able to play in any position on the pitch. Michels pioneered this system as manager of Dutch club Ajax between the years 1965 and 1976, and also Barcelona, which he managed for two periods between the years 1971 and 1978. Michels managed the Netherlands national side four times, and won the 1988 European Football Championship with the team. He also worked for brief stints as club manager for FC Koln, Bayern Leverkusen, and the Los Angeles Aztecs. Michels was known to be a solitary man who did not like to spend money but enjoyed the odd practical joke.

BORA MILUTINOVIĆ

(born September 7, 1944)

Greatest success: 1986 quarter-finals (Mexico)

Milutinovic is one of only two men to have led five different countries to the World Cup finals and the only manager to have led four into the knockout stages. A Serb, he spent his playing career in Europe but coached Mexico in their home tournament in 1986, leading them to the quarter-final where they were eliminated on penalties by finalists West Germany. Four years later, he took over Costa Rica just before the Italy finals and took them into the second round, having beaten Sweden and Scotland, losing narrowly to Brazil. He led USA in 1994 to their first knockout stage since the 1930s and then took Nigeria past well-fancied Spain at France 1998. Milutinović then led China to their first World Cup in 2002, for the first time leaving the tournament without a victory. He has also coached Honduras, Jamaica and Iraq.

AYMORÉ MOREIRA

(born 24 April 1912, died 26 July 1998)

Greatest success: 1962 World Cup (Brazil)

One of three coaching brothers, Moreira had been a Brazilian international himself, beginning his career as a winger before becoming a goalkeeper. Appointed to the post in 1961, he successfully defended Brazil's 1958 crown despite the absence of star player Pelé through injury for much of the 1962 tournament in Chile. The forward had injured himself in a group game against Czechoslovakia and it was against the same opposition in the final that his replacement, Amarildo, equalised after Brazil had fallen behind, before a sensational display from Garrincha led the holders to a memorable 3-1 victory.

JOSE MOURINHO (born 26 January 1963)

Greatest success: winning the league title in four different countries.

Mourinho's trophy-laden managerial career began with Portuguese team Porto, which won the Primeira Liga, the Taca de Portugal, the UEFA Cup, and then the UEFA Champions League in 2002-03. Mourinho then won the English Premier League as Chelsea manager in 2004-05, and led the team to an FA Cup and League Cup double in the following season. In 2008, Mourinho took over Italian side Internazionale, and won the Supercoppa Italiana and then the treble of the Serie A, Coppa Italia and UEFA Champions League in the next season. Mourinho joined Real Madrid in 2010, winning the Copa del Rey that season and then La Liga in the next. In 2013, Mourinho re-signed with Chelsea, and took the side to a Champions League semi-final in 2014 and Premiership Champions in 2015.

CARLOS ALBERTO PARREIRA

(born 27 February 1943)

Greatest success: 1994 World Cup (Brazil)

Parreira is the only man to coach at six World Cups and one of two on this list to lead five different countries at the tournament. He lifted the trophy with his home nation in 1994, their first title since 1970 when he had been in the coaching setup. Parreira led Kuwait and the United Arab Emirates to their first finals tournaments in 1982 and 1990 respectively and was then sacked after two games when in charge of Saudi Arabia at the 1998 tournament in France. Despite links with the Brazil job once more, he sat out in 2002 before returning to the position in 2003 and led his country to the quarter-finals in 2006. He then managed South Africa, the hosts, in 2010, but they became the first hosts to be eliminated at the group stage. He retired after the tournament, his sixth World Cup as a head coach, but remains involved with the Brazilian national team.

MANUEL PELLEGRINI

(born 16 September 1953)

Greatest success: 2014 Capital One Cup (Manchester City)

The former defender managed club teams in his native Chile for 16 years before taking over at Spanish side Villarreal. In 2004, Pellegrini led Villarreal to third place in the league and secured the club a Champions League spot for the first time. In the following campaign, Villarreal reached second in the league and played in the Champions League semi-final, where they lost 1-0 to Arsenal on aggregate. Following these successes, Pellegrini became manager of Real Madrid in 2009. He led the team to a record 97 points in the league, but was still sacked in 2010 for coming below Barcelona. After a spell with Malaga, Pellegrini replaced outgoing Manchester City manager Roberto Mancini in 2013 and signed a three-year contract with the club.

BELOW Jose Mourinho

GREAT MANAGERS

VITTORIO POZZO

(born 12 March 1886, died 21 December 1968)

Greatest success: 1934 and 1938 World Cups (Italy)

Pozzo, who was also a journalist, learned to love football during a period of study in England. In 1934 he had no doubts about using former Argentina internationals, such as Luis Monti and Raimundo Orsi, to strengthen his first World Cup-winning side. Ruthlessly, he then scrapped almost the entire team to build a new side for the 1938 competition. In between these triumphs, Pozzo guided Italy to gold medal success at the 1936 Olympic Games. Sadly, Pozzo retired in 1949 after the Superga air disaster wiped out the entire playing staff of Torino, around whom he was planning to build a team for the 1950 World Cup.

RIGHT Vittorio Pozzo

BELOW Sir Alf Ramsey

SIR ALF RAMSEY

(born 22 January 1920, died 28 April 1999)

Greatest success: 1966 World Cup (England)

Ramsey will always hold a special place in the hearts of England fans as the only manager to have brought the country success in a major competition. A tactical pioneer, Ramsey's side was built, unusually for the time, without wingers, instead having four narrow midfielders. The 'Wingless Wonders' began poorly with a 0-0 draw against Uruguay before springing to life with 2-0 wins over Mexico and France. Argentina were beaten 1-0 in a bad-tempered encounter before the great Eusebio's Portugal were knocked out in the semis. The final brought more controversy, with arguments continuing to this day on whether Geoff Hurst's third goal for England had crossed the line, but the forward added another to claim the first World Cup final hat-trick. A year after his achievement, Ramsey was knighted, and went on to lead England to the quarter-finals in Mexico in 1970.

HELMUT SCHÖN

(born 15 September 1915, died 23 February 1996)

Greatest success: 1974 World Cup (West Germany)

Under Schön's 14-year-leadership, West Germany won the World Cup on home territory in 1974, after finishing third at Mexico in 1970 and runner-up to England in 1966. West Germany hosted the World Cup finals as worthy winners of the 1972 European Championship under Schön. No coach has overseen more than Schön's 25 World Cup matches, or won more than his 16.

ABOVE Luiz Felipe Scolari

LUIZ FELIPE SCOLARI (born 9 November 1948)

Greatest success: 2002 World Cup (Brazil)

Scolari holds the record for both consecutive wins, 11, and games unbeaten, 12, at the World Cup. Brazil coach in 2002, he utilised a system to bring the best of Ronaldinho, Ronaldo and Rivaldo, with attacking full-backs Roberto Carlos and Cafu becoming important parts of the Brazilian attack. After disappointment four years earlier, they were excellent in Japan and Korea, winning all of their games, including the quarter-final against England with 10 men. After lifting the trophy, Scolari took over Portugal and turned them into contenders in 2006, leading them to the semi-finals where they were beaten by France. He was back in charge of Brazil for 2014.

ALBERTO SUPPICI (born 20 November 1898, died 21 June 1981)

Greatest success: 1930 World Cup (Uruguay)

Suppici was the first coach to win the World Cup, doing so in his own country as Uruguay followed up their 1928 Olympic victory with the inaugural world crown in Montevideo. Nicknamed 'the professor', Suppici was actually technical director and masterminded an excellent comeback against Argentina in the final. Trailing 2-1 at half-time, the Uruguayans scored three second-half goals in front of 93,000 supporters to become champions. Having left the position in 1932, Suppici returned three years later, and coached Uruguay until 1941.

MARIO ZAGALLO (born 9 August 1931)

Greatest success: 1970 World Cup (Brazil)

Mario Zagallo is a Brazilian icon, having enjoyed a magnificent career in football, both as a player and a coach. He played as an industrious left winger in the World Cup-winning sides in 1958 and 1962, then graduated to manage the side in 1970, winning in Mexico. With this victory, he became the first person to win the World Cup as both a player and a coach. His career with Brazil has continued in various roles, including the post of technical director at the 2006 World Cup finals. His Brazilian team won the World Cup in 1994 but finished as runner-up to France in the 1998 World Cup finals.

ABOVE The Germany players celebrate World Cup 2014 victory after beating Argentina 1-0, after extra-time.

PICTURE CREDITS

2014 World Cup update written by Ben Hubbard.

The publisher would like to thank the following for permission to reproduce the following copyright material:

Endpapers: Thinkstock, Getty Images

Mirrorpix: 17 (bl, cr), 90 (tr, tl, c, bl, br), 91 (tl, tr, c, bl, br), 96, 99, 101, 130, 131 (br), 133 (tr), 138 (tr, br), 139 (tr), 141.

Getty Images: 6, 7, 8, 10 (cl), 10–11 (main image), 12, 13, 14, 15, 16, 18, 19, 20, 21, 23, 24, 25, 26, 27, 28, 29 (t, b), 31 (t, b), 32, 33 (t, b), 34, 35, 36, 37, 38, 39 (t, b), 40 (bl, bc), 41, 42, 43 (t, b), 44 (t, b), 45 (t, b), 48 (cl), 48–49 (main image), 51 (t, b), 52, 55, 56, 57, 58, 59, 60, 61, 62 (t, b), 63, 64, 65, 66, 67, 68 (cl), 68–69 (main image), 70, 71, 72, 73, 74, 75, 76, 77, 78, 79, 80, 81, 82, 83, 84, 85, 86, 87, 88, 89, 91 (cr), 92, 93, 94, 95, 97, 98, 100, 102–103 (cl, main image), 104 (cl, br), 105, 106, 107, 108, 109, 110, 111, 112, 113, 115 (t, b), 116, 117, 118, 119, 120, 121, 122, 123, 124, 125, 126 (bl, tr), 127, 128, 128–129 (main image), 131 (tr), 132, 134, 135, 136, 137, 138 (tl, c, bl), 139 (tr, c, bl, cr, br), 140, 142, 143, 144, 145 (t, br), 146 (cl), 146–147 (main image), 148 (t, b), 149, 150, 151 (t, b), 152 (t, b), 153, 154 (t, b), 155, 156 (t, b), 157 (t, b), 158 (t, b), 159 (t, b), 160, 161 (t, bl, br), 162 (t, b), 163 (t, b), 164 (cl), 164–165 (main image), 166 (t, b), 167 (t, b), 168 (t, b), 169, 170, 171, 172 (t, b), 173, 174 (main image).

All additional images courtesy of iStock, Getty Images.

Every effort has been made to obtain permission to reproduce copyright material, but there may be cases where we have been unable to trace a copyright holder. The publisher will be happy to correct any omissions in future printings.